WALKING IN
MY MIND

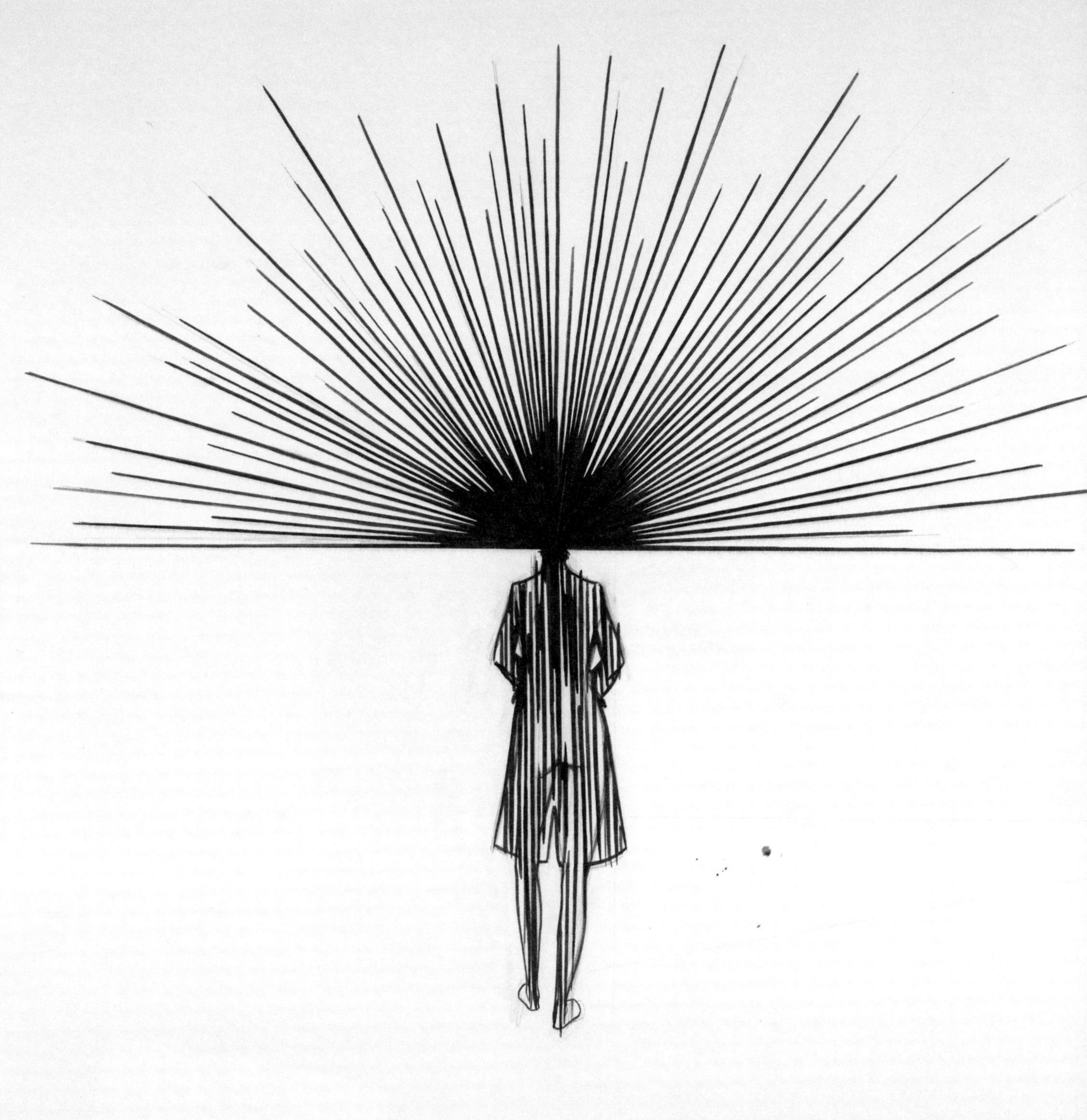

Charles Avery
Thomas Hirschhorn
Yayoi Kusama
Bo Christian Larsson
Mark Manders
Yoshitomo Nara
Jason Rhoades
Pipilotti Rist
Chiharu Shiota
Keith Tyson

WALKING IN MY MIND

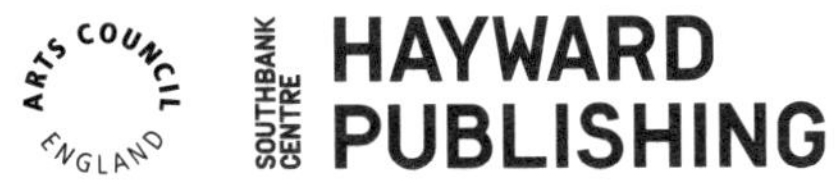

Published on the occasion of the exhibition *Walking in My Mind*
Hayward Gallery, London
23 June – 6 September 2009

Exhibition Curators: Stephanie Rosenthal and Mami Kataoka
Assistant Curator: Richard Parry
Exhibition Assistant: Vanessa North
Scientific Consultant: Dr Mark Lythgoe

Art Publisher: Mary Richards
Publishing Co-ordinator: Sarah Auld
Sales Manager: Deborah Power
Catalogue designed by APFEL (A Practice for Everyday Life)
Translators: Fiona Elliott (pp. 10 – 23); Jeffrey Hunter (pp. 26 – 33)
Produced in the UK by fandg.co.uk

Front cover: Yayoi Kusama, *Dots Obsession*, 2009
Back cover: Bo Christian Larsson, *Welcome to the Jungle*, 2008
Title page: Charles Avery, *Untitled (As I look into space, I meet the eye
of my creator, as she is watching me, as I am in her eye)*, 2002 – 2009

Published by Hayward Publishing
Southbank Centre
Belvedere Road
London SE1 8XX,
www.southbankcentre.co.uk

ISBN 978 1 85332 277 8

Distributed in North America, Central America and South America by D.A.P. /
Distributed Art Publishers, 155 Sixth Avenue, 2nd Floor, New York, N.Y. 10013,
tel: +212 627 1999, fax: +212 627 9484, www.artbook.com

Distributed outside North and South America by Cornerhouse Publications, 70
Oxford Street, Manchester M1 5NH, tel. +44 (0)161 200 1503; fax. +44 (0)161
200 1504, www.cornerhouse.org/books

CONTENTS

Art is the product of creative thinking within an aesthetic context. Rather than merely mirroring our social experience or the times we live in, art can actively 'think' about a broad range of cultural and social issues, engineering and giving form to new perspectives that have the potential to change the way we perceive not only our surroundings, but also our own cognitive activity. Art can illuminate, in other words, the unseen processes by which we make sense of the world as well as our own interior life.

Walking in My Mind examines this crucial dimension of contemporary art practice. Bringing together a diverse group of international artists whose work maps, models and explores the workings of the creative mind, it highlights the idea that art is an alternative way of thinking things out and ultimately of apprehending reality, especially aspects of our experience that are often otherwise closed or inaccessible to us. Besides investigating their own perceptual and creative processes, the artists in the exhibition also engage more generally with the question of how individuals process information and understand their surroundings. Their work, which often takes the form of immersive installations, invites us to become aware of own thoughts and feelings, and to reconsider the role these play in framing our relationships with external phenomena and the broader cultural context in which we live.

All art, of course, offer us the opportunity to see things through the eyes of its creator. But the works in this show go a step further: they lay out mental landscapes that we can inspect and reflect on as if we were walking around inside the artist's mind. The use of the word 'walking' in the exhibition title draws attention to the importance of our physical exploration of these works, as well as to the intimate link between bodily experience and creative thinking. It suggests that these artworks solicit both focused and unfocused ways of seeing, and that we should pay attention to the full range of our experience in responding to them. Rather than trying to find an answer to what they 'mean', we should allow ourselves to discover the different mental paths and ways of processing information that each work presents.

Walking in My Mind has been co-curated by Hayward Chief Curator Stephanie Rosenthal and Hayward International Curator Mami Kataoka. My deep thanks go to both of them for organising this compelling exhibition with intelligence, imagination and an acute sensitivity to the work of the artists involved. They have been ably supported throughout by Assistant Curator Richard Parry and Exhibition Assistant Vanessa North. I would also like to thank Southbank Centre Artistic Director Jude Kelly and Chief Executive Alan Bishop as well as Southbank Centre's Board of Trustees, for their support of a show which is logistically, as well as artistically, challenging, and which continues the Hayward Gallery's tradition of innovative exhibition-making.

Walking in My Mind would not have been possible without the generosity of all those who have loaned us valued works from their collections, and we are deeply grateful to all our lenders. For their vital financial support of this exhibition, we owe our immense gratitude to The Henry Moore Foundation, Pro Helvetia – Swiss Arts Council, Mondriaan Foundation, Swiss Cultural Fund (Great Britain), The Great Britain Sasakawa Foundation and Goethe Institute, London. We are also indebted to Steinle Contemporary, Munich and Marianne Boesky Gallery, New York for their additional assistance.

Early curatorial research for this exhibition included conversations with Mark Lythgoe, to whom we are indebted for freely sharing his insights and knowledge. In addition to the essays by the show's co-curators, this catalogue includes thought-provoking texts by psychologist Susan Blackmore and art critic Brian Dillon. Our thanks go to both of them for their excellent contributions, and to APFEL for their original design of this book. Both Charlotte Troy and Mary Richards, the head of Hayward Publishing, deserve our appreciation for their fine work in organising all aspects of this publication.

Finally, all of us at the Hayward extend our most profound gratitude to each of the ten artists in this exhibition. They have enriched us all by creating adventurous works of art that engage us on many levels, and that mobilise our own creative thinking and looking.

RALPH RUGOFF
DIRECTOR, HAYWARD GALLERY

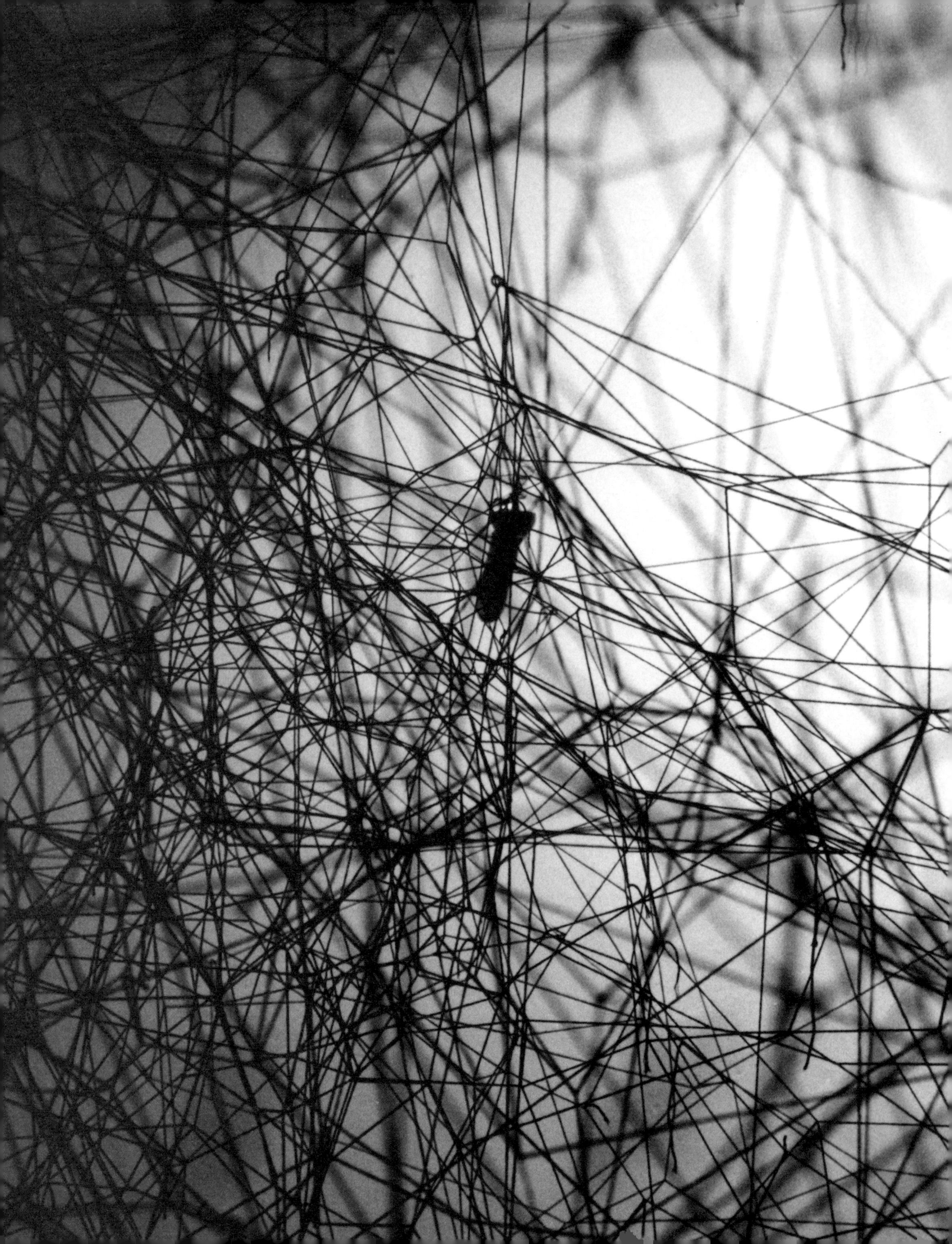

WALKING IN MY MIND

Stephanie Rosenthal

Like philosophers, psychologists and neuroscientists, visual artists can contribute to our understanding of the human mind and address the question: 'Where and what is my Self?'[1] As opposed to the written word used in these disciplines, however, the advantage of the work of art is that it can ignore logic and linearity in its answers, that it can make web-like connections, that it is not beholden to fixed sequences or hierarchies. As such, it can present a close approximation of the complex processes of the human brain and what we call 'the mind' (human consciousness).

Walking in My Mind presents ten immersive installations from the last decade that can be read as translations of the human mind into physical form. It offers some of the different ways in which artists construct images of their own or universal minds – which, for their part, draw the visitor into the artistic construct.

It was in 1969, exactly forty years ago, that Harald Szeeman realised the first major survey of Conceptual art, *Live In Your Head: When Attitudes Become Form*, shown in Bern and London. This show reflected the then growing conviction that art should be seen as a process or activity, as an experience or a state of mind. *Walking in My Mind* taps into this idea of showing works that have arisen from artists' experience of creative processes; however, the focus is not Conceptual art, but works that draw on a huge diversity of materials, on floods of images, and are constructed on a gigantic scale. These installations are the outcome of the artists' ability to create real, physically accessible 'mental' spaces that demand a response from the viewer. At the heart of the exhibition are works that envelop the visitor, making it all but impossible to distance oneself bodily from what one is seeing.[2] In this exhibition, the materialised mind of the artist meets the mind of each individual viewer. Hence the very deliberate choice of title: 'Walking in *My* Mind'.

★

Imagine the Hayward Gallery for a moment as the oversized head of some fantasy creature. It bids us enter its innermost sanctum, to wander around in the recesses of its mind. The various rooms, staircases, nooks and crannies are the forebrain, interbrain, midbrain and hindbrain, with their hemispheres and folds. You can imagine millions of nerve cells. The connections between these neurons, the synapses, are made by you, the visitor. As in the brain, our experiences shape possible connections, although here the route taken through the exhibition also determines the synapses.

The rhizome theory of Gilles Deleuze and Félix Guattari provides the perfect backdrop for this exhibition, which is itself like a rhizome, a profusion of roots. It functions by dint of connections, mental leaps, horizontal juxtapositions, with no need for hierarchical interpretation. The visitor – entering from outside – becomes part of this exhibition-rhizome, encountering the installations and potentially connecting with them, being affected by them, being asked to take a particular stance.[3]

Installations frequently involve viewers so that they become part of the work, an element in the composition, even a participant. Artists have been actively exploring this phenomenon since the late 1950s. Allan Kaprow famously called for participants rather than spectators for his 'environments'.[4] However, in this new role, the viewer could also by definition become an intruder, as in the work of Bruce Nauman. In 1968, Nauman showed a paradoxical sound installation with the title *Get Out of My Mind, Get Out of This Room*; the viewer was invited to enter an empty room – that Nauman equated with his mind – only to be told to leave again.[5] When reference is made to the viewer's participation in the works in the present exhibition, it is in the sense of the meeting of minds rather than of some form of interaction that may or may not be required to 'complete' a

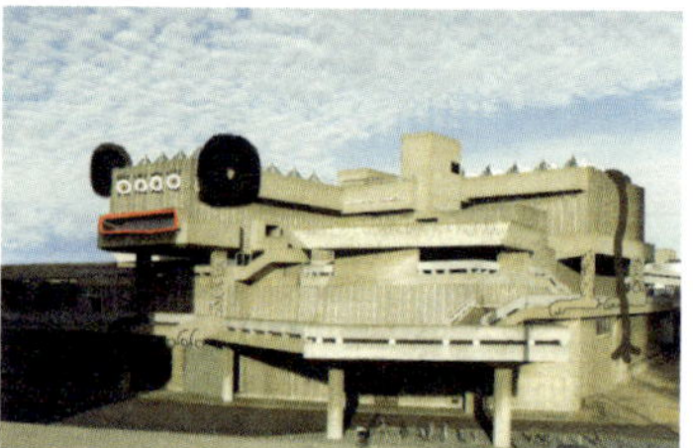

Gelitin, *Psycho Hayward*, 2008

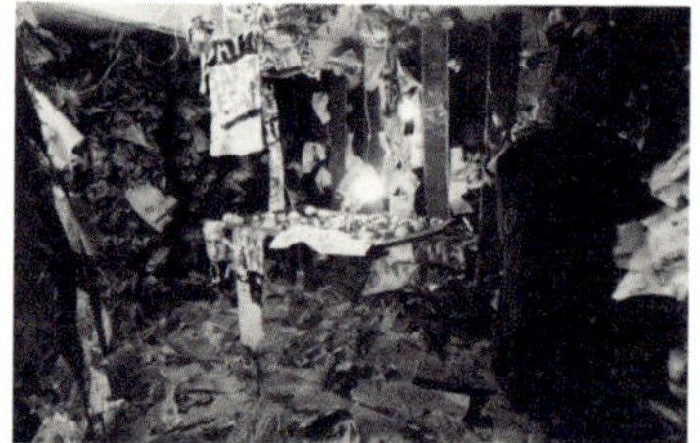

Allan Kaprow, *Apple Shrine*, 1960
Photo: © Robert R. McElroy / Licensed by VAGA, New York, NY

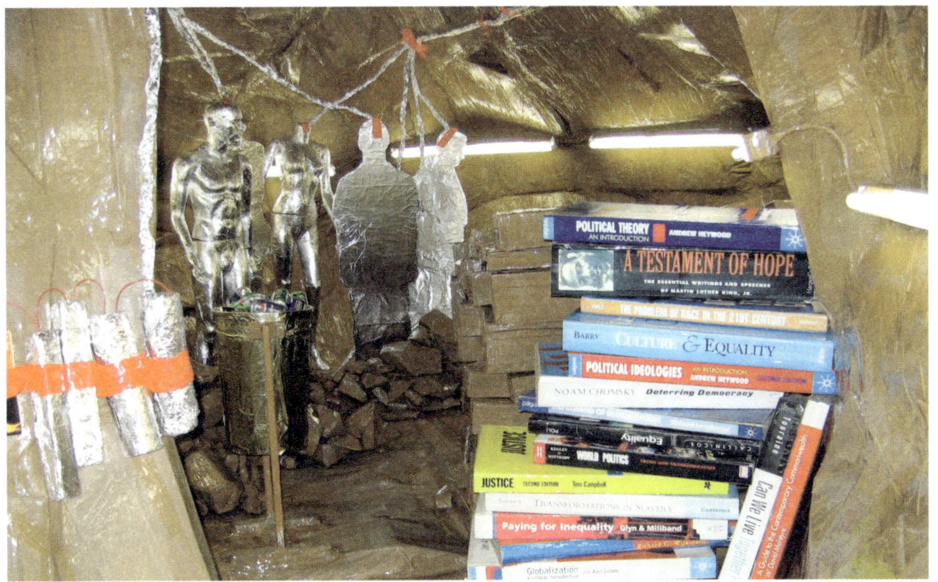

Thomas Hirschhorn, *Cavemanman*, 2002 (detail)

particular work. It is the viewer who makes the relevant connections within and between individual installations. In the words of Thomas Hirschhorn: 'I want my work to walk into the mind of the spectator (the Other) … I want to create a dialogue or a confrontation in the mind of the Other. I see it as the noble task of a work of art to link the creator's mind to the Other's mind. A work of art aims to enter and to occupy the mind of the Other.'[6]

★

In Hirschhorn's *Cavemanman* of 2002, visitors mentally and physically lose their way in a series of chambers. Behind a long white wall, there are four 'caves' made from a framework of spars covered with adhesive tape. These are filled with a huge array of data, objects and pictures, traces of an absent inhabitant. An uneven path leads through the passageways into caverns liberally dotted with images and texts. There is no hierarchy defining this series of rooms and their contents, although the fact that there is just one possible route through the chambers means that visitors have to conform to a choreography of sorts. In the first chamber, which has two rooms, there are paper clocks showing the time in different cities, and a room complete with posters, bookshelves and a bed. Throughout the complex of caves, mannequins wrapped in silver foil are connected to each other by foil arteries, while individual books (such as Noam Chomsky's *Reflections on Human Nature and the Social Order*, Thomas Paine's *Rights of Man* and Michel Foucault's *Use of Pleasure*) are tied to foil sticks of dynamite. Repeatedly scrawled on the wall behind the mannequins, in black spraypaint, is the phrase: '1 man = 1 man'. To quote the artist: 'A cave belongs to everyone; there are no specific occupants, and the inscription on the walls of *Cavemanman* says: 1 man = 1 man. All generations of occupants and all motivations of occupants are equal. All hypotheses are possible. The cave is a space of the possible.'[7]

One of Hirschhorn's inspirations for this work was the story of a young man in France convicted of defacing with graffiti a site on which prehistoric signs were carved. 'Why are the wall drawings that were made thousands of years ago considered art and the recently sprayed slogan considered vandalism?', Hirschhorn asked.[8] The piece also evokes the French caves of Lascaux and Chauvet, Bin Laden's hideout at Tora Bora, the Swiss tunnel system and church altars.

In the midst of the *Cavemanman* labyrinth we find ourselves both tangled up in our own thoughts and confronted with the artist's thoughts. The situation is not quite comprehensible and yet seems familiar. Although the feeling of being overloaded with information can have a certain appeal, it can also induce in us a desire to define our own boundaries. How do we fit into this deluge of familiar images and found materials? 'I want to do too much', explains Hirschhorn, 'because it is only when the eyes and the brain get exhausted that there are no lies any more and you can get the truth. I want to give from myself, in an offensive and aggressive manner. I want to create space and time within my work. This is why there are often massive amounts of information. This is the exchange my work wants to propose.'[9]

The way in which pictures relate to each other here may cast some light on Hirschhorn's view of and attitude to the world, revealing the workings of the human mind. His labyrinth is a biomorphic sculpture; it is beautiful, it opens out in different directions, it exists quite apart from its own contents. It constitutes an image of the mind, both individual and universal, the mind of Thomas Hirschhorn and the mind of the viewer. 'I believe there is the possibility to structure your mind in a cave with cavities where you put something inside, with garbage, with unspeakable things. We think there's no light on, we think they're forgotten … it's a metaphor for the space in the mind'.[10]

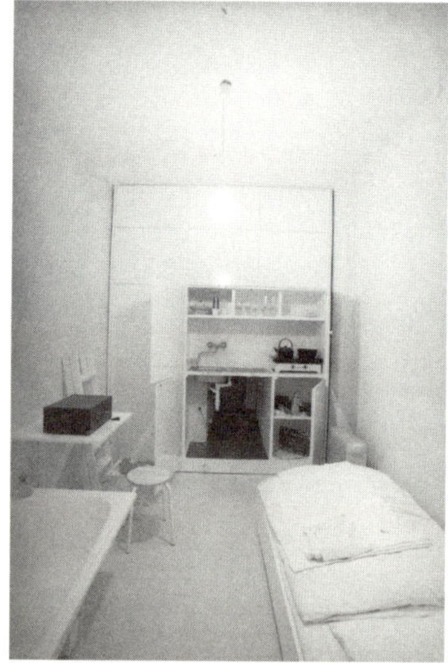

Gregor Schneider, *Haus Ur*, 1985–

The mind that Hirschhorn presents functions like a collage. There is a connection here to Georg Wilhelm Hegel's concept of the subjective mind ('in the form of self-relation'); the objective mind ('in the form of reality: realized, i.e. in a world produced and to be produced by it: in this world freedom presents itself under the shape of necessity'), and the absolute mind ('In that unity of mind as objectivity and of mind as ideality and concept, which essentially and actually is and for ever produces itself, mind in its absolute truth').[11] While Hirschhorn presents a three-dimensional collage made up of images taken from reality (objective mind), we also create our own reality (subjective minds) from the knowledge and experiences we bring to the piece, which might create what Hegel calls the 'absolute mind'.

Perusing this installation – and the environments created for this exhibition by Jason Rhoades and Yoshitomo Nara – is not unlike paying a visit to an artist's studio. Like an installation, a studio can also be read as the reflection of a mental space.[12] In Hirschhorn's case, the materials leave his studio to become embedded in an environment that minimises one's usual sense of being in an exhibition space. He creates the context for his materials and in effect makes up for the fact that his works have left the context in which they were made. In many ways this harks back to the late 1950s and early 60s when Allan Kaprow and some of his contemporaries abandoned their studios and relocated their artistic activities in a variety of public spaces. During the 1970s, artists such as Daniel Buren set an example by giving up their studios altogether, working 'in situ' in order to avoid the problem of having to show works in a context other than that in which they were created.[13] By the same token, artists like Ilya Kabakov took their studios to the viewer in the form of installations, to create the right context for their art. This is done more explicitly by Gregor Schneider in his *Haus Ur* (1985–), for which he turned his parents' house – in its entirety – into a constantly changing installation and, as such, into a studio. And it is similarly explicit in Paul McCarthy's *The Box* of 1999, an oversized wooden 'box' with the same dimensions as his studio and containing all the items that had once been in it, now fixed in the exact positions that they had previously occupied. The only major difference was that the replica 'studio' was tipped on its side, and the floor and the ceiling became the walls.

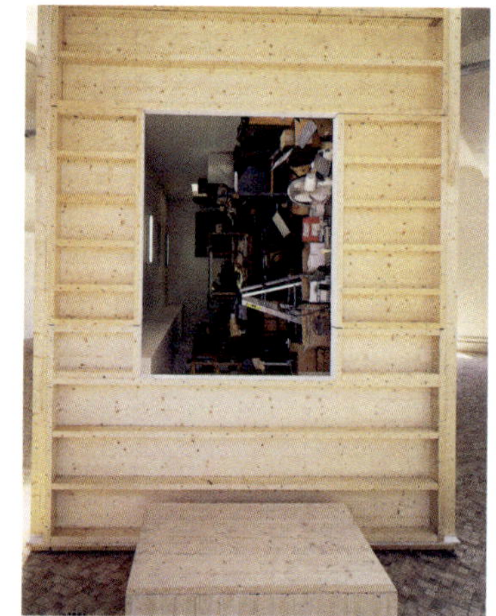

Paul McCarthy, *The Box*, 1999

Jason Rhoades' *The Creation Myth* (1998), subtitled 'The Mind, the Body and the Spirit, the Shit, the Prick and the Rebellious Part', is in essence a laboratory in which he

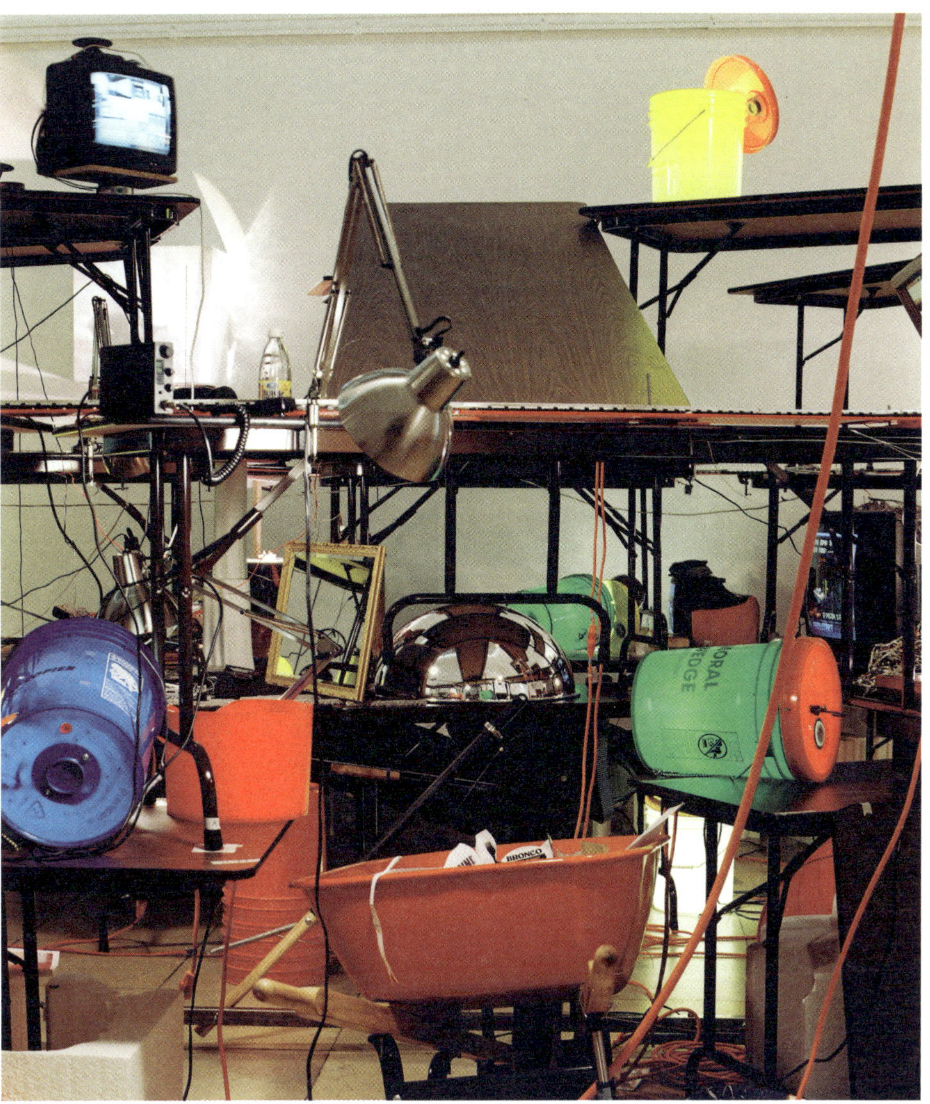

Jason Rhoades, *The Creation Myth*, 1998 (detail)

investigates the creative powers of human beings in general and of the artist in particular. It could perhaps be read as his answer to Michelangelo's fresco *The Creation of Adam*. Like Michelangelo, Rhoades was also interested in creating an image that would both depict and explore the moment of creation. In this piece, Rhoades portrays the mind as a 'psychobiological' mechanism,[14] metaphorically represented by the functioning of the digestive system (taking in food and emitting waste matter). He also outlines an essential function of the brain: the acquisition of knowledge. Despite its chaotic appearance, there is an underlying order here. The component parts of the work are arranged around the 'switching centre', the brain, which forms the core of the installation. The 'inner child' and the 'subconscious' are located directly below the 'everyday' area.

The various elements that make up this piece are connected by an arterial network of cables. Photographs taken by Rhoades, along with films and reproductions of his works, are seen side by side with images from pornographic magazines, in amongst a host of brand-new everyday items. Data is transported along paths into the mechanism, where it is processed and evaluated, and eventually leads to the creation of a new work. For

Rhoades, this does not have to be an object; it could equally well be an idea, a moment, a concept, a process. Acts such as chopping wood, playing computer games and operating a railway engine all serve here as metaphors for transforming knowledge and making information more readily digestible, as well as for intuitively childlike behaviour. Rhoades creates never-ending chains of associations and, like a modern-day alchemist, is constantly transforming one thing into another.

Rhoades' sculpture *The Prick* is positioned in *The Rebellious Part*, where its sharp prong has cut slits into the wall. It is as though the inner world – the world of feelings, desires and fears – were slowly emerging into the outside world. Smoke emits from the 'arse' of this sprawling, anatomical installation, relating to Rhoades' 'third subtitle' of the work: 'Yes I can blow smoke rings out of my Ass.'[15] In other words, as Rhoades himself has said, 'really creating is doing the impossible'.[16] And, in his view, it is the practice of art that makes it possible for the artist to experience this ideal.[17]

As the neurobiologist Semir Zeki has shown, 'concepts emerge in the brain, be they simple or more complex, as a result of neuronal processes that basically always take much the same course'. While art is an expression of the brain's neuronal functions, he explains, it also stems from the parts of the brain devoted to the formation of concepts.[18] One of the brain's particular capacities is to operate in abstract terms: 'Abstraction produces ideas and concepts, but beneath these there are yet more concrete experiences, which do not always perfectly chime with the ideas that our brain has developed. The creation of a work of art is one way to harmonise the two, and to turn the idea formed by the brain into something else.'[19] Rhoades' installation invites us to wander through the information-processing channels of the human brain. He makes a connection between pragmatic, technical processes and the act of creation, thereby unmasking creativity as a neuronal process and destroying the myth of the wondrous, mystical moment of sudden inspiration that is the seed of creation.

We find something very different in the inner worlds of Yoshitomo Nara and Keith Tyson. For *My Drawing Room (bedroom included)* (2008) Nara's small-format drawings in graphite and coloured pencil are on show in a wooden shed, spread out on tables, on the floors and on the walls. Once again, for the visitor it is as though one has been allowed a glimpse into an artist's studio, the source of the creative process.[20] Nara's shed is a metaphor for his inner Self, to which the visitor has no access and can only see by peering in through the window. All his drawings are self-portraits and, like the objects, refer to his childhood influences, to his own personal interests and preferences. A mixture of curiosity and voyeurism compels us to press avidly up against the window.

A rather different situation pertains in Tyson's installation. On the right and left side of the room are seventy-five *Studio Wall Drawings* (2000–2009). These are multi-layered paintings on paper, each with its own title and date. The titles refer to themes that forced their way into his studio from outside and left their mark on and in his works. Tyson has referred to these drawings as a kind of diary, reflecting ordinary occurrences in his studio, current political events and childhood memories. He has described the process of their making as follows: 'When I am absorbed and involved in the work, then all that stuff is automatic … It's like being a pianist. They just play.'[21] We can see in these works how Tyson's interests, his acquired knowledge, first-hand experience and imagination interlock and overlap. 'It is much more that I've been cursed or blessed with so many ideas and so many observations about the world. As if I had a mild form of autism, I find everything interesting.'[22] Here, too, viewers find themselves gazing into a reflection of the artist's creative process and into his thoughts about the human mind in general. Such themes have been an ongoing concern for the artist. In the centre of a previous work,

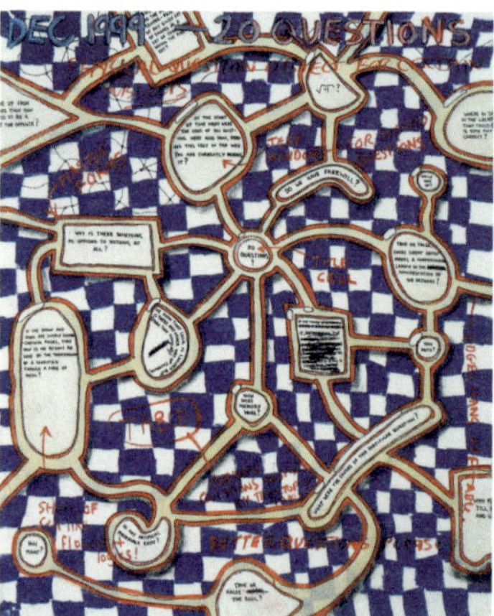

Keith Tyson, *Studio Wall Drawing: Dec. 1999 – 20 Questions*, 1999

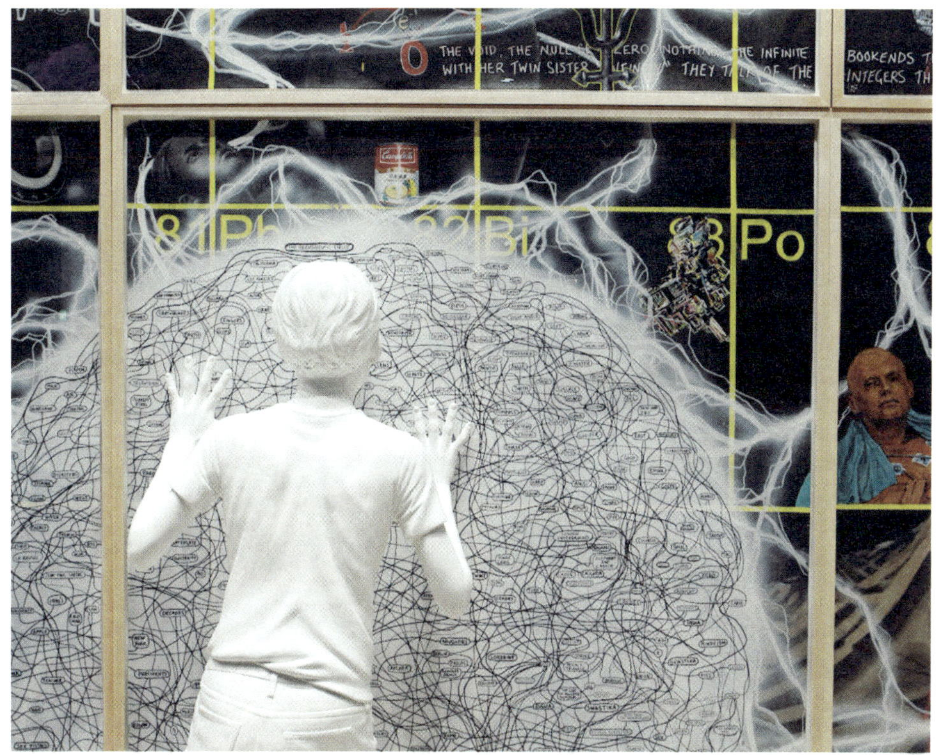

Keith Tyson, *Studio Wall Drawing: Jan 2009 – Locked Out of Eden – Viewing The Children Playing In The Garden From The Safety Of My Cerebral Fortress*, 2009 (detail)

Studio Wall Drawing: Dec. 1999 – 20 Questions, we can read: 'Do we have free will? How does memory work?' or 'If the brain and mind are simply electro-chemical pulses, then how do we account for love or the transmission of a condition through a piece of music?'

On the entire far wall of the room we find *Studio Wall Drawing: Jan 2009 – Locked Out of Eden – Viewing The Children Playing In The Garden From The Safety Of My Cerebral Fortress* (2009), a 21-panel work made specially for this exhibition. The point of departure for the work, a representation of a 'hellish paradise' and a gigantic brain, is the idea that it can be 'hellish' to try to understand one's own thoughts and emotions, however promising the idea of 'finding oneself'. Here Tyson conflates Heaven and Hell; not for the first time, he attempts to come to terms with the limitless wonder and horror of reality. The work can be read as a multi-layered self-portrait.[23] The artist appears in the work as a three-dimensional child figure seen from behind, pressed up against a diagram illustrating the web-like connections of the formative themes, experiences and events that have shaped his personality. It is as though the whole work has evolved from the figure, with the network of connections spreading and growing new shoots across the walls to the right and left. Internal and external space, internal and external worlds, all but meet in this work, with only the thin membrane of Tyson's mind to separate them. And at the same time, it is the mind that allows information to flow in both directions. In the wake of his *Artmachine* and other works,[24] it seems to be the culmination of his exploration of his own creative powers.

Creating a three-dimensional self-portrait through taking on other personas is a recurring theme in this exhibition. Bo Christian Larsson's installation *The first cut is the deepest and the division of seven* (2009), which is on show in the stairwell and was created for this exhibition reveals various personas of his Self.

When I first heard the title *Walking in My Mind*, an image appeared in my head of small people in rubber boots stepping around on my brain, trying to experience something beyond all that grey brain matter. I know this might sound silly, but in a sense, this is metaphorically what I think people would like to do. So with this in mind for my installation, I want to provide people with a rough map so that they can navigate through the mind's environment, and explore a general picture of someone else's inner landscape. I essentially want this, the walk in my mind, to be a real physical experience for anyone who decides to join. [25]

In any encounter with Larsson's work, we find ourselves entangled in the dense thickets of his internal visual landscape. Usually his installations are 'initiated' by a performance. Having sketched out the main stages in the action, Larsson then allows the performance to develop of its own accord: 'My drawings are pure inner visions that I use as blueprints for the installations. The installations function as an arena for the performance, and the performance is an act where objects are being created. Information has to enter your mind and become part of you before you can process it and use it in a creative way, so naturally everything comes from inside.' [26]

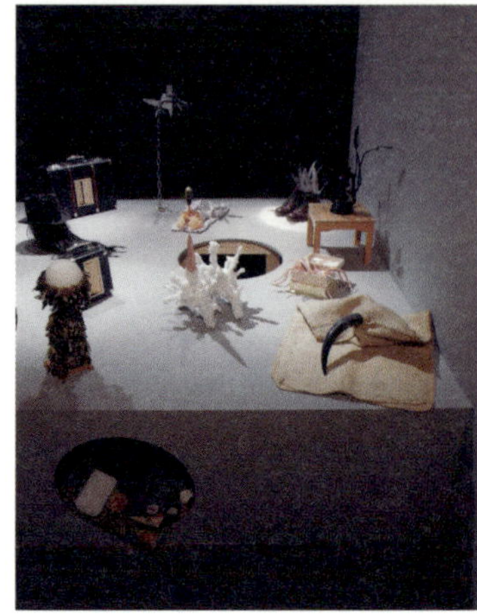

Bo Christian Larsson, *The first cut is the deepest and the division of seven*, 2009 (detail)

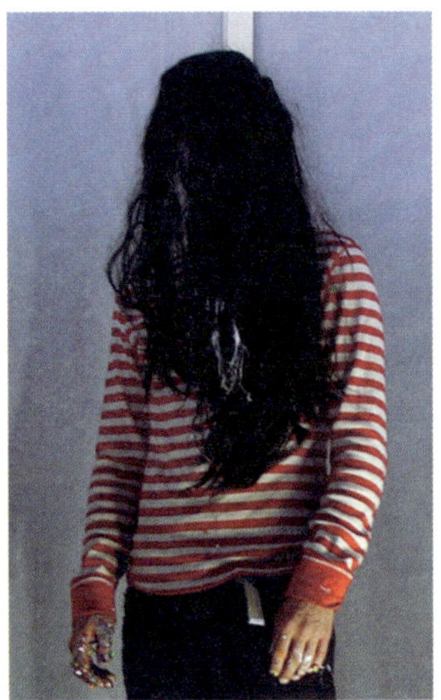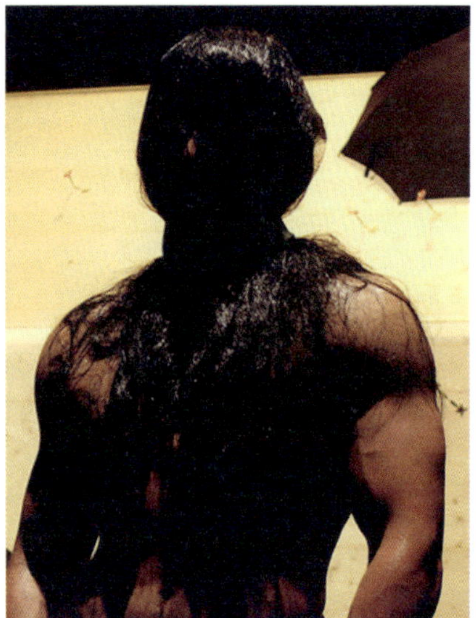

Bo Christian Larsson's characters Sonuvabitch and Mr. Empire

Thus *The first cut...* bears the marks of a performance – a series of initiation rites involving a range of different characters, most of whom have already appeared in earlier installations: Sonuvabitch – 'the constant hunter, on the search for the inner verve'; Mr. Empire – 'the silent warrior and guardian of the human idea'; Pentaman – 'the indistinguishable hermit; known best as a figure never to be seen. Sometimes the Sceptical Owl represents him'; The Redeemer – 'the voice of minorities and a judge without a court'; The Shadow – 'also known as The Worried Man'; The Poet – 'a perceptive soul and a proud bodyguard of the intellect' and The Worldhater – 'a disgusted, miserable complainer'. [27] Larsson's protagonists appear in his installations either as sculptural figures, or are represented symbolically as a wig, a piece of writing or some other objects.

Larsson himself played the character of Sonuvabitch and, as in most of his performances, wore a long wig that covered his eyes. As a result of this artificially induced 'blindness', he finds himself wandering round in darkness. In fact, Larsson, like mystics such as Johannes von Kreuz (1542–1591), believes that pursuing a path through darkness is the only way for the human spirit to come fully into its own.[28] Darkness paves the way for change, because it encourages us to confront the alien and the unfamiliar. Even as it reduces visual perception, darkness also sharpens our other senses and throws the human being back on his or her own resources. This also explains the veil of darkness surrounding his installation.

As exhibition-goers make their way up the dark staircase, they feel the presence of Larsson's shadowy nocturnal figures. The darkness enhances the feeling of physically being 'inside' another person's thoughts. A golden cage, constructed from tree trunks, on the ground floor could be read as a representation of the control mechanisms by which we take ourselves prisoner, day after day. And the process of feeling one's way forwards may remind visitors of trying to free oneself from one's own thoughts. At the top of the staircase, a parliament of owls is enthroned on a gallows. Having escaped the dense forest and reached the summit, we may feel a sense of liberation. The owl, which can see in the dark, is a metaphor for the intuitive human capacity – despite our not-seeing and our intellectual not-understanding – to make connections. Larsson has chosen it as the symbol of the 'Secret Society', but it may also be symbolic of his own persona and his inquiry into his intrinsic Self. Thus his characters act as representatives of control mechanisms, thoughts, experiences, desires, patterns of behaviour and personal concerns – all the things that both make us what we are and limit what we can do. And although the figures that appear here as Larsson's protagonists represent facets of his individual personality, they may well be related to the ones with which we, too, have to negotiate in our own fight for freedom.

Mark Manders also has an alter ego (called Mark Manders), whose imaginings are made concrete in *Self-Portrait as a Building*, a group of works that he has been developing since 1986. 'You could see … this self-portrait as a building', he states, 'as an enormous three-dimensional photograph of a mind. Not my mind though. It's a place where my thoughts are frozen together.' He has also stated that: 'The building is fiction, but everything inside exists in reality.'[29] For the ensemble realised for *Walking in My Mind*, Manders has

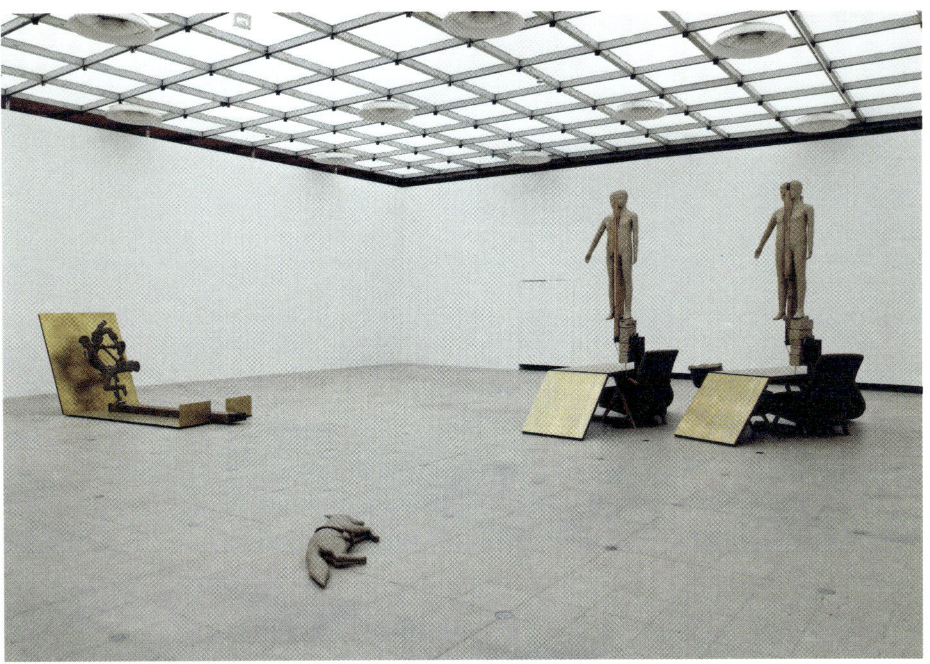

Mark Manders, installation view with *Life-Size Scene with Revealed Figure*, 2009
Fox/Mouse/Belt, 1992 and *Livingroom Scene*, 2008

characteristically combined works from different phases of his career (1990 and 2009). As always, this presentation adds another element to his self-portrait, revealing new rooms in his imaginary edifice. Manders makes no distinction between elements made today and those made twenty years ago. 'Like an encyclopaedia, the building is always ready, even though it keeps on changing and growing or shrinking.'[30]

We find ourselves walking through a world of different-sized objects drained of colour, taking them in from various perspectives. We observe some from a bird's-eye view, with a sense of detachment, and in front of others we are overcome by a sense of our own smallness as we roam through a field of oversized figures that seem foreign yet strangely familiar. Manders creates archetypes, forms that are redolent with associations: emergent life, loneliness, community, unity, mystery, calm, wide-open spaces, close confinement. Recognition vies with alienation as we prowl through the installation. It is as though we have been left alone in the building, and the objects in it are starting to come to life, but we sense that we are invading someone's privacy, pushing our way into a place where we don't belong, a world that we explore like an inquisitive yet uncertain guest, treading softly, careful not to catch the occupant unawares.

By contrast, Charles Avery does not set out to plunge viewers into his world, but rather to use aspects of it to set their imaginations alight. In this exhibition he is showing works from *The Islanders*, a project that has been ongoing since 2004. A model of an imaginary world, it could be – but is not necessarily – a vision of the future. He does no more than hint at how this other world might look, providing just enough detail – vivid marks or patches of colour in his drawings, for example – to unlock our imaginations, encouraging us to add to the colours, breathing life into them little by little. And although he shows us fantastic creatures, his reports seem neutral compared to the emotional travel journals of an explorer such as Alexander von Humboldt (1769–1859). Avery's drawings are caricature-like, the sculptures look as though they could have come from a natural history

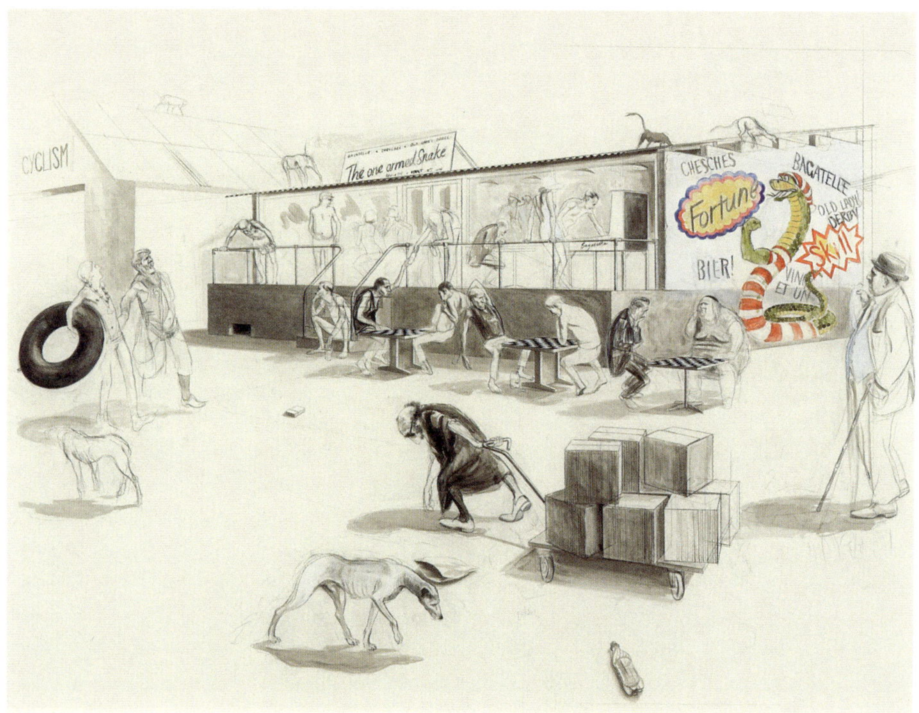

Charles Avery, *Untitled (The Bar of the One-Armed Snake)*, 2009

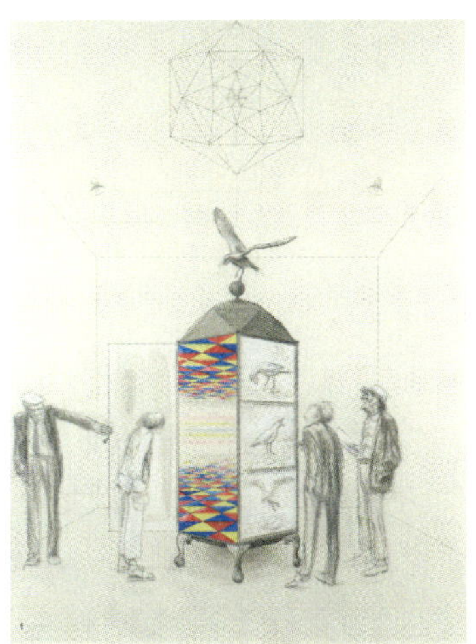

Charles Avery, *Untitled (Artist's Impression of the Eternity Chamber)*, 2007

or anthropological museum and the texts are written like factual observations. While we know that the subjective nature of historical travel journals means that we must exercise caution in assessing their 'truthfulness', the question of what is real and what is not real is of no concern to Avery. His stated principle is to make 'no difference between mind and matter … everything is real'.

Avery's Island can be read as an image of how the human mind functions. According to the artist, the land conquered by The Hunter symbolises the objective realm of perception, understanding and the ordering of our own surroundings, while the territories that are as yet unexplored and uncultivated represent the subjective realm. But things can change in an instant, since the Island can suddenly revert back into its wild state. Thus Avery takes the notion of objective reality to an absurd extreme, showing how subjectivity is constantly breaking new ground, and by analogy, how we are unable objectively to understand either our surroundings or ourselves.

The Islanders describes how, despite this, human beings go out hunting day after day for knowledge, how we strive to understand the world around us in an endeavour to give it a comprehensible form. The Hunter, whose occupation is the 'original and most august profession on the Island', came there, we are told, 'in pursuit of an elusive beast called the Noumenon'.[31] According to Plato, the *noumenon* is that which can be understood by the human spirit, as opposed to that which can be seen by the human eye. In the philosophy of Immanuel Kant, a *noumenon* is an unknown, indescribable reality that forms the basis of an observed phenomenon. In Avery's work, The Hunter's search for the *noumenon* can be equated with our search for ourselves – a search that will never succeed but that will also never cease.

★

Yayoi Kusama, Chiharu Shiota and Pipilotti Rist each create an image of the mind that refers on different levels to the web-like structures of neuronal processes. Tyson's work includes imagery of electro-chemical pulses. In the installations of both Rist and Kusama, viewers lose their orientation, one way or another, and – in a metaphorical sense – find themselves caught up in a network of neurons and synapses. Meanwhile, in Shiota's work, the interconnections of thought processes find visual form in a web of black threads.

In Kusama's installation *Dots Obsession* (2009), made up of mirrors and balloons decorated with red and white polka dots, we are in danger of losing our way, but in a manner that is entirely different from the experience of the other installations.[32] One has a sense of being absorbed into this artificial scenario, of losing touch with the limits of one's own body. Lost amid the balloons and mirror images, we cannot see the end of the passage. When we make our way through the space and step out onto the terrace of the Hayward Gallery and are confronted with her work *Guidepost to the New World* (2005), in which polka-dotted sculptures are scattered over an Astroturf lawn, it is as though we are seeing the outside world through Kusama's eyes. This impression is reinforced by the trees between Hungerford Bridge and Waterloo Bridge, which Kusama has clad in polka-dot fabric. As Kusama herself has said: 'A polka dot has the form of the sun which is a symbol of the energy of the whole world and our living life, and also the form of the moon which is calm, round, soft, colourful, senseless and unknowing … Our earth is only one polka dot among the million stars in the cosmos … Polka dots are a way to infinity.'[33]

This representation of infinity conveys a notion of the mind as something ungraspable and indefinable. And if we read her installations as images of her mind, then the dots could be taken to represent the millions of neurons that exist in the brain. As viewers wander amongst these 'neurons', they create the synapses. These polka-dot works are, in formal terms, the opposite of Kusama's *Infinity Net Paintings*, where our thought patterns take the form of web-like structures, similar to those in her early drawings.

Something similar happens in Chiharu Shiota's *After the Dream* (2009). She, too, creates a diagrammatic image of the human mind, and our thoughts can easily become snarled up in her installation of taut, black threads. Like our thoughts, the threads in Shiota's installation are not linear, but more like a root system, with multiple knots and inter-connections existing side by side. The arrangement of the threads recalls diagrams of neurons and synapses in the human brain,[34] as well as Deleuze and Guattari's rhizome, which serves to illustrate the notion of non-hierarchical yet interconnected simultaneity as opposed to hierarchical thought patterns.[35]

Pipilotti Rist's sense that film (like the canvas of a painting) can be read as a metaphor for human skin, which separates us from the outside world, informs many of her works. In the case of *Extremitäten (weich, weich) [Extremities (smooth, smooth)]* (1999/2009) projections of body parts are shown on the walls, floor and ceiling of the gallery. Visitors plunge into this pool of images – or swim with the images in a pool of darkness. Curtains surround the room, creating an intimate atmosphere. Lying on the seating area in the centre of the installation, we see larger-than-life images of a breast, foot, penis, ear and mouth, which loom out of the blackness only to disappear again. A female voice is heard singing, soothingly guiding us forwards: 'You are a butterflower / you are a mammal / you are a molecule / you are a woman mouse / you are a mouse / you are different from me / you are nothing / you are the king / you are a pollen / you are full of pain / you are the cerebellum / you are like you / you are normal / you are a friend / I will become like you.'

Ever since she started making video works, Rist has used sensual images and, on occasion, psychedelic music to create the impression that we are looking into ourselves, confronted with images that could well have come from within us. Rist equates video installations with the optical systems and brain processes inside our skulls.[36] For, as she says, 'The way we think and feel is not just flat and rectangular. I try to take this factor

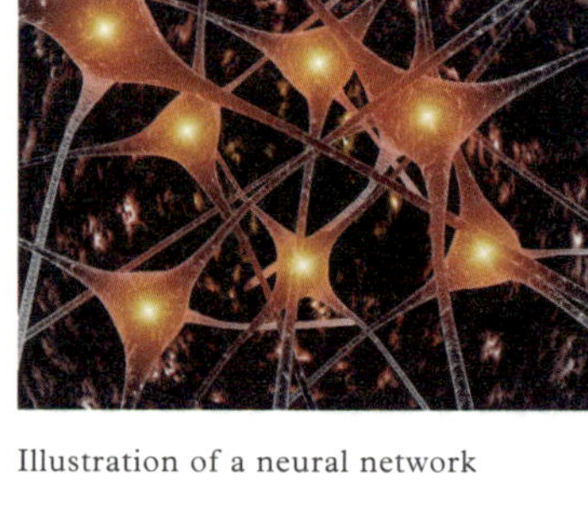

Illustration of a neural network

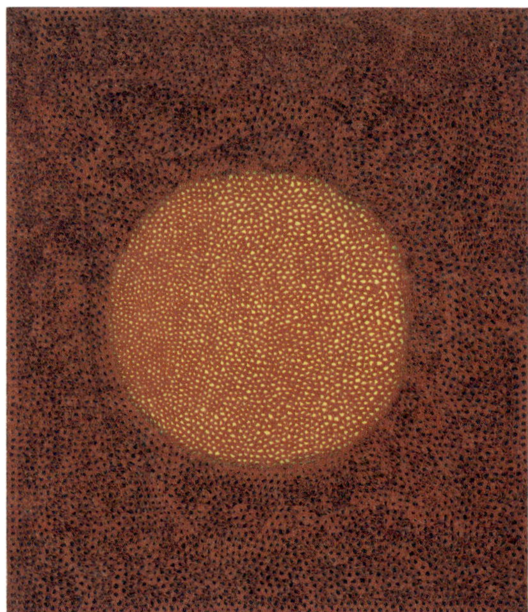

Yayoi Kusama, *Infinity Net*, 1965

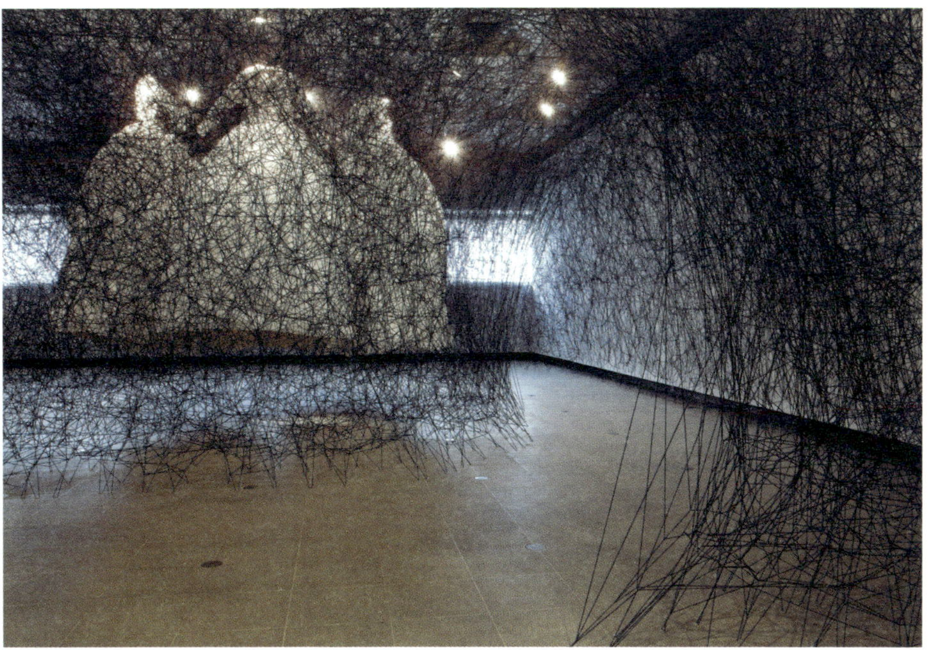

Chiharu Shiota, *After the Dream*, 2009

into account when I make works in space.'[37] Her videos draw us in so persuasively that we can become reluctant to move on. One has the growing feeling of being both in one's own body and in that of some other person – or perhaps of lying in bed at night with one's eyes closed, when it can seem that the limits of one's own body are no longer clearly defined. The sensations experienced by the viewer are not unlike those that arise through autogenic training (a relaxation technique), which Rist knows first hand.

> *Extremities (smooth, smooth)* talks-walks around in the areas where the 'felt' sizes of our body parts become relative – a cold hand can be perceived as one centimetre, or a foot touched by another body becomes as big as a mountain. The work relates to the scientific fact that every sun, every star, every planet is ephemeral, and will either implode or explode after a certain period of time … every cell, every molecule, every atom of us has been in several suns before it became a part of our planet, before it became us. Impossible to understand, but walkable in our mind.[38]

The generosity with which Rist lays bare her own personal thought processes and vulnerability encourages the viewer to identify with the content of her works: 'The more honest and vulnerable I am, the more painful the process is, the better the outcome and the less it is important who I am … I work on showing my internal landscape, full of natural and self-made catastrophes, ambivalences, contradictions, escapes, hopes and utopias as precise as artistically and physically feasible.'

Elsewhere, she has compared poor video resolution to her own mental condition: 'I don't even try to copy reality. What I'm really interested in are the painterly qualities that are intrinsic to that deficiency; for example, tones of red that bleed (since the norm for sharpness is based on green), the hysterical fuzziness, or the brilliance of the buzzing. I love this nervous light. I keep working at my material until it resembles my own synaptic activities and mental states.'[39] As we contemplate Rist's work, it is almost as though our own internal images merge with the images created by the artist; we seem to be both in our own minds and in hers, entirely at one with the work.

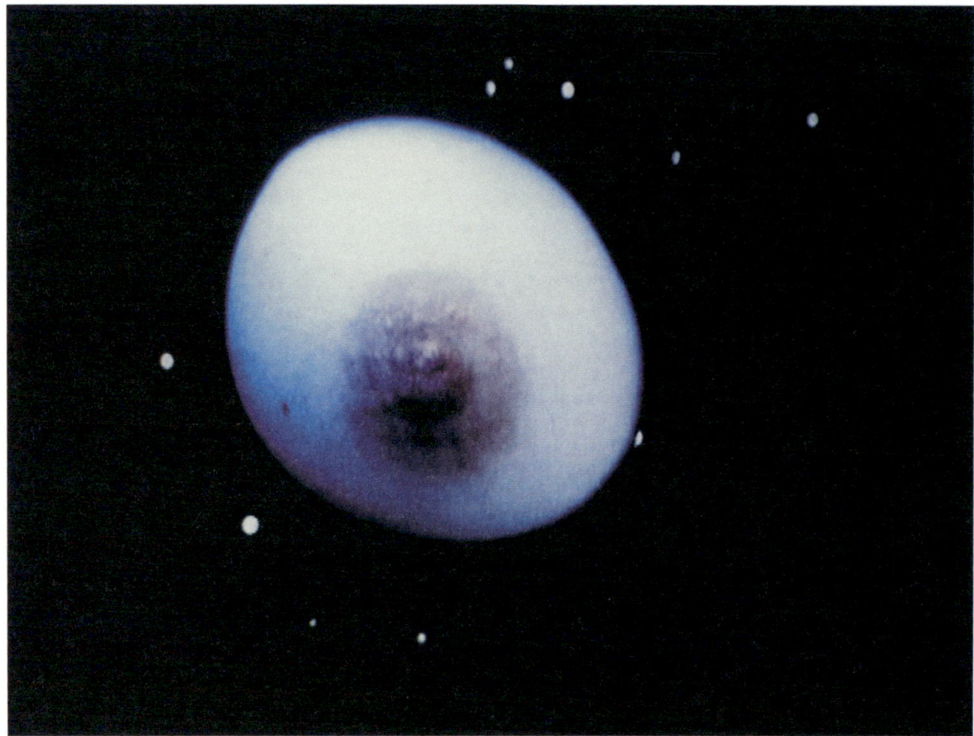

Pipilotti Rist, *Extremitäten (weich, weich) [Extremities (smooth, smooth)]*, 1999/2009 (detail)

The environments evoked by the works in this exhibition – the artist's studio, the three-dimensional self-portrait, abstract world views, patterns of synapses and neurons – can be interpreted as metaphors for the human mind. Their compelling nature and appearance physically confronts the viewer. In some, the relationship between the viewer and the work casts the former in the role of subject. One is showered with data and this may encourage one to reinforce one's own defences, and seek out one's own position. In others, one's own boundaries become blurred. Lost in infinity, in space that is designed to dissolve distinctions, one no longer knows where one's Self ends and the Other begins. It may be that at the end of our tour of the show, we will feel a little like the characters in the film *Being John Malkovich* – thrown out of the minds of the artists, landing with a bump, shaking our heads, dazed and bewildered, wondering if we are still in one piece and if the experience was real. As we step out of the Hayward back into the real world, the question is whether we want to use this illuminating sense of bewilderment to delve deeper into the human mind.

[1] In her essay in this catalogue, Susan Blackmore vividly demonstrates the difficulty of understanding the way in which the human mind works, and suggests that we can only portray or describe things that we feel we understand or have experienced ourselves. Thus our imaginations are limited by our knowledge of the mind. And it is only because of this that we still believe 'we are the mind that inhabits our body' (see pp. 35–40).

[2] This development in art has been discussed in publications such as *Installation Art: A Critical History* by Claire Bishop (Tate Publishing, London, 2005) and *Understanding Installation Art* by Mark Rosenthal (Prestel Verlag, London and New York, 2003).

[3] 'There may be nothing to understand in a book, but much that you can do something with. A book must combine with something else to create a mechanism, it must become a handy tool for "an outside". The book is not a root-tree, but part of a rhizome, the plateau of a rhizome for the reader it suits. The combinations, permutations and instructions for use are never found within the book itself for they depend on the connections with this or that "outside". Feel free, take what you like!' Translation of text by Gilles Deleuze and Félix Guattari on the jacket of the German edition of their book *Rhizom*, Merve Verlag, Berlin, undated.

[4] Kaprow wrote that 'The term "environment" refers to an art form that fills an entire room (or outdoor space) surrounding the visitor and consisting of any material whatsoever, including lights, sounds, color.' Passage from the accompanying pamphlet *Words*, 1962, Allan Kaprow Papers, Getty Research Institute, Los Angeles, Box 7, Folder 5.

In his typewritten score for *A Service for the Dead*, 1962, Kaprow wrote: 'Connected with this kind of thinking, of course, were the gallery-goers; for since they were encompassed by the environment in which they found themselves, their bodies, colors of clothing, movements, and voices became a part of the whole (whether or not they realized it in those days). It seemed clear to me that a passive and separated onlooker was not only undesirable for my needs, but was literally impossible.' Allan Kaprow Papers, Getty Research Institute, Los Angeles, Box 7, Folder 1. A modified version was published in *Art International 7*, no. 1, 1963, pp. 46–47.

[5] There are also other areas where the mind or the body are given a real space, with the conceit being that one can spend time in it and move around in it. Gaston Bachelard, for one, has written a book on this topic: *The Poetics of Space*, Beacon Press, London, 1992; first published 1958.

[6] Email communication with the artist.

[7] Thomas Hirschhorn, conversation with Philippe Vergne, in *Heart of Darkness: Kai Althoff, Ellen Gallagher and Edgar Cleijne and Thomas Hirschhorn*, Walker Art Center, Minneapolis, 2006, p. 113.

[8] Thomas Hirschhorn, in *Hans Ulrich Obrist Interviews Volume 1*, Charta, Milan, 2003, p. 394.

[9] Thomas Hirschhorn, interview with Iris Mickein, in *Common Wealth*, Tate Modern, London, 2003, pp. 62–63.

[10] Thomas Hirschhorn, interview with Paul Schmelzer; http://mnartists.org/work.do?rid=126081

[11] Georg Friedrich Wilhelm Hegel, trans. William Wallace; www.hegel.net/en/enz3.htm

[12] The artist has said: 'For me, my atelier is not only a practical place to work, but a mental space too... My atelier is a space in my head more than anything else. That's why I would never consider not having one.' 'Atelier in the Mind, or Form Versus Chaos', interview with Michael Diers, *Checkpoint*, Arndt & Partner Gallery Magazine, no. 2, May – Aug 2007, p. 25.

[13] See Daniel Buren in Jens Hoffman and Christina Kennedy (eds.), *The Studio*, Dublin City Gallery The Hugh Lane, Dublin, 2006, p. 104: 'It is a place where works are produced which later will be exhibited in an entirely different context, for example, a gallery or a museum, and through that shift of location fundamentally changed their meaning.'

[14] See Rhoades' map of *The Creation Myth*, 1998, pp. 114–115.

[15] The second subtitle is: 'what one sees and How one Files. How one sees Files and How one Files seeing'.

[16] Jason Rhoades, interview in video produced to aid the installation of *The Creation Myth*, 1998.

[17] Ibid.

[18] Semir Zeki, *Iconic Turn: Die neue Macht der Bilder*, DuMont, Cologne, 2004, p. 78.

[19] Ibid., pp. 83–84.

[20] See the essay by Mami Kataoka in this publication, pp. 26–33.

[21] 'It's Like an Organic System', conversation between Ethan Wagner and Keith Tyson, *Parkett*, no. 71, p. 112.

[22] Ibid., p. 113

[23] In contrast to the classical self-portrait, showing the artist's face and giving an impression of his or her personality, here the focus is very much on the latter function. See Ernst van Alphen, *Art in Mind*, University of Chicago Press, Chicago, 2005.

[24] *Artmachine* was a method Tyson developed during the 1990s, which functions like a random generator to create his artworks.

[25] Email communication with the artist.

[26] Ibid.

[27] Ibid.

[28] See Johannes vom Kreuz, *Die dunkle Nacht, Sämtliche Werke*, vol. 2, Johannes Verlag, Einsiedeln, 1992.

[29] Mark Manders, in *The Absence of Mark Manders*, Hatje Cantz Verlag, Ostfildern, 2007, p. 22.

[30] Ibid.

[31] Charles Avery, *The Islanders: An Introduction*, Parasol unit foundation for contemporary art and Koenig Books, London, p. 23.

[32] See Claire Bishop's discussion of Jacques Lacan's paper on 'The Mirror Stage', in Bishop 2005, op. cit., p. 90.

[33] *Yayoi Kusama*, Phaidon, Press, London, 2000, p. 124.

[34] I would like to thank Mark Lythgoe, scientific consultant for this exhibition, for giving me advice on this subject matter.

[35] Deleuze and Guattari write: 'The tree and root inspire a sad image of thought that is forever imitating the multiple on the basis of a centered or segmented higher unity.' And some pages later: 'It is odd how the tree has dominated Western reality and all of Western thought, from botany to biology and anatomy, but also gnosiology, theology, ontology, all of philosophy.' See Deleuze and Guattari, 'Introduction: Rhizome' in *A Thousand Plateaus: Capitalism and Schizophrenia*, Continuum, London and New York 2004, pp. 18, 20.

[36] Ibid.

[37] *Parkett*, no. 71, supplement, p. 15.

[38] Email communication with the artist.

[39] *Parkett*, no. 71, supplement, p. 16.

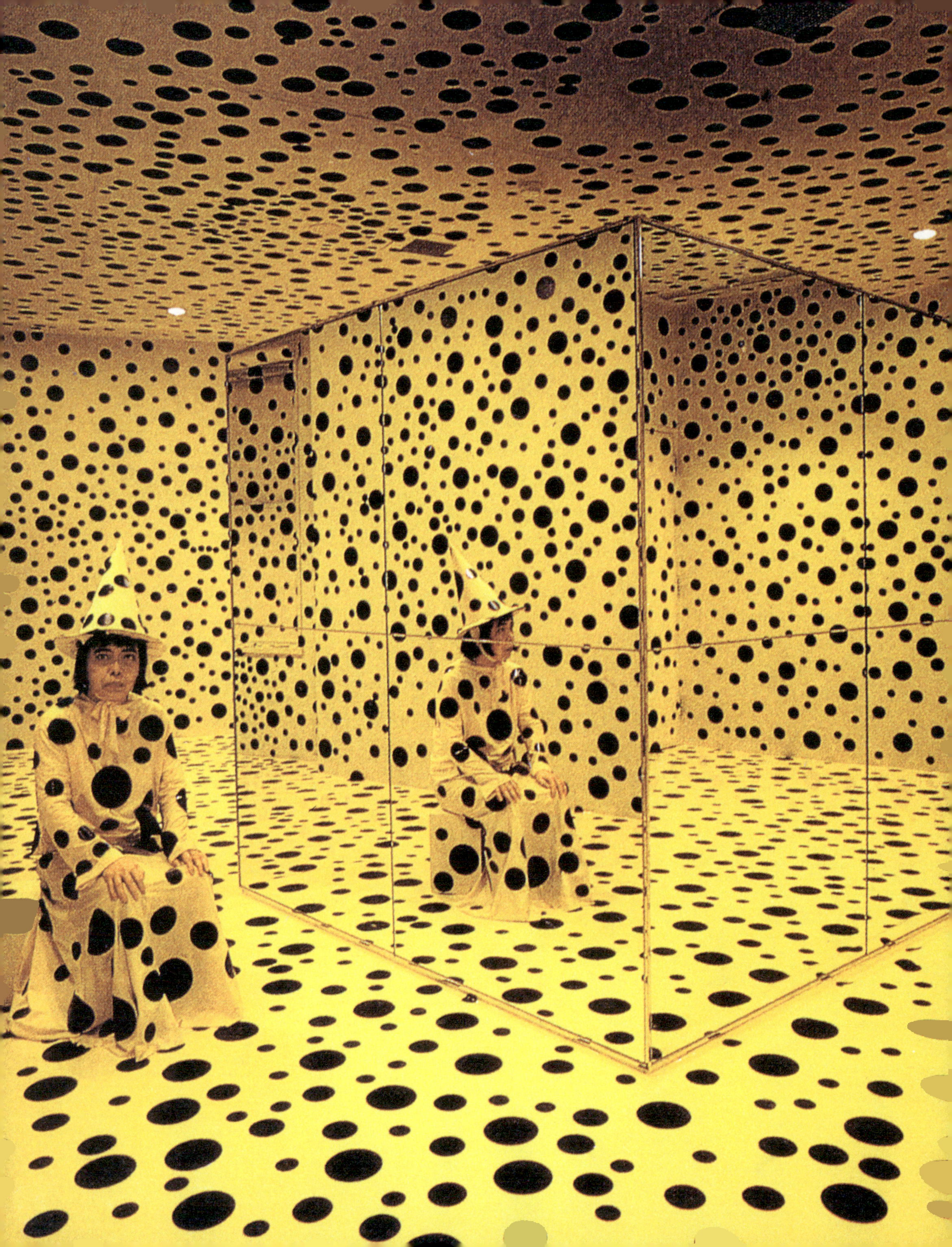

BETWEEN
THE MICROCOSM
AND THE MACROCOSM

Mami Kataoka

The title of this exhibition of installations by ten artists, *Walking in My Mind*, deliberately raises a question of interesting complexity: exactly whose mind are we walking in? The answer is multivalent, since the exhibition offers multiple points of view: that of the artists, who observe their own inner worlds from the perspective of a spectator, and that of the exhibition viewers, who experience this externalised representation of the artists' inner worlds, but also compare it with their own inner worlds.

The show attempts to examine the nature of installations not only from the usual standpoints – considering the physical relationship between the objects and images in the installations and the surrounding space, as well as the viewer's immersive bodily experience – but also in terms of exploring how the non-material, intangible elements that make up an installation – the artist's creative process, fundamental impulses, feelings, memories and imagination – can be represented in three-dimensional space. The Russian artist Ilya Kabakov, who in 1988 first created the 'total installation' – a work in which the walls, ceiling, floor and objects are united in a coherent artistic space – said that the museumgoer, upon entering such an installation, is at once its 'victim' and at the same time a viewer, judging and appraising the work. As such, he is simultaneously subject and object, a phenomenon that Kabakov compares to a book and its reader. The reader is drawn into the world of illusion created by the author as he reads, while at the same time comparing the author's literary style and skill to that of other authors; he may even begin to envisage the author actually writing the book. Kabakov has called this a double-action mechanism, 'the experiencing of the illusion and simultaneously the introspection on it'.[1] The present exhibition offers the same type of double-action. The visitor is the 'victim' of the physical, spatial reality of the installation while also attempting to share the artist's introspection. Indeed, the exhibition may even offer the possibility of a triple-action mechanism, for while both victim and viewer, he also finds himself beginning to take a walk through his own mind.

This essay considers the ways in which the creative processes of a selection of the artists in the present exhibition – Yayoi Kusama, Chiharu Shiota, Mark Manders, Charles Avery, Yoshitomo Nara and Keith Tyson – are given visual form and represented in three-dimensional space, stimulating this triple-action in the viewer.

YAYOI KUSAMA, RELEASING THE MIND INTO SPACE

> When I'm facing a canvas and painting a net of dots I see the dots continuing on from the desk to the floor until they even cover my own body. The dots repeat and repeat and the net of dots stretches out infinitely. In other words, I forget myself, and become lost in the net, until my arms, legs, my clothes, and the entire room is filled with dots.[2]

Yayoi Kusama began to experience visual and auditory delusions in her teenage years. Diagnosed as schizophrenic and manic-depressive by a psychologist who discovered her artistic genius during her adolescence, she continued to suffer from pronounced neurosis after moving to New York in the late 1950s. In a show of 1959, she exhibited her first *Infinity Nets*. The New York art scene at the time was dominated by Action Painting, but Minimalism, with which Kusama would compare her works, was beginning to emerge. With its distinctive visual rhythm and monochrome palette, Kusama's work attracted considerable attention. To the artist, the *Infinity Nets* released something indefinable and ineffable in her innermost depths 'into the chaos of the void'.[3] 'My life is a dot, in other words, one of a million particles. Through the white matrix of nothingness of dots connected on an astronomical scale, self and other and the entire universe is obliterated', she has explained.[4] She bases her aesthetic ideas on dissolution and combination, proliferation

previous page:
Yayoi Kusama, *Mirror Room (Pumpkin)*, 1991

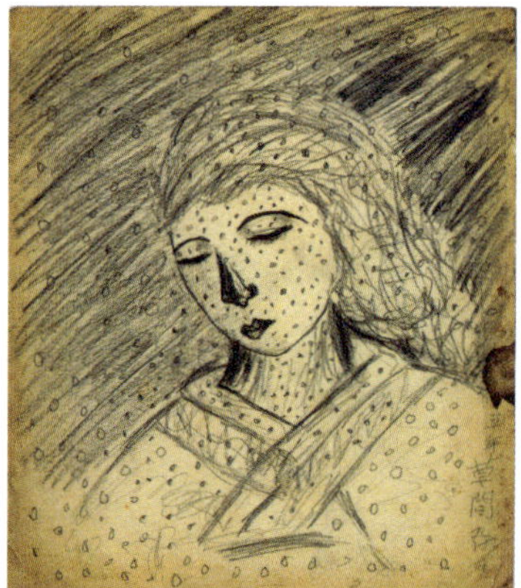

Yayoi Kusama, *Untitled*, 1939

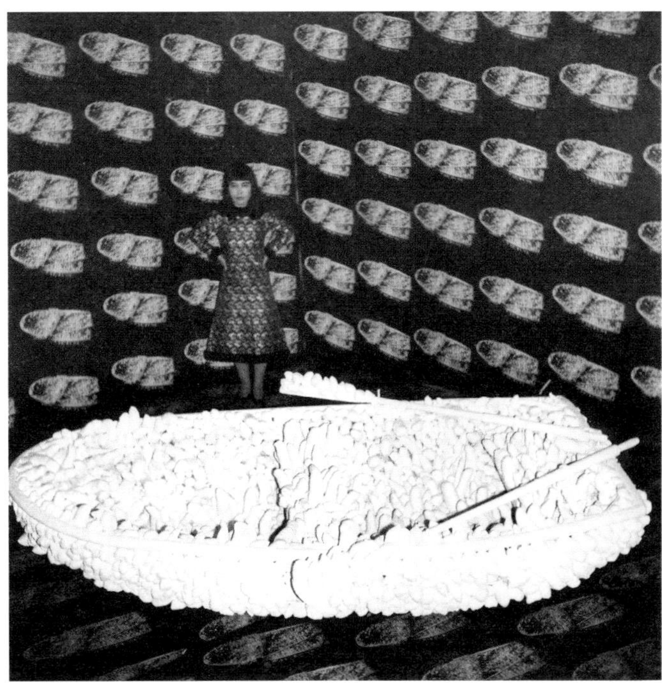

Yayoi Kusama, *Aggregation: One Thousand Boats Show*, 1963

and separation, a feeling of disintegrating into particles and of hearing messages from outer space. But this is not mere obliteration, for in the process, she elevates her self, like cosmic dust, into something eternal. Externalising her inner microcosm, she projects it onto a macrocosm far surpassing our powers of conception, and in doing so acquires an infinite mission. This is the source of the momentum that has sustained Kusama's creative energy for over half a century.

Kusama's first environmental work, *Aggregation: One Thousand Boats Show* was exhibited in 1963 at the Gertrude Stein Gallery. She filled a 10-metre-long boat with stuffed phallus-shaped objects and then covered the floor, walls and ceiling of the gallery with 999 black-and-white photographs of this sculpture. She went on to produce environmental works employing the phallus – a symbol of her terror of sex – and macaroni, standing for the food mass-produced by American consumer society. In *Driving Image Show* (1964), she covered the gallery floor with macaroni, and in *Infinity Mirror Room – Phalli's Field* (1965) she created an environment out of mirrors and plastic. Mirrors were also employed in the 1966 *Kusama's Peep Show*, where she exhibited the *Endless Love Room*, a hexagonal, mirrored space illuminated by flashing red, white, blue and green lights, creating visual equivalents of such immaterial and intangible things as 'mechanization, repetition, threatening ideas, impulses, vertigo, and all-encompassing, non-existent love'.[5]

Kusama returned to Japan in 1973, and after several retrospective exhibitions during the 1990s, mostly in the United States, began to create much larger installations that have been exhibited around the world. She continues to employ the mirrors featured in *Endless Love Room*. In *Fireflies on the Water* (2002), 150 tiny lights hang down from the ceiling, creating an effect of infinite repetition on the mirrored walls and the pool in the centre of the floor. The result is a scene of great serenity and ethereality. The three-dimensional objects, repeated endlessly and illusionistically in the two-dimensional mirrored surfaces, visible to the eye but impossible actually to reach out and touch, are the perfect embodiment of Kusama's art of phantasms and hallucinations, evoking the indefinable and ineffable.

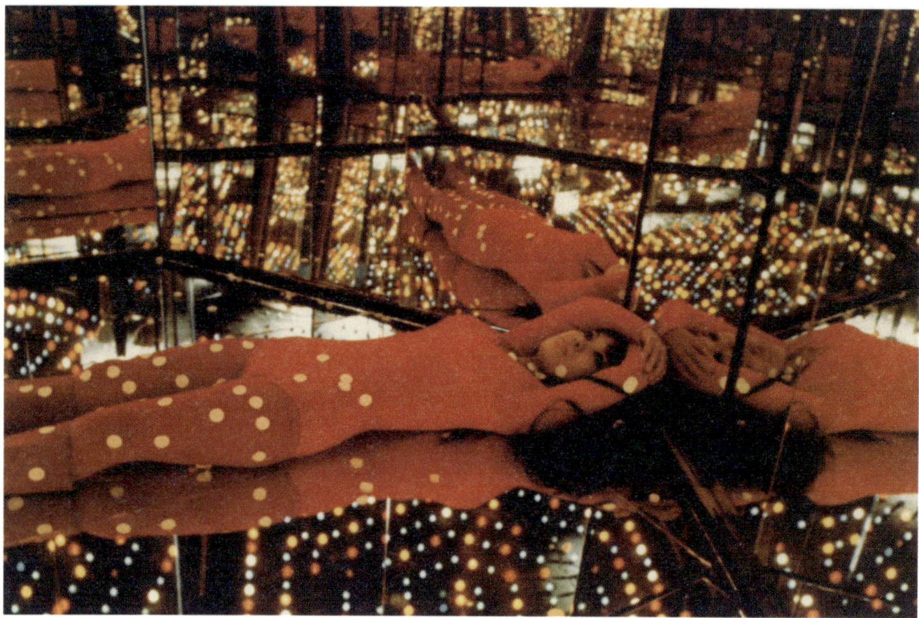

Yayoi Kusama, *Kusama's Peep Show*, 1966

RELEASING SENSUAL MEMORIES INTO SPACE

Kusama's childhood experiences instilled in her a fear of male sexuality, which she later sought to overcome by using the phallus as a repeated motif in her art – a process that she called 'psychosomatic art'.[6] A similar memory of fear and uncertainty has motivated the art of Chiharu Shiota, a Japanese artist who has made Berlin her base since 1996. 'In my childhood,' the artist has said, 'I remember the fear and the physical sensation of terror I felt when plucking weeds growing on top my grandmother's grave … I was afraid to pull the weeds, and I felt as if I could hear the person buried in the grave still breathing, so the memory of that experience, along with earth, greenery, and death all play an important role in my work.'[7]

The memories and anxieties of childhood are powerfully linked to the artist's feelings regarding the uncertainty of existence and her rootlessness as an expatriate. 'There are times when I wake up in the morning and don't know where I am. When I'm worried about something, I wake up at four or five o'clock in the morning … It also seems to me that if I didn't have this feeling of insecurity, I couldn't create, which only gives me something additional to worry about.'[8]

Shiota's anxiety as a resident in a foreign land triggers a chain reaction, her anxiety about her identity and place leading to anxiety about where she is going and a fear of death (she contracted cancer several years ago). She has also talked about a dread of losing her voice and the ability to communicate, as well as a fear of the dark, which began when she was nine years old following a fire in which her neighbour's house burned down during the night. She vividly recalls seeing one of the remnants of the fire, a piano that had been rendered silent in the destruction. All of these concepts – memories, death, sleep, the darkness of the night – are immaterial and uncertain. This fear of, and at the same time, attraction to, the abstract and intangible exist simultaneously in Shiota's work.

Her early performances were influenced by the work of Ana Mendieta, who used her body in her performances in combination with such materials as gunpowder, fire and

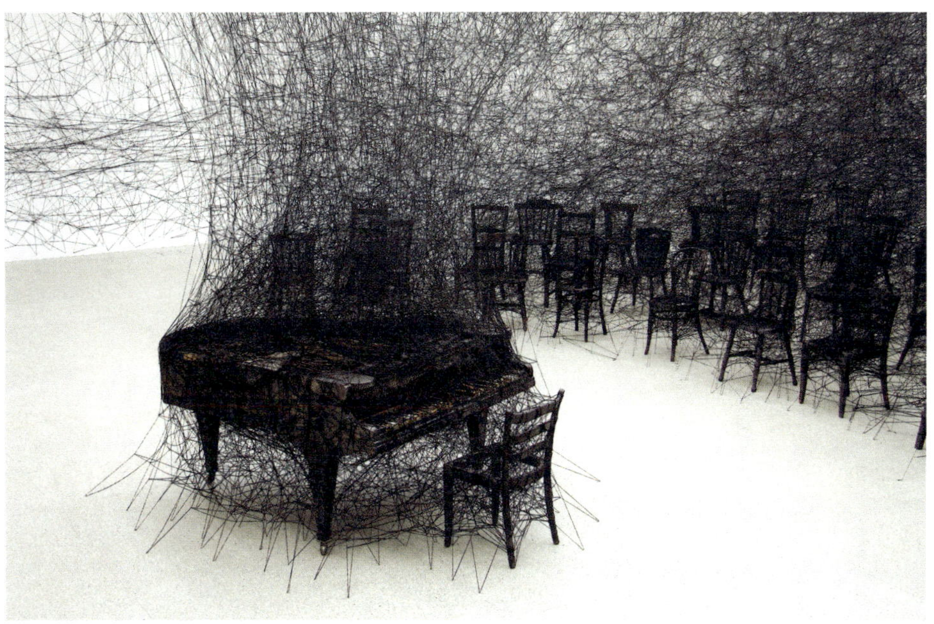

Chiharu Shiota, *In Silence*, 2002

mud to suggest pain, death and mortality, and who died tragically young at the age of thirty-six. Shiota's initial performances included *bathroom* (1999), in which she constantly washed her body in a bathtub full of mud, and the installation *Memory of Skin* (2001), where she dipped five oversized dresses in mud and hung them from the ceiling. Her focus has now expanded to a merging of the individual with the cosmos, also a theme in Mendieta's work.

Since 2000, Shiota has given her abstract ideas three-dimensional form in her installations employing black threads. In this series of works, she releases her ideas into space by stretching the threads like spider webs over the walls, floors and ceilings of the room. Her first work in the series included several hospital beds set in a darkened space. Shiota engaged in a performance, sleeping or sitting naked in the beds. 'It seems to me that there is no way back, no matter where I go to. I feel there is something common between the silence of the burnt piano and the silence on my way home, and this is deeply hidden in my heart. The threads are interwoven into each other. Get entangled. Torn apart. And disentangle themselves.'[9]

In the spaces that Shiota creates, the overlapping of such opposites as the conscious and unconscious, reality and dream, the body and the universe, and the vague space between, is given visual incarnation by the intertwined black threads. This approach not only presents a visual model of the concept of the rhizome as articulated by Gilles Deleuze and Félix Guattari in their famous *A Thousand Plateaus*,[10] but also expresses the nonverbal, non-logical, physical and sensual memory that drives Shiota's creative process.

HAVING A ROOM IN THE MIND

The attempt to grasp intangible emotions, memories and the imagination through spatial means is reminiscent of what the British historian Frances A. Yates has called 'the art of memory', which flourished prior to the development of printing.[11] Yates's history of the practice of memorisation from the Classical period to the Renaissance, draws attention to the 'technique of impressing "places" and "images" on memory' – and, in particular,

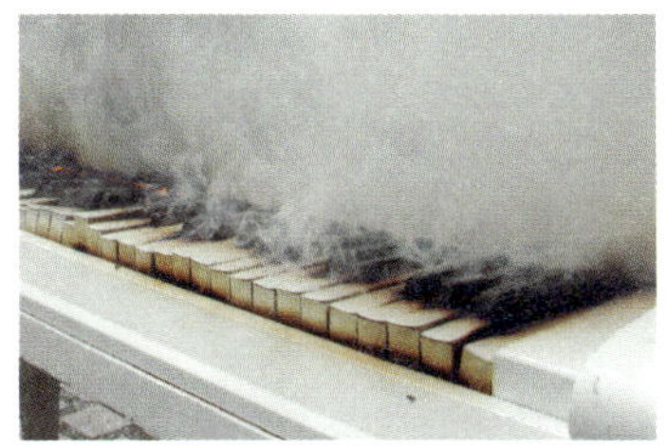

Chiharu Shiota, *In Silence*, 2002 (detail)

the correspondence of specific images to particular parts of architectural space and the way they are ordered in that space.[12] As a result, memorisation was not merely a rote exercise, but involved various mental skills, including sensation, cognition, imagination, perception and the recollection of ideas. Virtues and vices, heaven and hell, were linked with concrete images and places, and they were arranged in a grand cosmology of the heavens, the universe and 'supercelestial' realms. For example, referring to the 'memory theatre' created by the sixteenth-century Italian architect Giulio Camillo, Yates writes: 'The theatre is thus a vision of the world and of the nature of things from a height, from the stars themselves and even from the supercelestial founts of wisdom beyond them.'[13] In other words, the power of memory is summoned by ordering and arranging all the phenomena and ideas of the universe, whether visible or not, and creating a series of connections linking them in a chain so that one leads to the next in an unbroken series.

This is a process that one can see operating in *Self-Portrait as a Building* (1986–) by the Dutch artist Mark Manders. While Manders calls the work a self-portrait, it is an expression not of the artist per se, but of an alter-ego Mark Manders, a created persona, in the form of a house plan. This alter ego is 'a character who lives in a logically designed and constructed world which consists of thoughts that are halted or congeal at their moment of greatest intensity. It's someone who disappears into his actions. He lives in a building that he continually abandons; the building is uninhabited, in fact.'[14]

Manders' sculptural works are a product of this fictional house plan, and he describes the relationship between drawing and sculpture as 'a kind of "thought structure" that allows me to construct a particular emotion in poetic form'.[15] In his exhibition *The Absence of Mark Manders* at S.M.A.K., Ghent, in February 2009, a succession of rooms were carpeted with flooring fabrics used in ordinary living spaces, as if one were walking through the home of the fictional Mark Manders while he was out. While moving through the rooms, spectators sensed the existence of the actual Manders – the artist who created the installation – as well as the fictional Manders who is imagined to inhabit the space. Hence the viewer witnessed an overlapping, imaginary encounter between the artist and his fictional double, even though both were absent from the space.

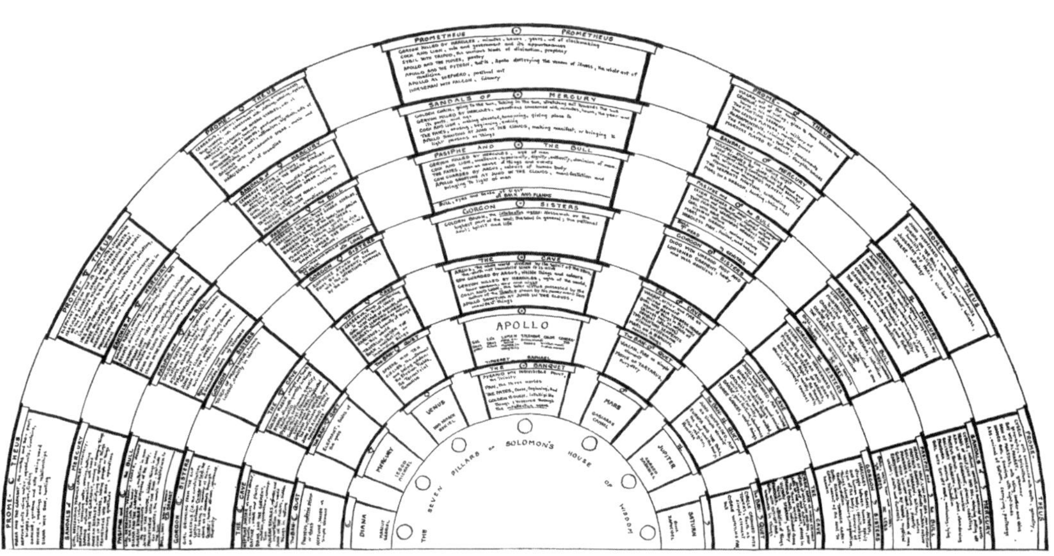

Frances A. Yates, *The Memory Theatre of Giulio Camillo*, 1966

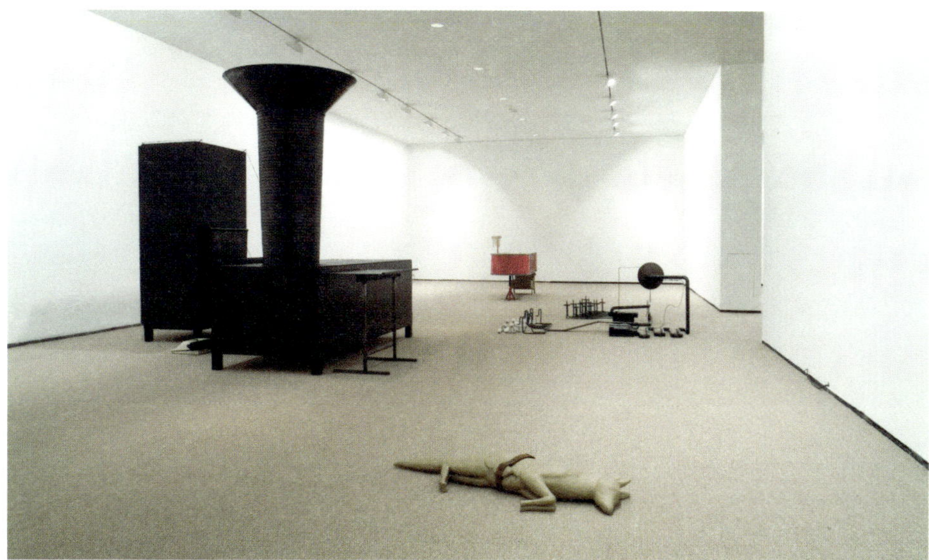

Mark Manders, installation at S.M.A.K., Ghent, with *Fox/Mouse/Belt*, 1992, in the foreground

The Scottish artist Charles Avery also creates a fictional place, in this case an Island, through drawings and sculptures. Avery terms the fictional resident of his Island 'The Hunter'. A link between the island and the outer world, The Hunter 'represents all men and women who choose to identify with him', he says.[16] At the same time, he is the artist's avatar. Avery also identifies another character who recurs in his art, Miss Miss, as his 'anima' – his unconscious or true inner self, as opposed to his 'persona', the outer aspect of his personality. In the unconscious of the male, the anima finds expression as a feminine inner personality. The Island, says Avery, is a place where he can locate the complex and interwoven philosophical issues, thoughts and ideas in his mind, 'and rationalize them spatially as opposed to logically'.[17]

The idea of observing the Island – the world – from a separate perspective is similar in some ways to Camillo's explanation of the world in terms of the edifice of the memory theatre. As Avery has himself indicated, his main avenue of expression is not the installation itself, but the three-dimensional space that he creates in the viewer's mind through the media of drawing and sculpture. In his *Eternity Chamber* and *Eternal Forest*, in particular, he creates images that suggest a land of eternity, an unknown space, connected somehow to his imaginary island, similar to the way in which the wardrobe leads to the land of Narnia in C.S. Lewis' books. His drawings, combining precise lines drawn with a straight edge and overlapping geometrical shapes made with soft pencil, also create an enigmatic, immaterial feeling. Another character on his island, *Coscienza* (consciousness), never shows her face, which remains obscured by a large hat like that worn by a Vietnamese peasant. This also suggests that the Island is an inner, spiritual realm.

CONNECTING THE MICROCOSM AND THE MACROCOSM

Yoshitomo Nara is another artist who expresses his inner world through drawing. The essence of his art is to be found in his drawings of little girls with huge heads and eyes, holding knives, accompanied by texts that convey a venomous side to the infantile or childish, as well as pointing to the contradictions of adult society. His drawings can be seen as self-portraits reflecting his memories, his conscious and unconscious mind. They also reflect the influence of American comic books and music, which he experienced as a result of the American military base near his home, which had its own radio station. In

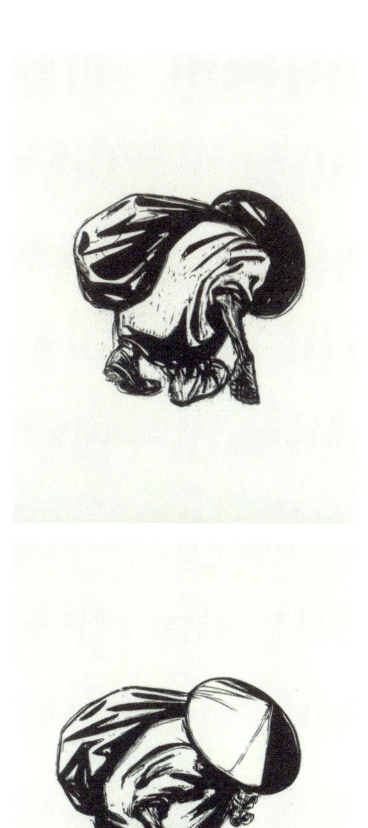

Charles Avery, *Coscienza*, 2008

2003, the drawings evolved from paintings and sculptures into a full installation, when Nara engaged in a collaborative project with the 'creative unit' graf, based in Osaka. Graf constructed a small shed, which represents Nara's childhood home, the only house on the top of the hill when he was a small boy, and visible from his school. However, during his adolescence, as Japan went through its rapid economic growth, this specific landscape disappeared and the hill became filled with new, modern-style houses. Now the image of the house remains only in his memory. Inside the shed, Nara has recreated his studio, which can be seen as a representation of his recollections and consciousness. The interior of this private space, into which the viewer can look through the windows or even sometimes enter, contains half-completed paintings, drawings, artists' materials, palettes, notepads, accessories and cigarettes, all creating a kind of monologue that communicates the artist's raw emotions and impulses, imparting a feeling of loneliness and isolation.

In its replication of an individual's memories and thoughts, Nara's installation functions in a similar way to Ilya Kabakov's 'total installations'. In 1988, when the new era of *perestroika* was already underway, Kabakov exhibited his first total installation *Ten Characters* in New York. For Kabakov, a total installation is not simply a spatial creation but also a theatre equipped to recreate social and cultural memories and experiences. He commented that unlike in the West, where objects are central, in Russia, with its shortage of material goods, space was the decisive factor. *The Man Who Flew into Space from His Apartment*, depicts a communal flat. The walls are plastered with posters and Soviet propaganda. In the centre of the room is a catapult underneath a large hole in the ceiling, from which the character has flown into space – leaping instantaneously from the microcosm to the macrocosm. Thus the various elements of Kabakov's total installation function to communicate the social and cultural context. While the man who flew into space could represent Kabakov himself in his studio, dreaming of escaping from the restraints of his society, Nara's shed, which is also the artist's studio, is more personal in its focus, presenting his mental landscape, an introverted microcosm and a small, comfortable space from which he would not wish to escape.

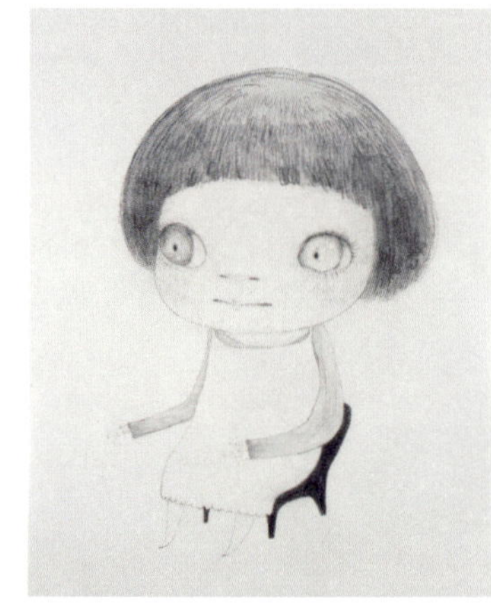

Yoshitomo Nara, *Untitled*, 2008

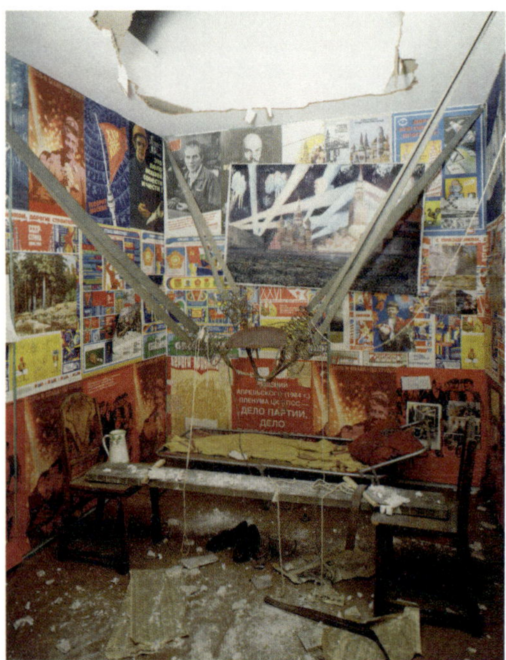

Ilya Kabakov, *The Man who Flew into Space from his Apartment*, 1988

The drawings of Keith Tyson are much more objective and extroverted. Though he employs the same two-dimensional medium of drawing, such elements as diagrams of space and, on a more quotidian level, clippings from newspapers and magazines, link his work to an astronomical, mathematical or scientific perspective on the universe. In that sense, Tyson's drawings (or paintings) that completely fill the space from floor to ceiling have something in common with Camillo's memory theatre, which attempted to bring order to the entire universe and superhuman realms, placing the viewer at their centre. This immersive quality contrasts with Nara's internal landscape, which is viewed from the outside. In Tyson's installation we find the white figure of a boy, which represents the artist's alter ego and is an embodiment of his childhood memories, while the complex diagram on his body symbolises his interconnection and relationships with the rest of the universe.

FROM THE UNIVERSE, THE FOREST AND SLEEP TO THE INFINITE

We can observe common motifs in the work of the artists discussed in this essay. One is an alter ego or avatar who shares the viewpoint of the artist. Another is the motif of an imaginary three-dimensional space resembling the theatre of memory, or undefined zones such as the cosmos, a forest, sleep or darkness. The alter egos, as agents for the artist's consciousness, live within the illusory world created by the artist but, through the mediating passageway of these zones, are able to shift back and forth between reality and illusion. An exception is Kusama, whose hallucinations caused her to experience her own life as a dot or a particle of the universe and motivated her to depict the feeling of 'releasing the ineffable into the chaos of the void'. She represents the rare case of an artist who can pass freely between illusion and reality without the need to resort to an avatar.

In reality, the introspective, spiritual dimension of the self is an infinite realm of unbounded consciousness that cannot be apprehended in its entirety. These artists offer representations of that ineffable microcosm. Given that, this indefinable zone of the microcosm – with the back of the closet or an eternity chamber as the gateway – can be seen as linked to the infinite macrocosm, whose limits also exceed our comprehension. This may indeed be the 'chaos of the void'. The double-action mechanism of victim and viewer identified by Kabakov, as well as the constant passage between reality and illusion and the simultaneous representation of subject and object in these installations, are all tied to this chaotic void. When one explores the exhibition, walking through its installations, the experience will trigger each individual's inner realm of memories, emotions and thoughts, drawing them into an even more profound zone of infinity.

NOTES

[1] Ilya Kabakov, *On the Total Installation*, Cantz Verlag, Ostfildern, 1995, p. 245.
[2] Yayoi Kusama, *Mugen no Ami Kusama Yayoi Jiden*, Sakuhinsha, Tokyo, 2002, pp. 21–22.
[3] Ibid., pp. 28–29.
[4] Ibid., pp. 24–25.
[5] Ibid.
[6] Growing up in a rigidly traditional Japanese household, Kusama has said that the education she received about sex in her adolescence, as well as the experience of meetings for an arranged marriage and of witnessing sexual intercourse when she was a child, caused her to have feelings of strong repugnance and fear associated with sex.
[7] *Chiharu Shiota*, Shiota Chiharu no Berlin Nikki, Asahi Graph, Tokyo, 2002, unpaginated.
[8] Ibid.
[9] Ibid.
[10] Gilles Deleuze and Félix Guattari, *A Thousand Plateaus: Capitalism and Schizophrenia*, University of Minnesota Press, Minneapolis, 1987 (first published 1980).
[11] Frances A. Yates, *The Art of Memory*, Pimlico, London, 1994 (first published 1966).
[12] Ibid, p. 148.
[13] Ibid.
[14] Mark Manders, interview with Marije Langelaar, 'It is disappointing that we seem to observe the world as through a membrane', Arnhem, 27 March 2001; http://www.markmanders.org
[15] Ibid.
[16] Charles Avery, in Tom Morton, 'An Interview with Charles Avery', *The Islanders: An Introduction*, Parasol Unit and Koenig Books, London, 2008, p. 157.
[17] Ibid.

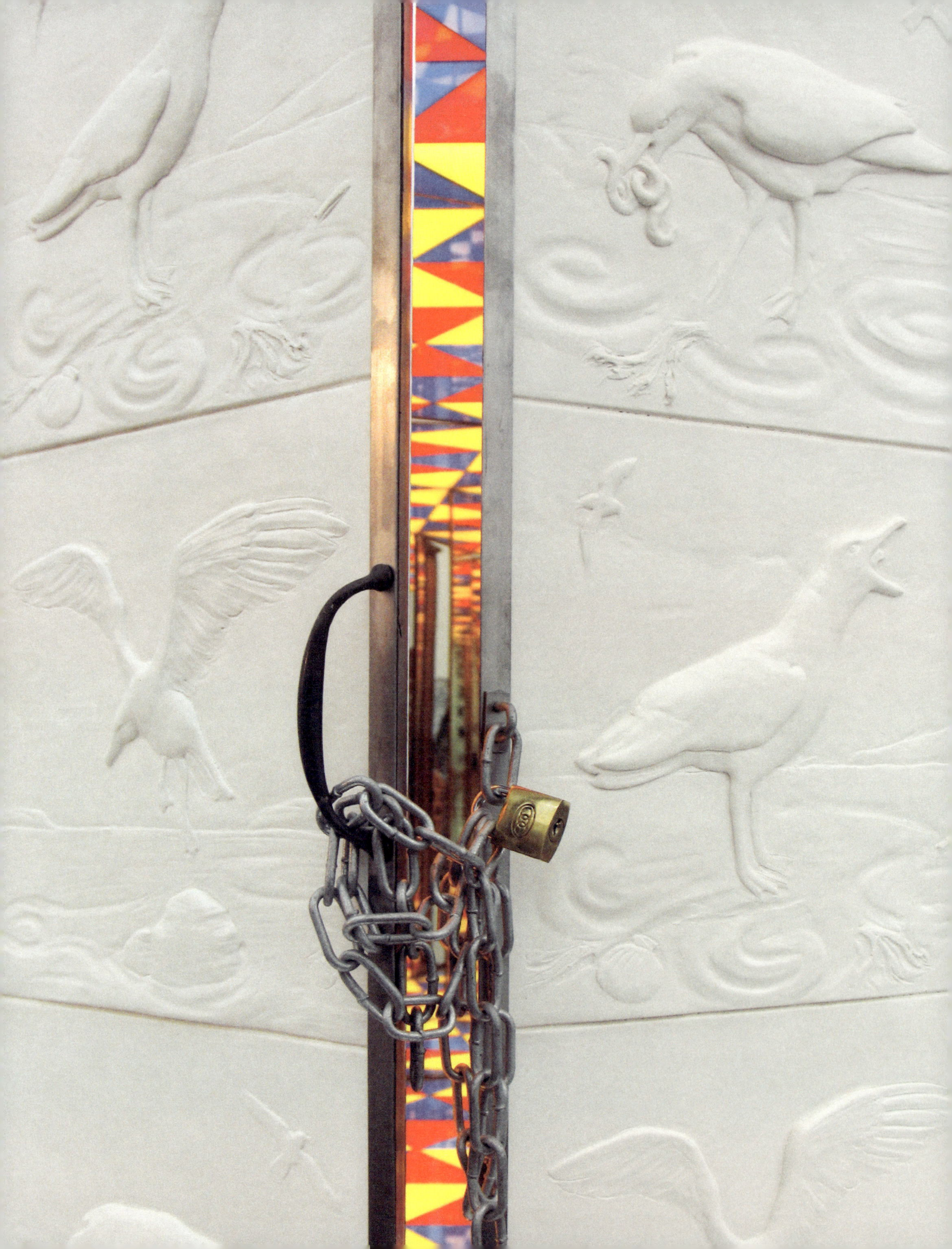

MYSTERIES

OF

THE MIND

Susan Blackmore

If I step inside my mind, do I leave the world behind? Can I turn my attention from the real world out there, to my own private inner world of thoughts, emotions and desires? It certainly feels as though I can. It seems to me, and probably to you, that 'I' am somewhere inside my own head; somewhere where I can think and feel and conjure up ideas and thoughts, and from where I look out through my eyes onto the real, objective, shared world of solid things and actual events. As I wander the galleries I am inspired with feelings and reactions. Images and thoughts well up in my mind, creating my subjective experiences – but can an artist ever convey their own mind to mine? And can I even know if they have succeeded? It *seems* as though there must be two completely different worlds: the mental world in which each person lives, feels, thinks and hopes in the privacy of their own subjective mind; and the shared, objective world full of towns, cities, galleries, works of art and the physical people who made them.

But, as we will see, scientifically this has to be nonsense. Philosophically it has to be nonsense. And even spiritually it seems to be nonsense. This puzzle – called the 'mind–body problem' – is very old, dating back to the ancient philosophers and probably beyond. It is easy to describe but apparently insoluble – at least so far.

To demonstrate the problem, take any object – this catalogue will do. Hold it up and look at it. Feel the paper as you turn it around in your hands, or stare at Yayoi Kusama's vivid red and white polka dots. By doing this you are having your own inner experience – the 'what it's like' for you to be looking at that particular shade of red, as it appears to you. No one else can see it exactly as you do in this moment. Not only is your precise physical view unique (in terms of the angle of gaze, lighting, shadows) but so too are the associations – based on your life's experience – that you make with this object. Some viewers may associate polka dots with a frightening experience; others with a favourite childhood toy. In addition, every visual system is different. Ten per cent of men are red-green colour blind: they cannot distinguish these two colours from one another. How can they imagine how red looks to me? Even more peculiar, how can I imagine what the colour red/green looks like to them? To raise an old conundrum, how can I know if your experience of red is just like my experience of turquoise? I might say 'red' because I've learned to do so, from my completely different subjective experiences. And you would never know. You could never know.

On the other hand, you happily assume that there really is a catalogue made of shiny paper with printing on it, and that if you dropped it now it would fall to the floor. You assume that other people would hear the noise of the catalogue hitting the floor, and maybe even pick it up for you. You happily assume that the other bodies you can see wandering around, and the ballons, drawings, wires and mannequins, are really there for all to see. Unlike your personal experience, they actually exist and other people can agree that they do.

How can this be? How can our private inner experiences be so different from, and yet connected to, the outer physical world? In the mid-seventeenth century, the French philosopher René Descartes struggled with the problem of mind, staring into his own experiences, doubting the existence of everything, and trying to find something to rely on. He argued that there was one thing he could not doubt: 'I think, therefore I am'. In this way he tried to get to the bottom of the problem but in the end he stuck with his intuitions and declared that there really are two kinds of 'stuff' in the world.

Today we call this concept 'Cartesian dualism'. The two kinds of stuff are extended or physical stuff (which exists in space) and mental or thinking stuff (which has no location and is private). The body is a machine made of the first type, but the mind or soul is non-physical and made of the second type; beyond space or location it can sense, think and feel. So when you look at your catalogue, the nerves in your body cause your 'soul' to experience the colour; if you then decide to drop it, the mental stuff causes your physical brain to respond and your muscles to move.

This scheme is hopeless, of course. If the two realms are totally different then one cannot affect the other – and if they interact they cannot be totally different realms. Descartes concluded that body and soul interacted in the pineal gland, but this is a cop out. The pineal gland is a physical part of the brain and there is no reason why it alone should take instructions from a non-material soul.

Cartesian dualism is false; it is doomed; it has failed. That, at least, is the opinion of almost all scientists and philosophers. And yet the vast majority of people, now and in the past, are and have been dualists. The theory has survived because it is so deep-seated – indeed, it can even be seen in very young children, who early on in infancy distinguish living things that move under their own power from inanimate things that do not. They readily attribute intentions, powers, feelings and desires to the living things, believing that they are driven by spirits or inner beings. This tendency makes sense in evolutionary terms, because we evolved to deal with other living creatures in a hostile world, yet it leads us as adults into scientific and logical lunacy.

We end up, as philosopher Gilbert Ryle so eloquently put it back in the 1940s, believing in 'the ghost in the machine', the inner self who inhabits our physical frame. Even though science has revealed that living creatures are made of matter just like everything else – that life itself can be explained by the chemistry of DNA rather than a 'life force', and that thinking goes on in the brain and emotions in the hormones – we still hang on to our ghost. Surely I am distinct from my body! I am the mind that inhabits my body! That's how we feel.

When psychology dawned, in the late nineteenth century, the mind–body problem soon returned. In 1890, William James, one of the great founders of psychology, described the 'chasm' between the inner and the outer worlds, the 'fathomless abyss' that separates mind from the mere motions of matter: '"A motion became a feeling!" – no phrase that our lips can frame is so devoid of apprehensible meaning.'

Gaze at Pipilotti Rist's smooth, evocative ear, or let yourself be drawn into Chiharu Shiota's entangled dresses, and you will see what he means. How can my perceptual experience or my strangled, trapped desire to run away be caused by the motions of molecules in my brain?

The fundamental difficulty of this problem was arguably responsible for the dark ages of psychology that lasted for most of the twentieth century. On the one hand Freud's baseless speculations about the nature of mind were wildly popular and distracted psychology from making any real progress. On the other hand, experimental psychology turned to behaviourism, a paradigm that successfully measured observable behaviours but at the cost of rejecting talk of inner worlds or minds. As more was learned about how the brain works, the concept of 'mind' was recast as 'what brains do', but that still left one more ghostly mystery, and it was simply not mentioned. For most of the twentieth century, including when I was a student in the 1970s, you could not mention the word 'consciousness'.

Then, finally, after all those dreary decades, the 'C' word was welcomed back. At last we could talk about and investigate mental imagery, subjectivity, imagination and creativity. At last scientists could tackle the mystery of consciousness without being laughed at.

But – of course – they hit the threat of dualism all over again. Paradoxically, the more we learn about the brain, the worse the problem becomes. We now have brain scans, single-cell recording techniques, transcranial magnetic stimulation, and many other ways of finding out how the brain works. We can peer into a living brain and see millions of cells communicating with each other through billions of connections, making ever-changing patterns and complicated recursive loops. We can detect specialised areas that do certain jobs, such as understanding language or constructing speech, seeing colour, recognising shapes, hearing tones, controlling fine muscle movements, planning actions or feeling pain. There are tiny brain parts that detect touch to the tip of your nose or move your right big toe, and a whole system dedicated to controlling eye movements. Because we are social animals we even have a special 'face area' devoted to detecting and recognising faces – which is why we are so much better at detecting tiny differences between human faces than much bigger differences between plants or rocks or birds.

But where does consciousness come in? The more we learn, the less role there seems to be for anything other than more brain cells, more recursive loops and more intricate connections. If this is all there is to our brains, why does it feel like anything at all? If we are just very cleverly designed machines why do we have the unique feeling of being 'ourselves'?

This is the modern version of the mind–body problem, now called the 'hard problem' of consciousness. David Chalmers was right at the forefront of the return of 'consciousness' when in 1994, as a young philosopher of just 28, he gave a paper at one of the first-ever consciousness conferences. As he tells the story, he planned to deliver a complicated philosophical argument that few people would probably have understood, so he prefaced it by clarifying what he was talking about. He didn't want to talk about the 'easy problems' of perception, learning, memory (all the things psychology and neuroscience were doing so well at exploring and explaining at that time) but the 'hard problem' of 'consciousness itself' – the problem of subjective experience, or 'what it's like to be me'. As Chalmers describes it, the hard problem is how subjective experiences can arise from the objective activity of the brain. Few remember the rest of his paper, but the term 'hard problem' stuck. Every scientist and philosopher working on consciousness now wants to solve the hard problem.

There are many theories and much confusion. Some think the problem is so hard that a really wacky solution is required. Among quantum theories, for example, mathematician Roger Penrose proposes that consciousness depends on quantum coherence in the microtubules of brain cells. If you know little about quantum mechanics (which is true of most of us) and little about the micro-structure of brain cells, this may sound impressive, but really it only substitutes one mystery for another. The philosopher Patricia Churchland describes this idea as 'about as explanatorily powerful as pixie dust in the synapses'. Then there are theories involving complex feedback loops, special brain areas and special processes. But the hard problem lurks untouched. Why should these processes, or these areas, give rise to subjective experience – to the very turquoise-ness of that colour, to the hurting-ness of pain – when they are just more physical activities in a brain?

Some think we are best to press on without worrying about the hard problem. Until his death in 2004, Francis Crick devoted himself to two great mysteries: that of life itself (he was awarded the Nobel Prize for discovering the structure of DNA in the 1950s), and that of consciousness. He began the hunt for the 'neural correlates of consciousness' (NCCs), the brain processes that correlate with conscious, as opposed to unconscious, perceptions. In the famous ambiguous image 'my wife and my mother-in-law', you are conscious either of the old woman's face, or of the young woman's face – you cannot see both at once. The purpose of searching for the NCCs is to see which parts of the brain's visual system change when the experience changes and which stay the same. These areas have indeed been identified, yet this still cannot explain how some brain events become conscious while others do not. Crick was undeterred, saying that science always starts with correlations before moving on to causes, and that eventually the hard problem will be solved.

Other theories skirt around the problem. For example, the popular 'Global Workspace' theory proposed by psychologist Bernard Baars argues that most information is processed unconsciously but some makes it into the 'global workspace', an area or process of the brain similar to working memory, whose contents are broadcast to the rest of the (unconscious) brain. This workspace is the theatre of the mind in which some things make it onto the stage, are lit by the power of attention, and so become conscious. There is evidence that the brain might be organised in this way, but what about my inner subjective experience? Why should the information being processed on the stage be different from the rest? Why does being broadcast turn some neural impulses into my experiences while others remain just that – signals passing along nerves in a physical brain?

Part of the appeal of Global Workspace theory is that it fits our intuitions. Our minds feel like a mental theatre. It's easy to imagine that somewhere in my head I am sitting and watching my own inner screen, onto which I can project images and fantasies – or I can create new ideas, or open my eyes and gaze out onto the exterior world. I feel as though I can turn the spotlight of my attention onto the stage of my mind and light up the things I want to think about. But is this really what is going on?

'No!' says the philosopher Daniel Dennett in his classic 1991 book *Consciousness Explained*. Rather, these intuitions merely lead us into imagining what he calls the 'Cartesian theatre'. Everybody says they reject Cartesian dualism, but in fact they still cling to the idea of an inner place where consciousness happens for the sake of 'me' – the conscious observer. They then go looking for the brain processes that correlate with this non-existent place. This is nonsense, he says, not least because of the way the brain is organised. There is no central place in which consciousness could happen, or where 'I' could sit and receive its impressions or give out the orders. The brain is a massively parallel system with information flowing around in all directions, for multiple purposes, all at once. It never all comes together to make the experiences I think I'm having. The show, the theatre and its inner observer are all illusions.

Think about the visual system. This is not really one system, but instead about forty separate systems doing different jobs. Among these are two great rivers of information: the dorsal stream (which processes incoming images extremely fast so as to coordinate quick actions) and the ventral stream (which, much more slowly, works out what it is you are seeing). This means that you can catch a ball using one stream before the other even knows it is a ball; you can jump out of someone's way before you've seen them as a person; you can reach out to touch a sculpture with your fingers accurately positioned before you have consciously seen its shape. But it doesn't feel like that!

Or take another example; say you decide to do something spontaneously and of your own free will. You might choose to raise your catalogue up in the air – go on, do it now, and do it several times to get the feel of acting voluntarily. It feels as though you first decide to act, and then the action follows – as though the inner you makes the conscious decision and then the body follows. But this isn't what happens at all. Many experiments, especially those done by the neuroscientist Ben Libet in the 1980s, show that brain activity leading to the action begins up to half a second before you get the feeling of wanting to move. In other words the brain gets on with its decisions long before you have the thought 'I'm going to lift my arm now'. The way it feels, and the way it is, are totally different.

Here, I think, lies the heart of the mystery. Our strong intuitions about the nature of consciousness lead us astray. Scientists and philosophers, as well as everybody else, find themselves making all sorts of false assumptions about their own minds. We can't resist thinking that there is some kind of inner self who is the source of creativity, who makes decisions, who is the subject of experiences and persists through a lifetime witnessing the ever-changing stream of consciousness. So they search for the stream of consciousness in the brain and – surprise, surprise – cannot find it.

Could the self – and, indeed, free will and even consciousness – all be illusions? I think so. That is not to say that they don't exist or that there are no experiences, but rather that experiences are not what they appear to be. If this is so where should our investigations go from here? Alongside our developing science I have begun to think we need to try something else.

Long ago, before I began working on the science of consciousness, I took up Zen meditation. Zen is a branch of Buddhism that appealed to me because it has little dogma or ritual, does not demand that you believe anything on faith, and emphasises working hard at meditation in order to see how things really are. According to these teachings the self is illusory – which is not to say it doesn't exist, but rather that it is not what we think it is – it has no permanence and no separate existence. Duality is illusory.

There are wonderful parallels between science and Zen. Both claim that our ordinary view is illusory, dualism is false and that the self is not separate from the physical world. Of course, there are also differences: science seeks to understand and intervene in the world, whereas Zen seeks freedom from suffering. Yet they have stumbled upon the same ideas.

Could each illuminate the other? I have come to think that we will never solve the problem of consciousness without putting our intuitions aside and looking again – really deeply – at our own experiences. And if we try hard enough, or in the right way, is it possible to leap out of the Cartesian theatre, to throw out the ghost in the machine? Might it not be possible to avoid the lure of dualism and see a way through the mystery?

I decided to have a go. I set aside time for several solitary retreats, in which I spent most of every day meditating on a series of questions. Hour after hour I sat and watched as the mind played its tricks, flitting from this to that, watching things and naming them, grasping at sounds and sights, but ultimately calming down to empty quietness. Then I asked the questions: Am I conscious now? What was I conscious of a moment ago? Who is asking the question? I wouldn't claim that this way I can solve Chalmers' 'hard problem' (in fact, I don't think that problem even makes sense) but I would say this has given me a totally different way of thinking about the mind.

In deep calmness the distinction between me and the world goes away. There really is no inner and outer, no subjective and objective. Sometimes in the midst of painting, composing or sculpting, artists get into a special state called 'flow' in which the work seems to be doing itself and the creator and the created merge. Yet when they return to 'ordinary' life, the Cartesian illusion proves as powerful as ever.

Consciousness is said to be the greatest mystery facing science today. We seem nowhere near to solving this mystery, and no one knows which path or method or investigation will eventually pay off. Yet surely arts, science, philosophy and spiritual practice can all contribute something as we try to grasp what is at once the most obvious, and yet the most elusive, of phenomena: our own minds.

ARTISTS

CHARLES AVERY

Charles Avery was born in 1973 in Oban, Scotland. His childhood was spent on the Hebridean island of Mull, which he has acknowledged as being 'the total basis of my subconscious'. Avery creates drawings, charts, sculptures and texts that combine to form museum-type displays. Few of his influences come from the arena of fine art; instead, his imagination has been touched by a diverse assortment of writers, artists and philosophers, including Jonathan Swift, William Blake, George Bernard Shaw, P.G. Wodehouse, J.D. Salinger, Jorge Luis Borges, Joseph Beuys, Woody Allen and Ludwig Wittgenstein. In 2007, Avery was one of six artists selected to represent Scotland at the 52nd Venice Biennale, as part of the *Scotland and Venice* exhibition. His work was shown in *Altermodern*, the fourth Tate Triennial, in 2009. He lives and works in London.

Untitled (One-armed Snake), 2009

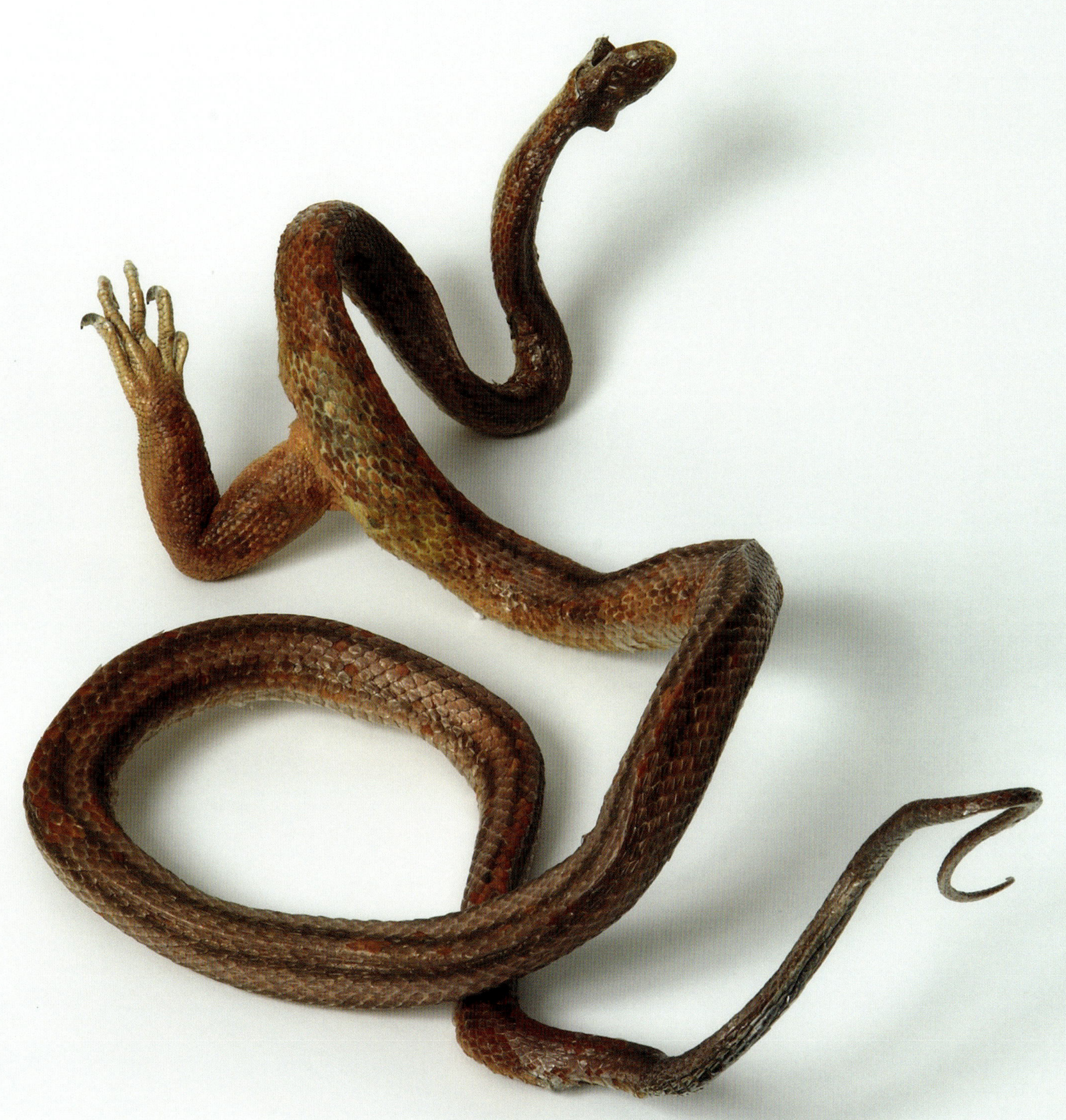

Since 2004, Avery's work has focused on a single, epic project, *The Islanders*. Described by the artist as a 'philosophical allegory', this is an encyclopaedic investigation of an imaginary island and everything it contains – its people, customs, mythology, topography, human history and natural history – as seen through the eyes of an explorer. The anonymous protagonist is also a hunter, whose elusive quarry is a mythical beast which no-one has ever seen. In periodic breaks from his never-ending quest for this creature, the explorer brings documentation and material evidence from the Island back to the known world. Avery's installation for *Walking in My Mind* consists of one such consignment, which is displayed at various points inside the gallery and on one of the outdoor sculpture terraces. Besides a hemispherical map of the Island, there are drawings that give us glimpses of the Island's landscape and its human inhabitants, plus an *Eternity Chamber* and specimens of the Island's bizarre fauna. Two of these creatures – a one-armed snake and a bejewelled hare – are products of a sort of 'rogue' taxidermy, like objects from a Renaissance cabinet of curiosities or a Victorian freak show, while the stone-mice are, as Avery explains, 'part rodent, part mineral', and it is difficult to distinguish them from real stones. The *Eternity Chamber* belongs to the Island's Cult of the Gulls, whose insane leader's extreme longevity is attributed to his having once witnessed eternity. The kiosk's monochrome exterior is covered with images of seagulls. Inside, the mirrored walls reflect the brilliantly patterned floor and ceiling, presenting a dazzling illusion of infinity. But we are only allowed to glance at this vision of eternity through a crack in the padlocked doors; if we were to enter the chamber, Avery warns, we would be driven mad.

foreground:
Untitled (Bejewelled Hare), 2009

background:
Untitled (The Three Trees), 2009 (detail)

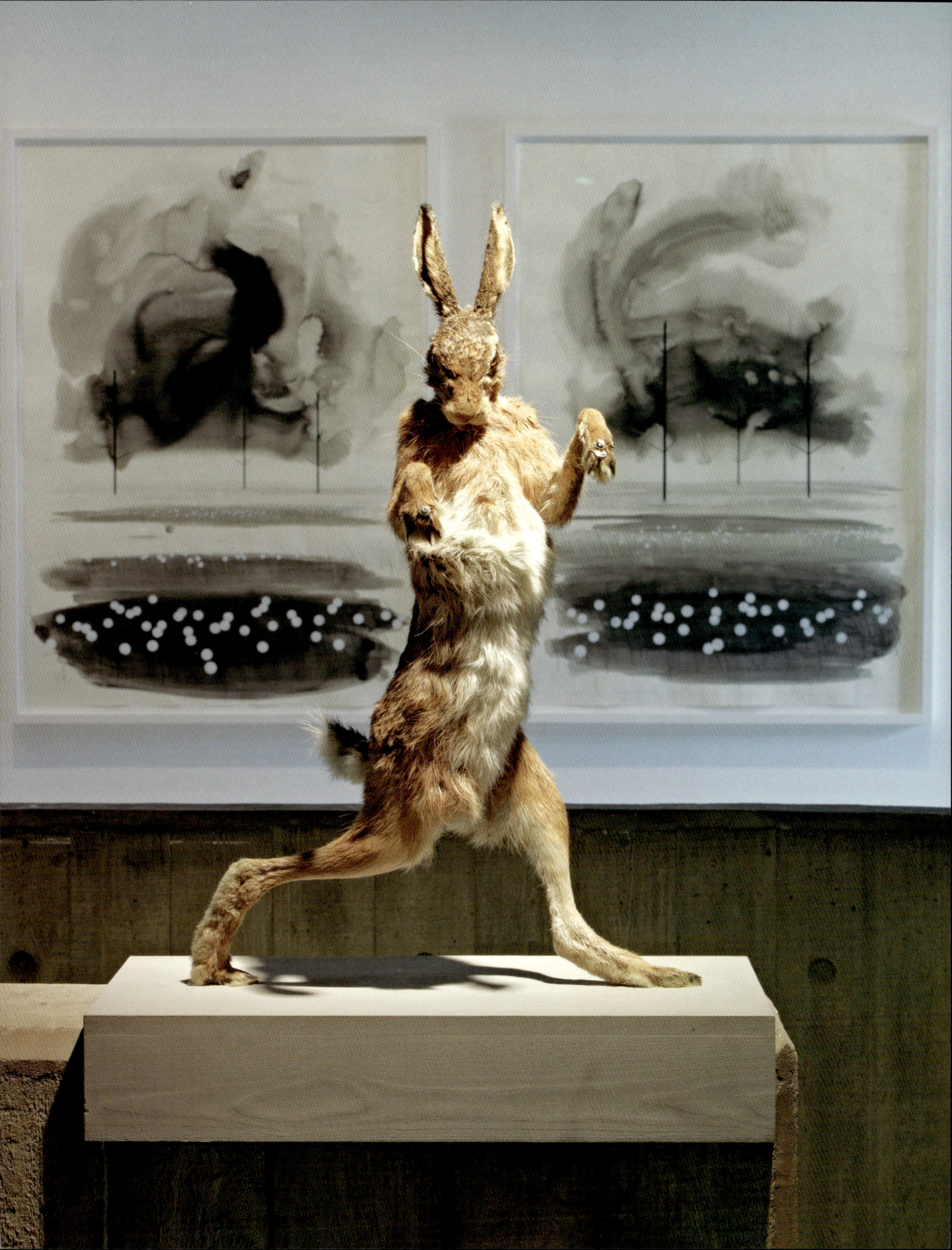

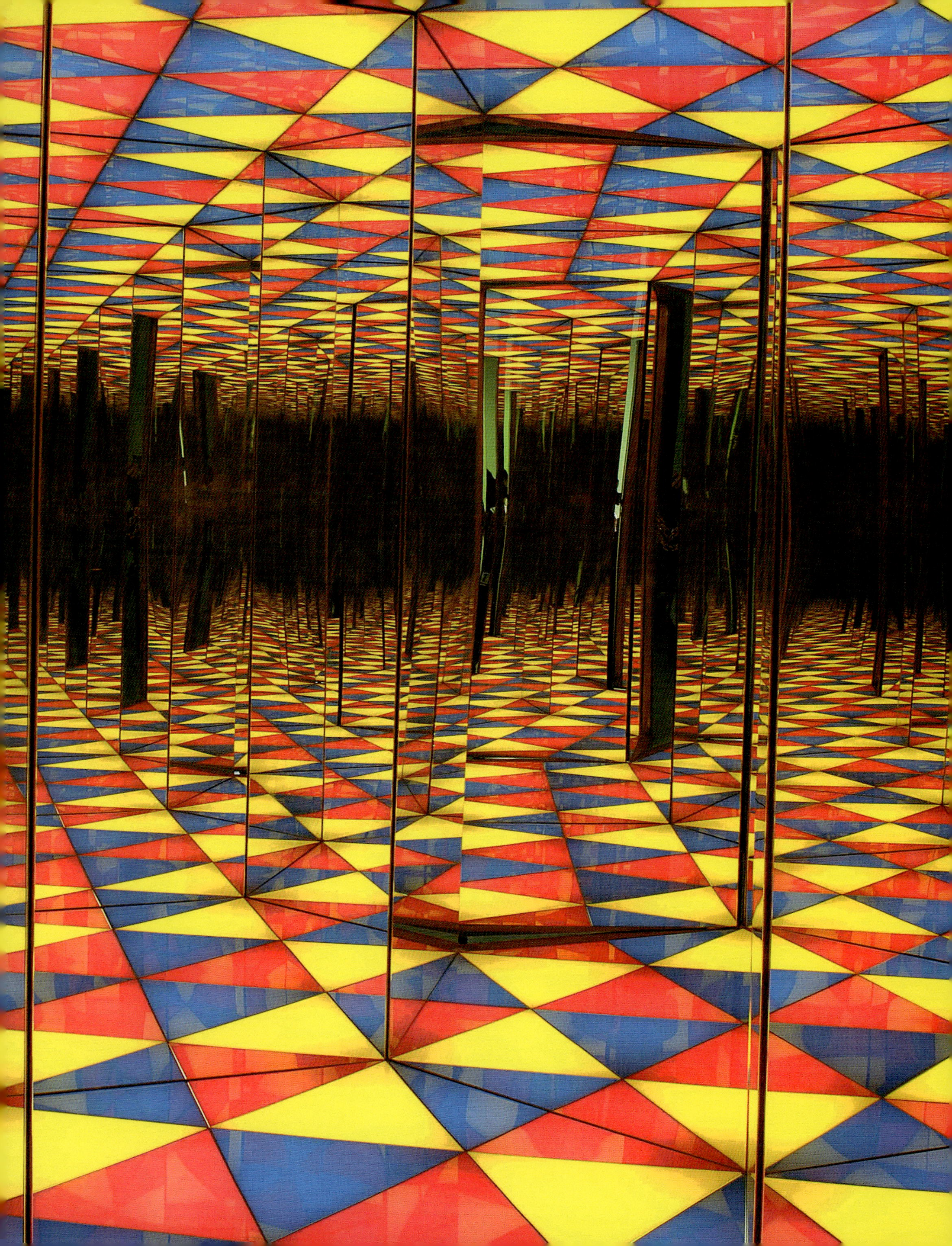

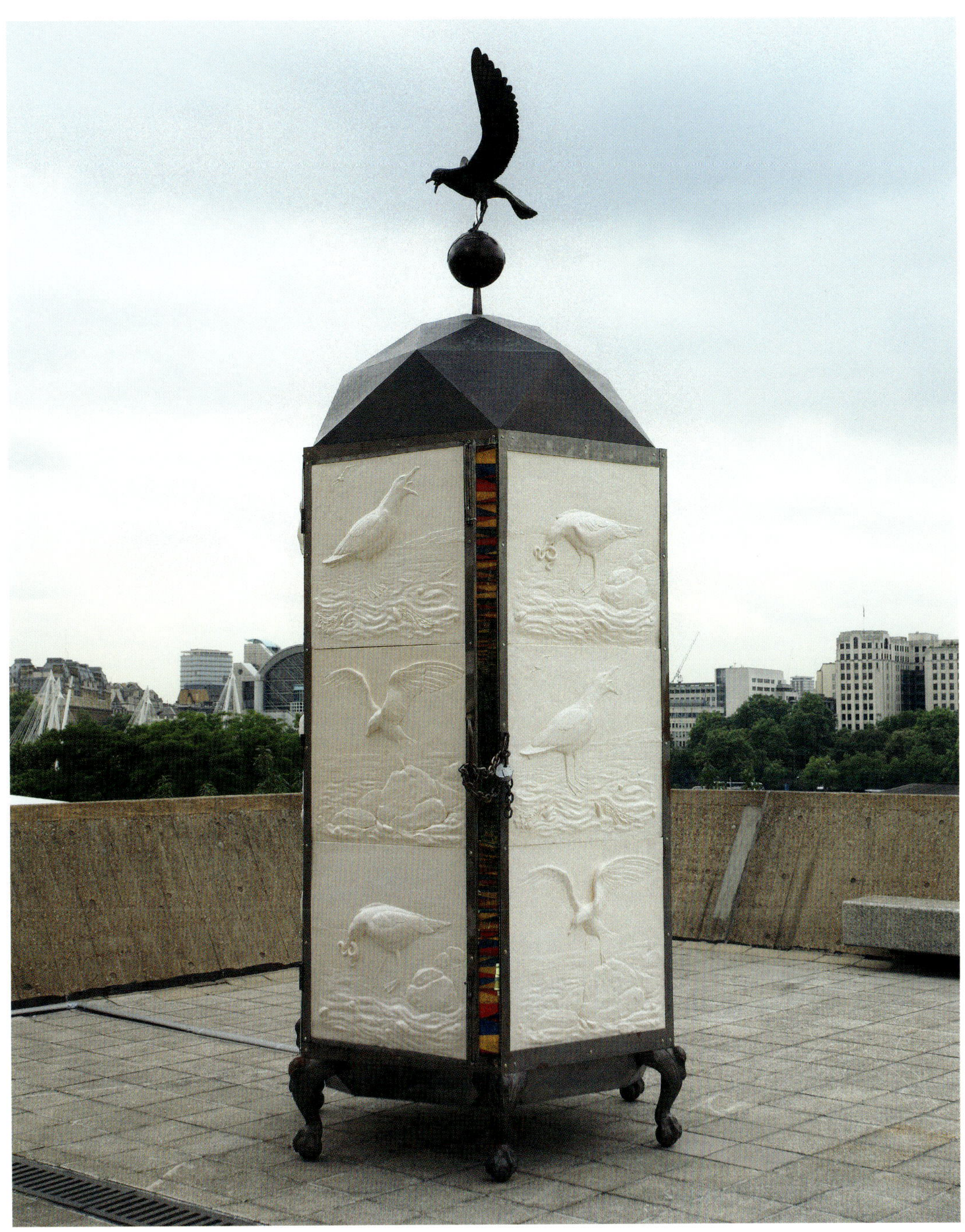

Untitled (Eternity Chamber), 2007

opposite:
Untitled (Eternity Chamber),
2007 (detail)

following page:
Installation views with *Untitled (Hat no.3)*, 2009 and *Stone-mice*, 2008 in the foreground

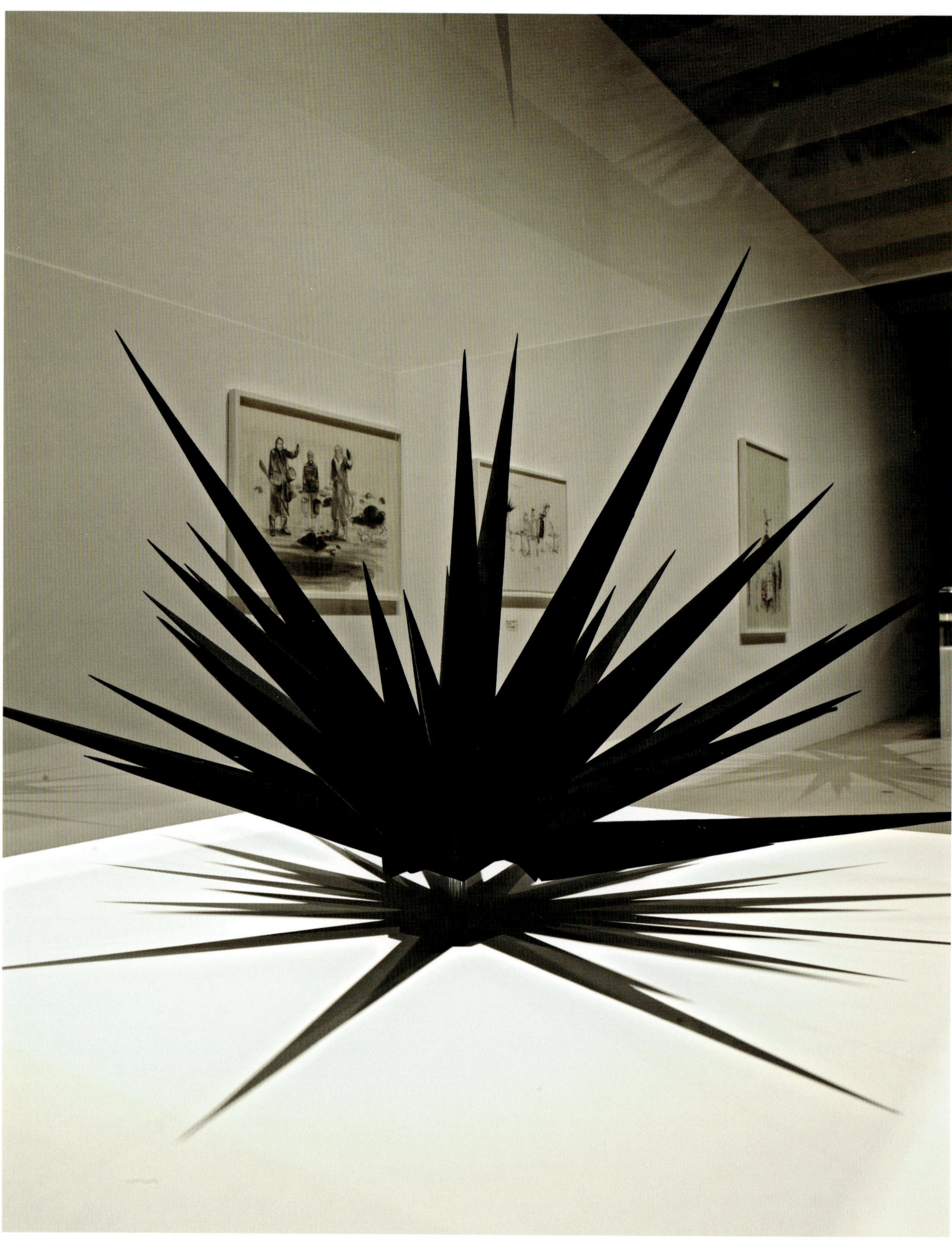

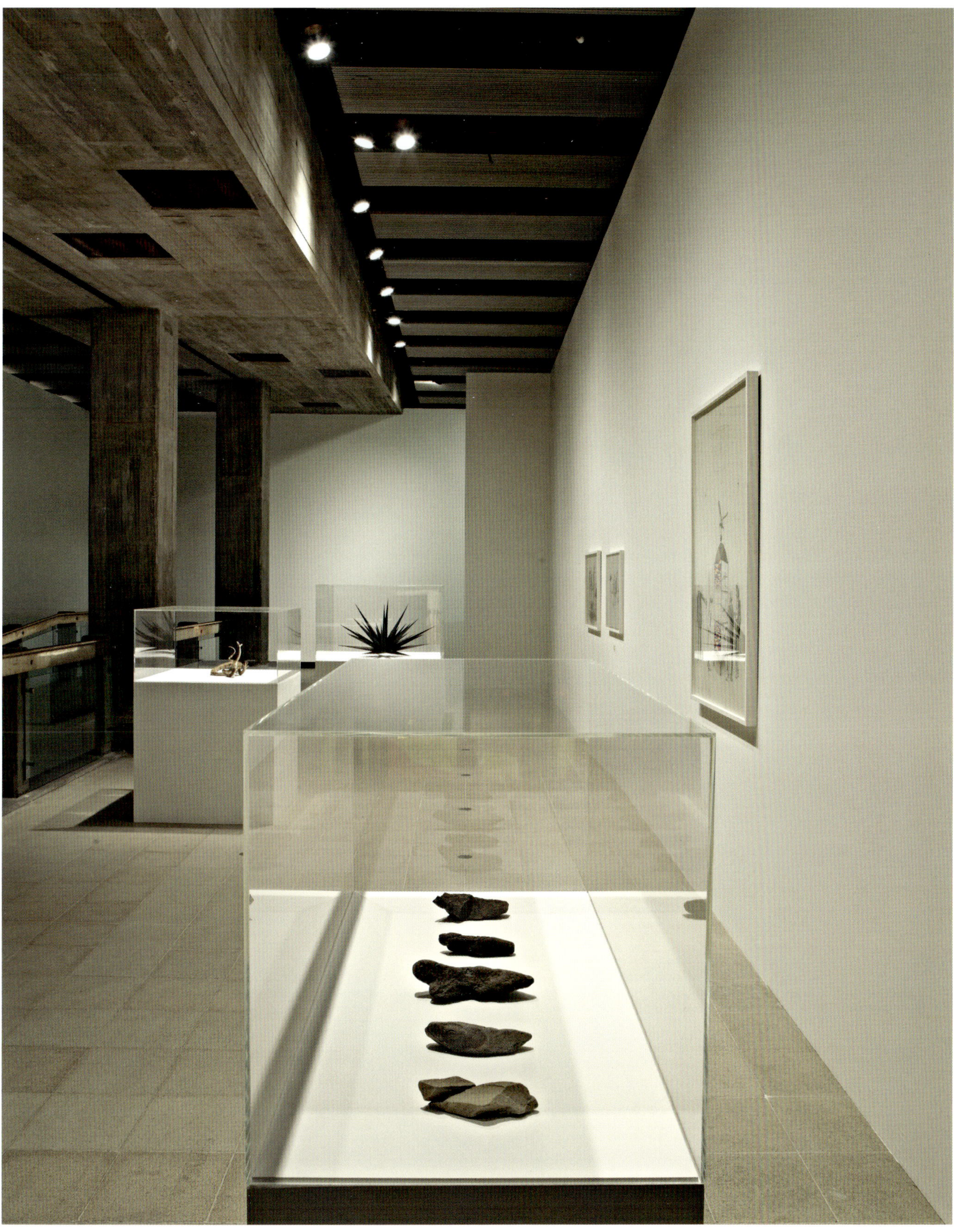

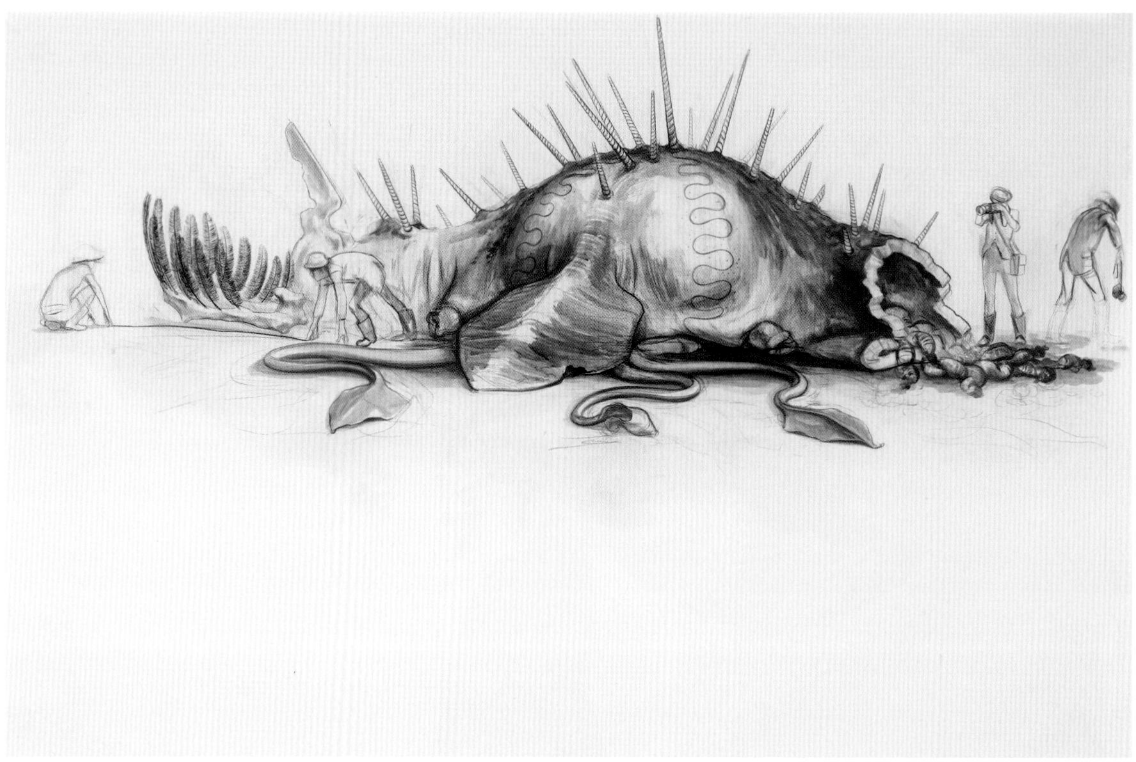

'Since I first came to the Island I have trodden the extent of
it, from Descartes' Axiom across the cold northern Plane,
through the alleyways of Onomatopoeia.

I have the trust of the Riders of the Invisible Reigns, as I do
the junkies and pushers who stalk the tourists.

I have remembered what I have seen in drawings and what I
have heard-say in writings. I have imported many specimens
and artefacts in order to evince the substance of that place.

Yet the drawings are but picture postcards of an ever-changing
world. The specimens are as fossils of their former selves once
expatriated from their realm. Subjected to the harsh light
of Reality the grass withers and dries and the Stone-mouse
becomes merely a stone that looks like a mouse.

I cannot tell you how the Island really is – I have no idea – I
can state only the facts as I perceive them. You must be satisfied
with this or you must travel there yourself sometime, and see
these beings in their natural environment, for the place is
utterly subjective.'

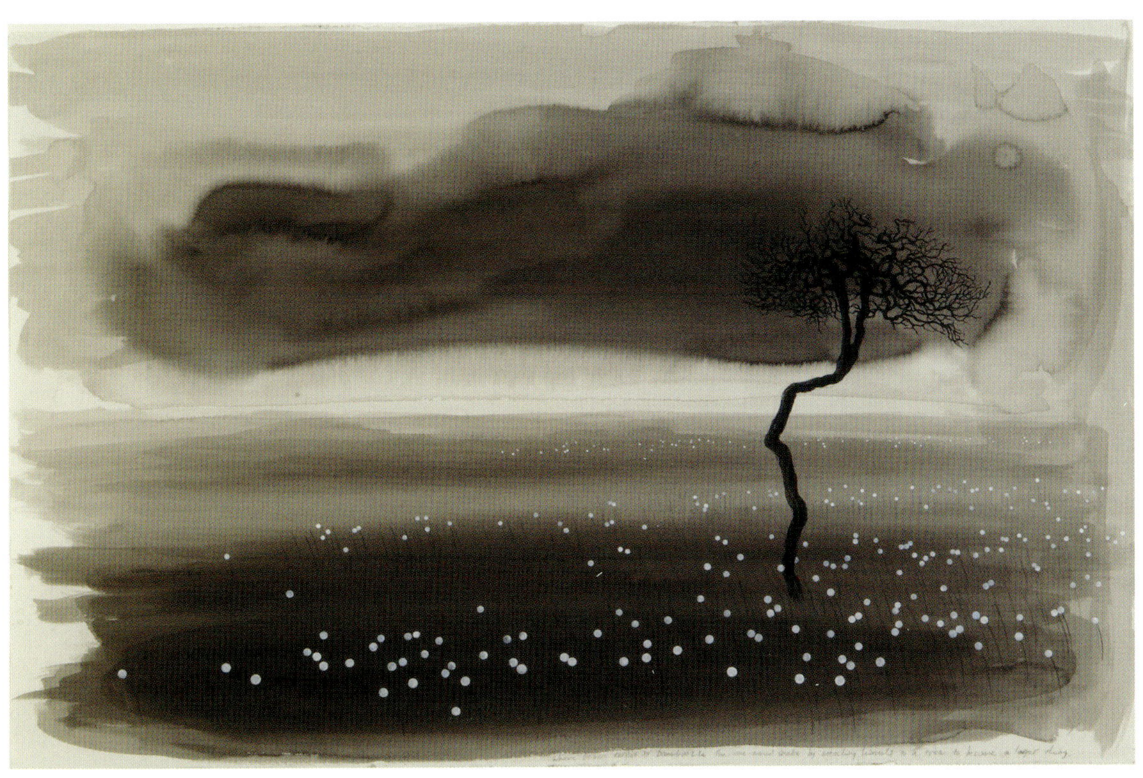

*Untitled (The Tree where Aeaen
sought to bamboozle the One-Armed
Snake)*, 2009

opposite:
*Untitled (Lionel Leslie's
Leviathan)*, 2009

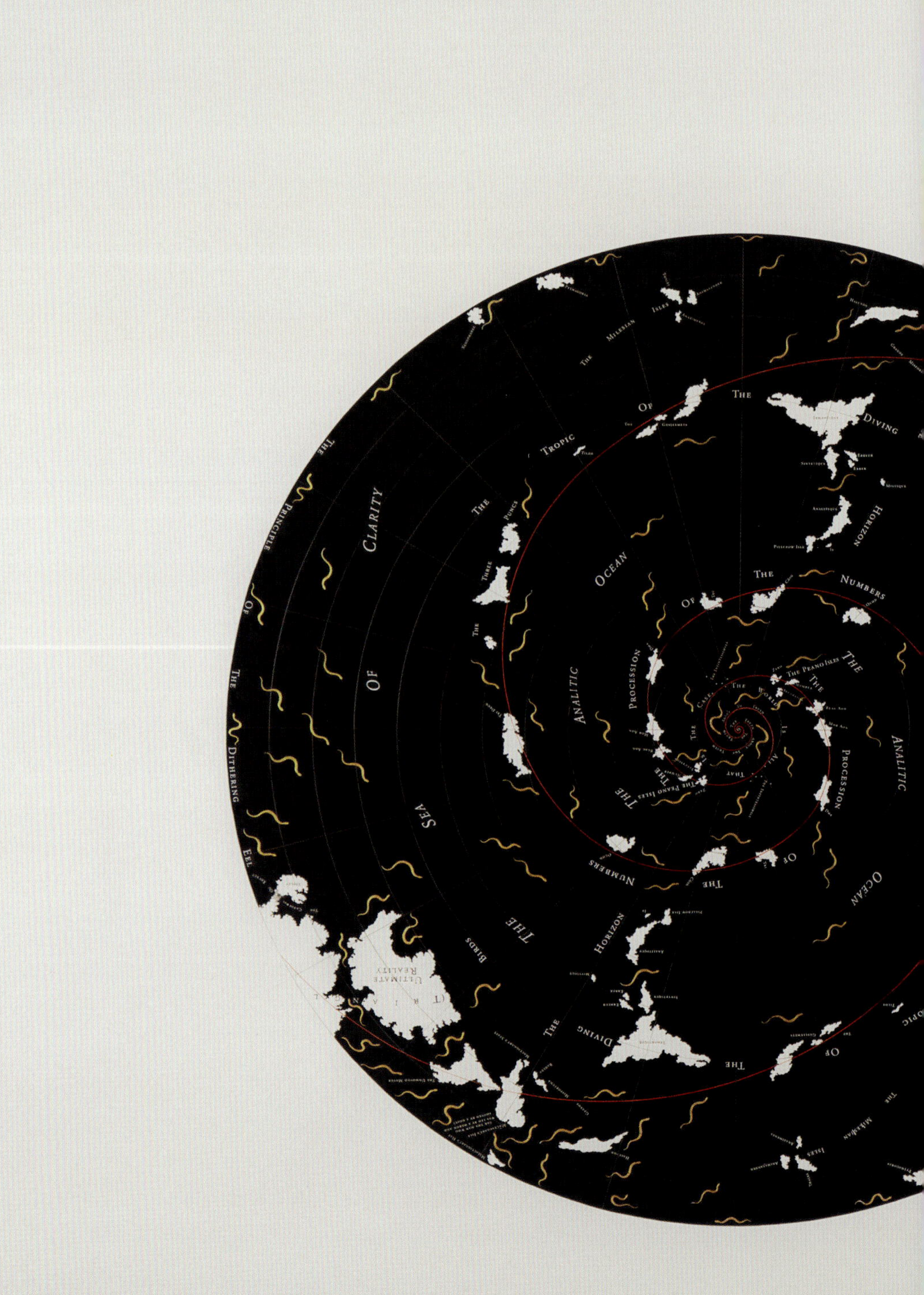
THE DIVING
TROPIC OF
THE MILESIAN ISLES
CLARITY
THE PRINCIPLE
OCEAN OF
THE HORIZON
NUMBERS
ANALITIC
PROCESSION
THE DITHERING
THE PRAND ISLES
ANALITIC PROCESSION
SEA
OF
EEL
NUMBERS
THE
THE BIRDS
HORIZON
THE ULTIMATE REALITY
DIVING
OCEAN
THE
OF

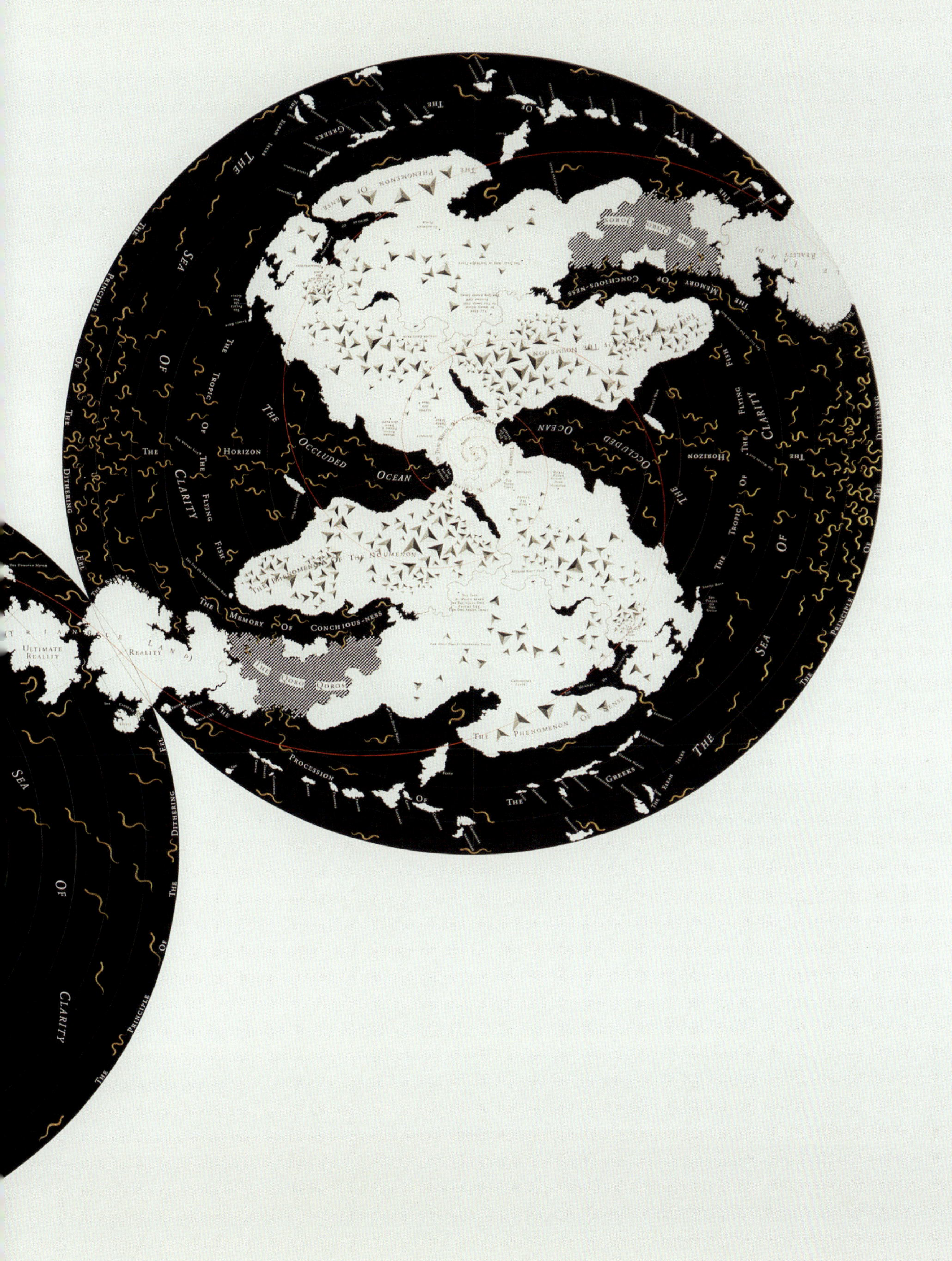
THE SEA OF PRINCIPLE OF CLARITY
THE TROPIC OF HORIZON
THE CLARITY
THE FLYING FISH
THE DITHERING EEL
THE OCCLUDED OCEAN
THE NOUMENON
THE MEMORY OF CONCHIOUS-NESS
THE PHENOMENON OF SENSE
THE GREEKS
ULTIMATE REALITY
REALITY
TRIANGLE LAND
THE PROCESSION OF
OCCLUDED OCEAN
HORIZON
THE SEA OF DITHERING EEL
THE PRINCIPLE OF CLARITY

THOMAS HIRSCHHORN

Thomas Hirschhorn was born in 1957 in Bern, Switzerland.
Before becoming an artist in the mid-1980s, he trained as a
graphic designer at the Schule für Gestaltung in Zurich. In
1984 he moved to France, intending to join the Grapus design
collective, a Marxist group that aimed to combine graphic
excellence with a social conscience. After working with them
for half a day, he realised that they – like all graphic designers
– had to carry out their clients' orders, whereas he wanted to
be free; responsible for his own work. His transition to 'artist'
took several years. Since then, many of his projects – such
as altars and kiosks dedicated to writers and artists – have
been intended for public spaces, while the larger monuments
to his chosen philosophers (for instance the *Bataille Monument*,
made for *Documenta 11* at Kassel in 2002) have involved
interactions with the communities in which he was working.
In 2009, he created the *Bijlmer Spinoza Festival*, a collaborative
multimedia art project based on Spinoza's *Ethics*, which was
made in co-operation with people living in the Bijlmer area of
Amsterdam. He lives and works in Paris, France.

following pages:
Cavemanman, 2002 (details)

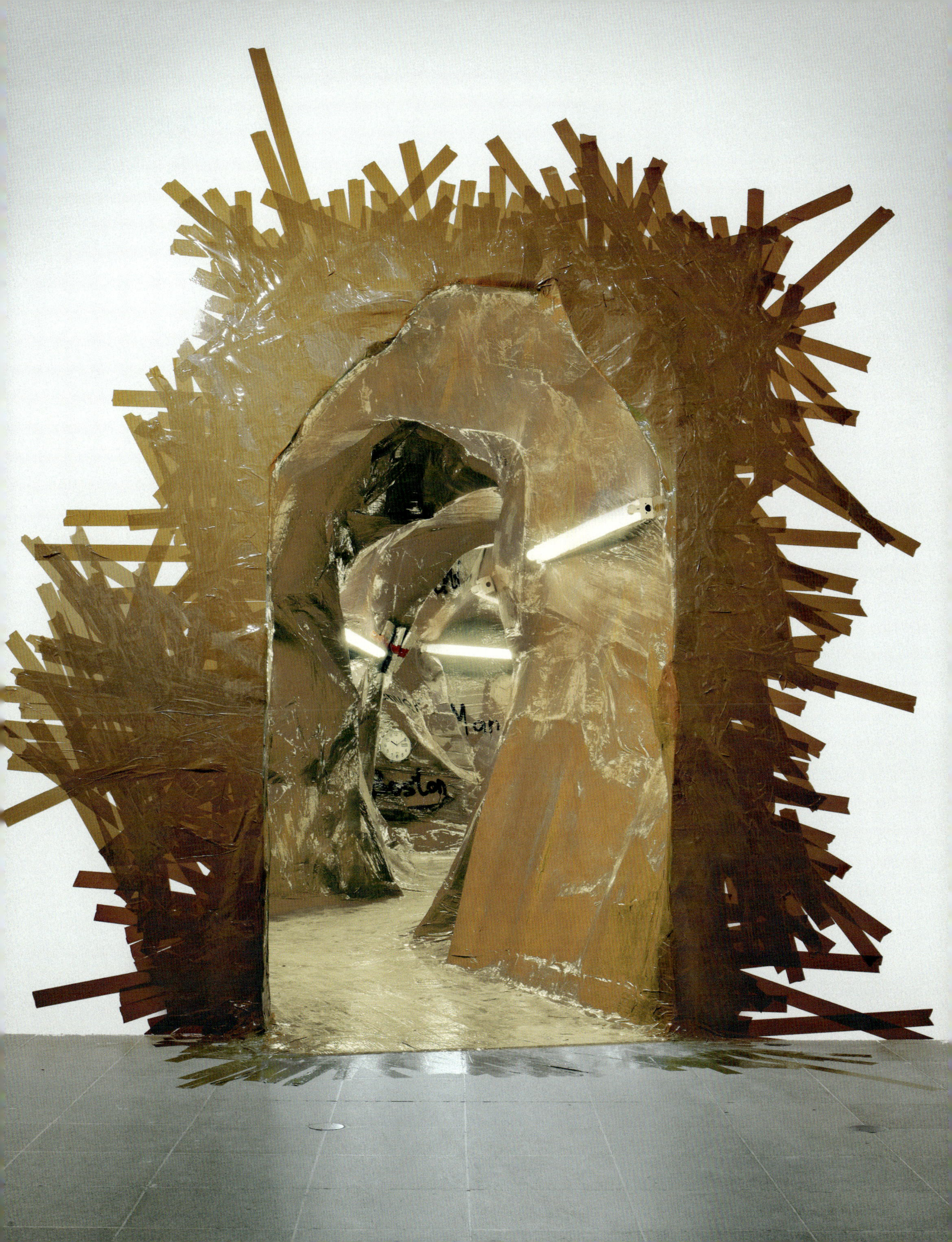

Originally shown at the Barbara Gladstone Gallery in New York, and since redisplayed in various international exhibitions, *Cavemanman* (2002) is a sprawling complex of caves and linking tunnels made from cardboard and glossy brown packing tape which, like all Hirschhorn's materials, have been chosen because they are things 'everybody knows and uses in their everyday life, not for doing art'. Each of the four caverns is crammed with information of different sorts and peopled by wired-up, foil-covered shop dummies and cardboard cutouts, the floor littered with empty drink cans and fallen tape-and-cardboard rocks. One of the caves is given over to media images of 'people at work'. Another houses a plethora of identical clock faces from different cities across the globe, all of which tell the same hour, minute and date, as if time has stood still all over the world. Further in, other spaces are devoted to a collection of hugely enlarged copies of volumes such as *Class Warfare, Justice, Can We Live Together?, Culture and Equality, Oppression and Liberty*. Normal-sized books line a fourth cave, a bedroom with pin-ups and posters on the ceiling and a television showing a film about Lascaux II – the replica of the famous French caves made when the original site was closed to tourists in 1963. The innermost space is covered in graffiti; the words '1 Man = 1 Man' are repeated obsessively and insistently all over the walls and ceiling. Everywhere, floors are uneven and the tunnels and caves are illuminated by harsh strip lighting. Some of the tunnels are plastered over with photocopied excerpts from philosophical writings and articles about social justice. Here and there are bundles of fake dynamite, some attached to books and some to bodies, giving the impression that the whole cave system is – or was – the lair of some reclusive and paranoid philosopher who has left it booby-trapped. At the same time, the individual chambers correspond to the four major lobes of the cerebral cortex, the 'grey matter' of the human brain.

following page:
Thomas Hirschhorn, Map of
Cavemanman for the Hayward
Gallery installation, 2009

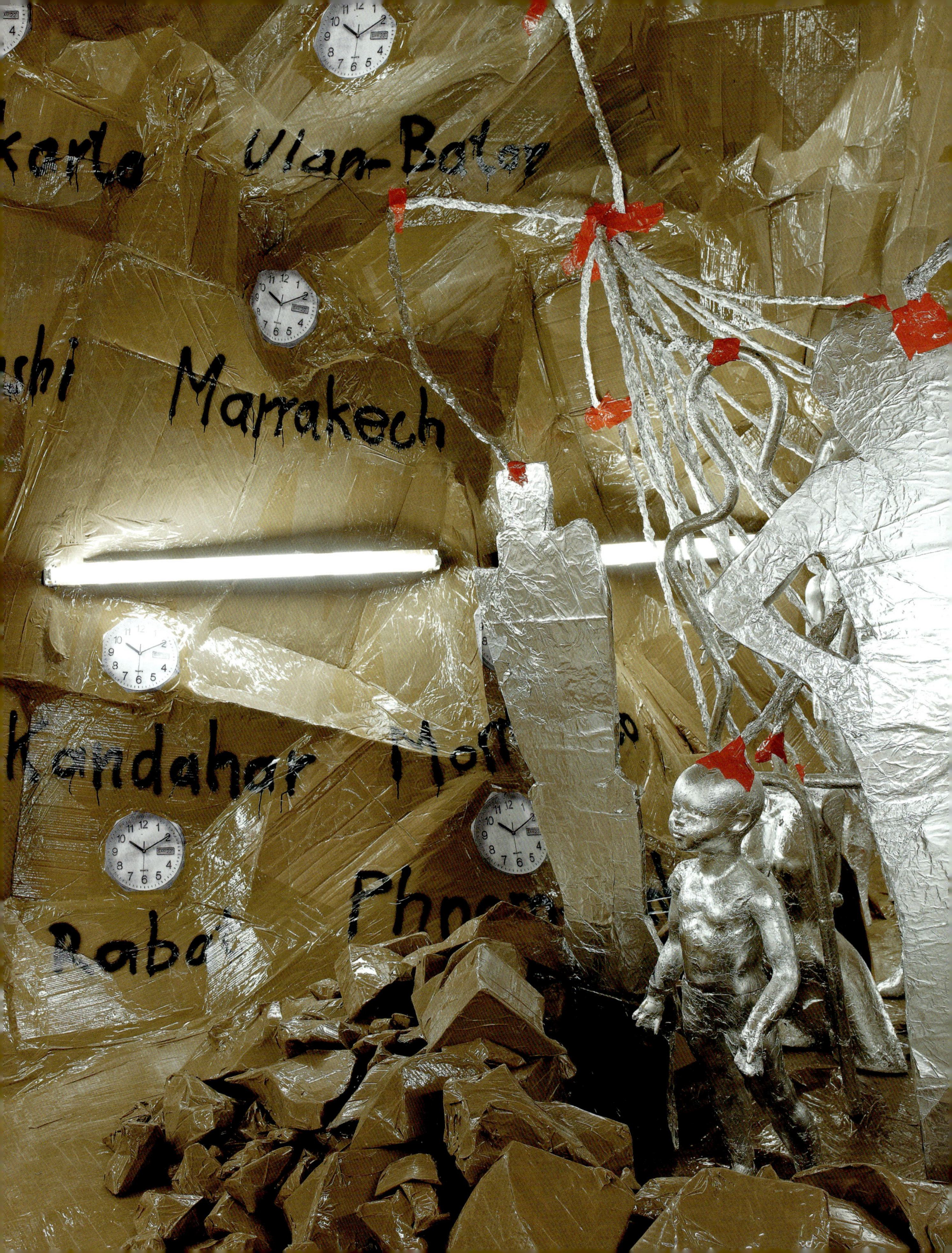

Ulan-Bator
Marrakech
Kandahar
Rabat
Phnom

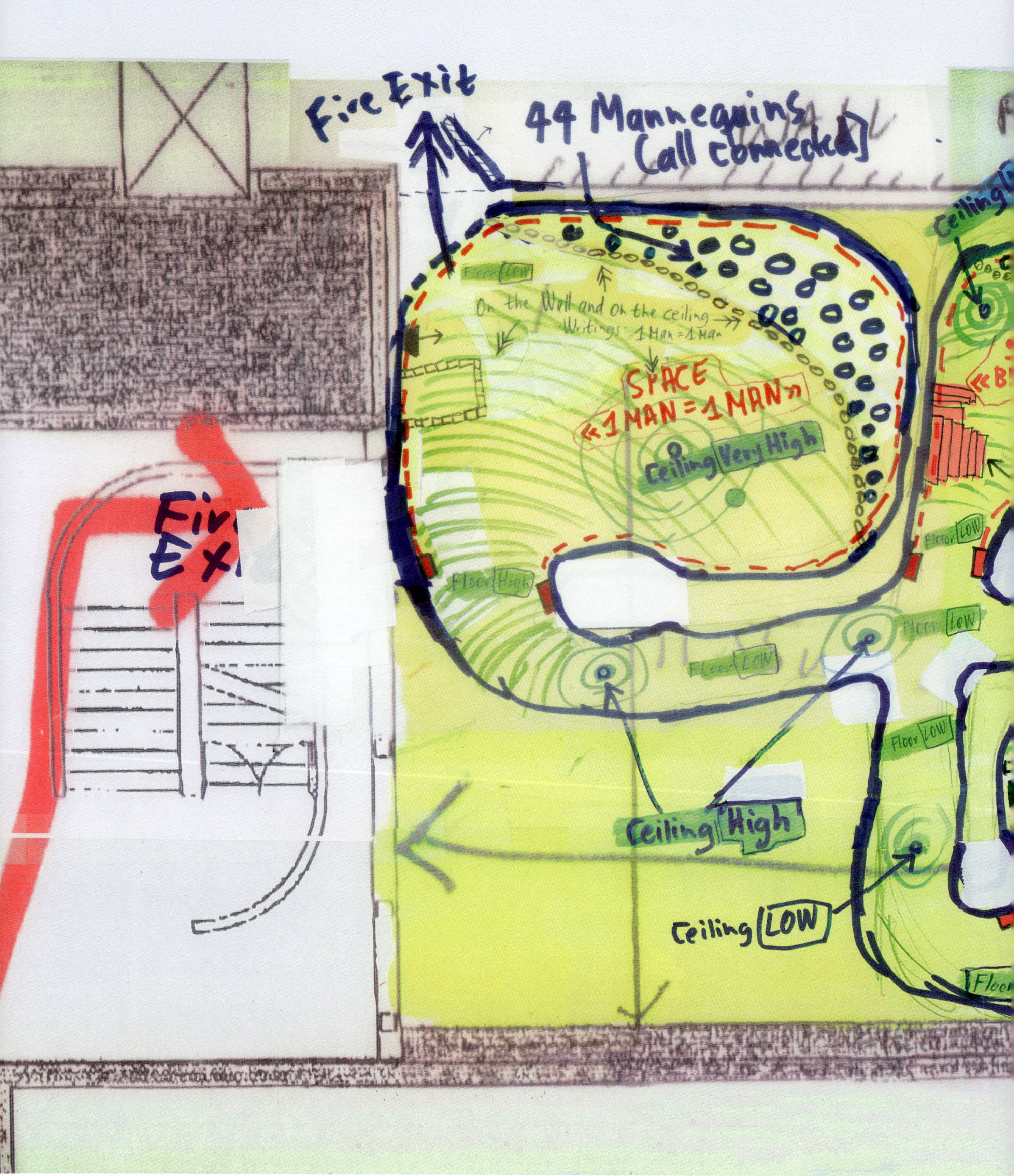

Fire Exit
44 Mannequins (all connected)
Floor LOW
On the Wall and on the ceiling Writings: 1 Man = 1 Man
SPACE «1 MAN = 1 MAN»
Ceiling Very High
Fire Exit
Floor High
Floor LOW
Floor LOW
Floor LOW
Floor LOW
Ceiling High
Ceiling LOW
Floor

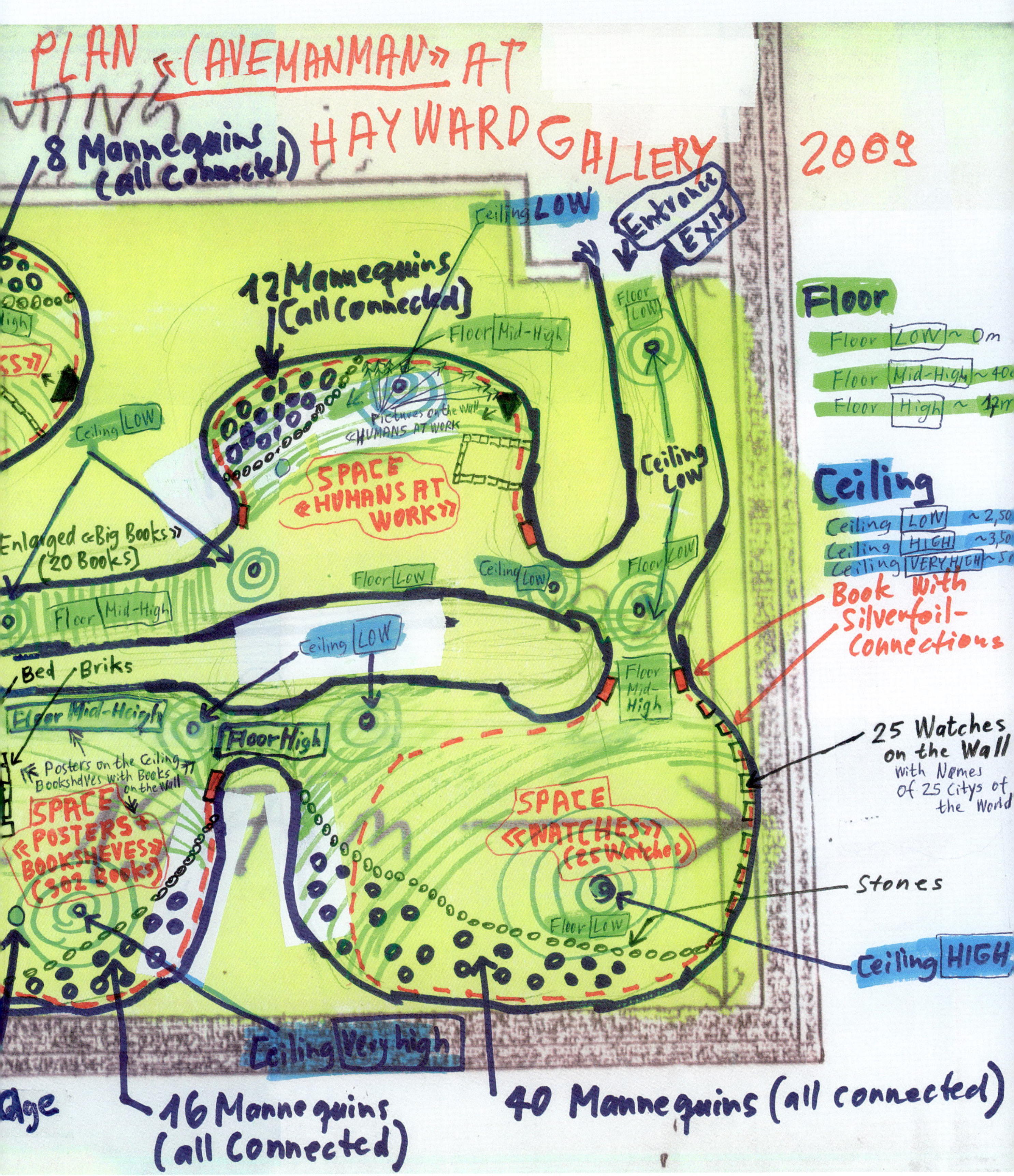
PLAN «CAVEMANMAN» AT HAYWARD GALLERY 2009
8 Mannequins (all connected)
12 Mannequins (all connected)
Ceiling LOW
Entrance Exit
Floor LOW
Floor Mid-High
Pictures on the Wall
«HUMANS AT WORK»
SPACE «HUMANS AT WORK»
Ceiling LOW
Ceiling LOW
Enlarged «Big Books» (20 Books)
Floor LOW
Floor Mid-High
Floor LOW
Ceiling LOW
Ceiling LOW
Bed Briks
Floor Mid-High
Floor High
Posters on the Ceiling Bookshelves with Books on the Wall
SPACE «POSTERS + BOOKSHELVES» (302 Books)
Floor Mid-High
SPACE «WATCHES» (25 Watches)
Floor LOW
Stones
Floor
Floor LOW ~ 0m
Floor Mid-High ~ 40
Floor High ~ 1m
Ceiling
Ceiling LOW ~ 2,50
Ceiling HIGH ~ 3,50
Ceiling VERY HIGH ~ 5
Book with Silverfoil-Connections
25 Watches on the Wall with Names of 25 Citys of the World
Ceiling HIGH
Ceiling Very high
16 Mannequins (all connected)
40 Mannequins (all connected)

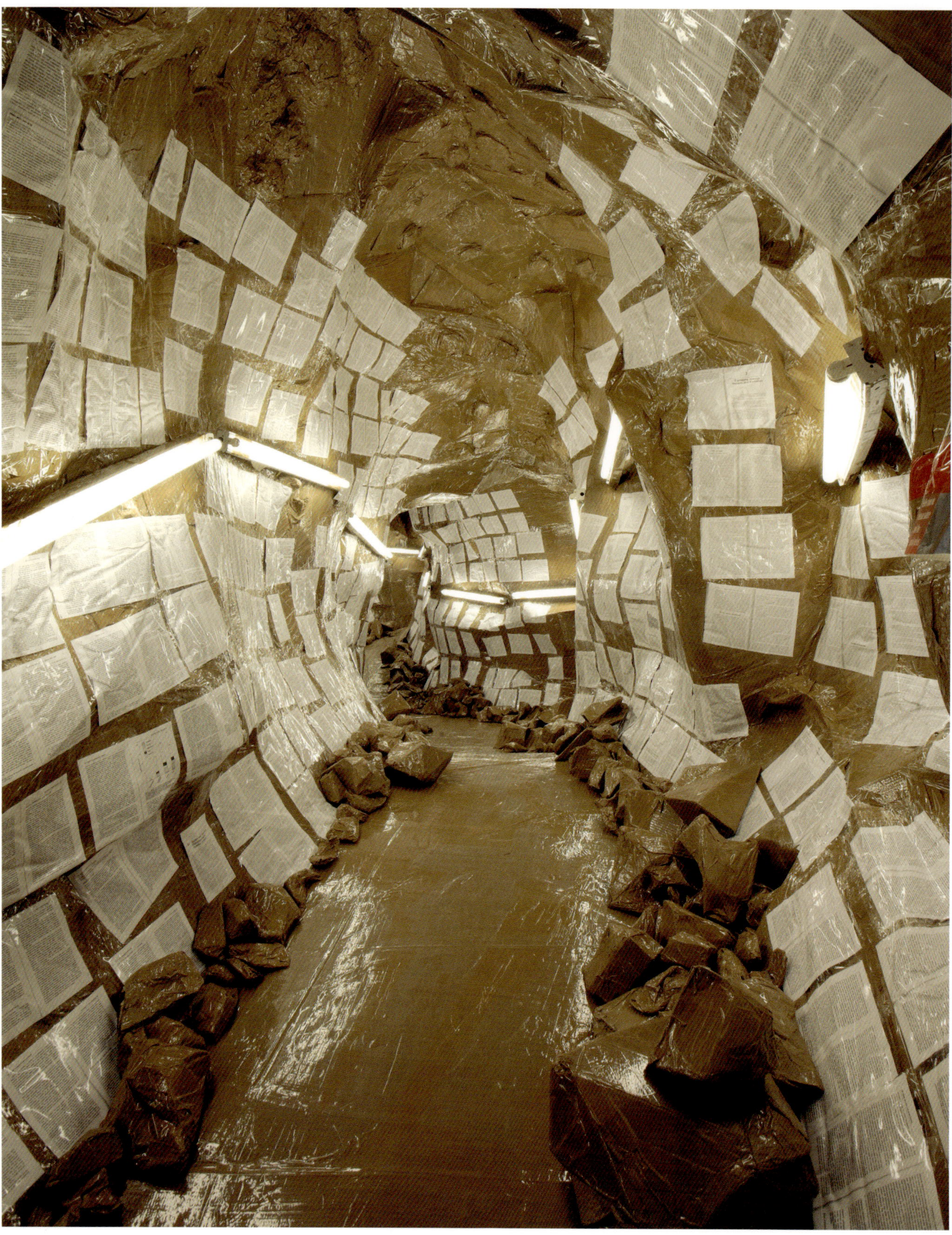

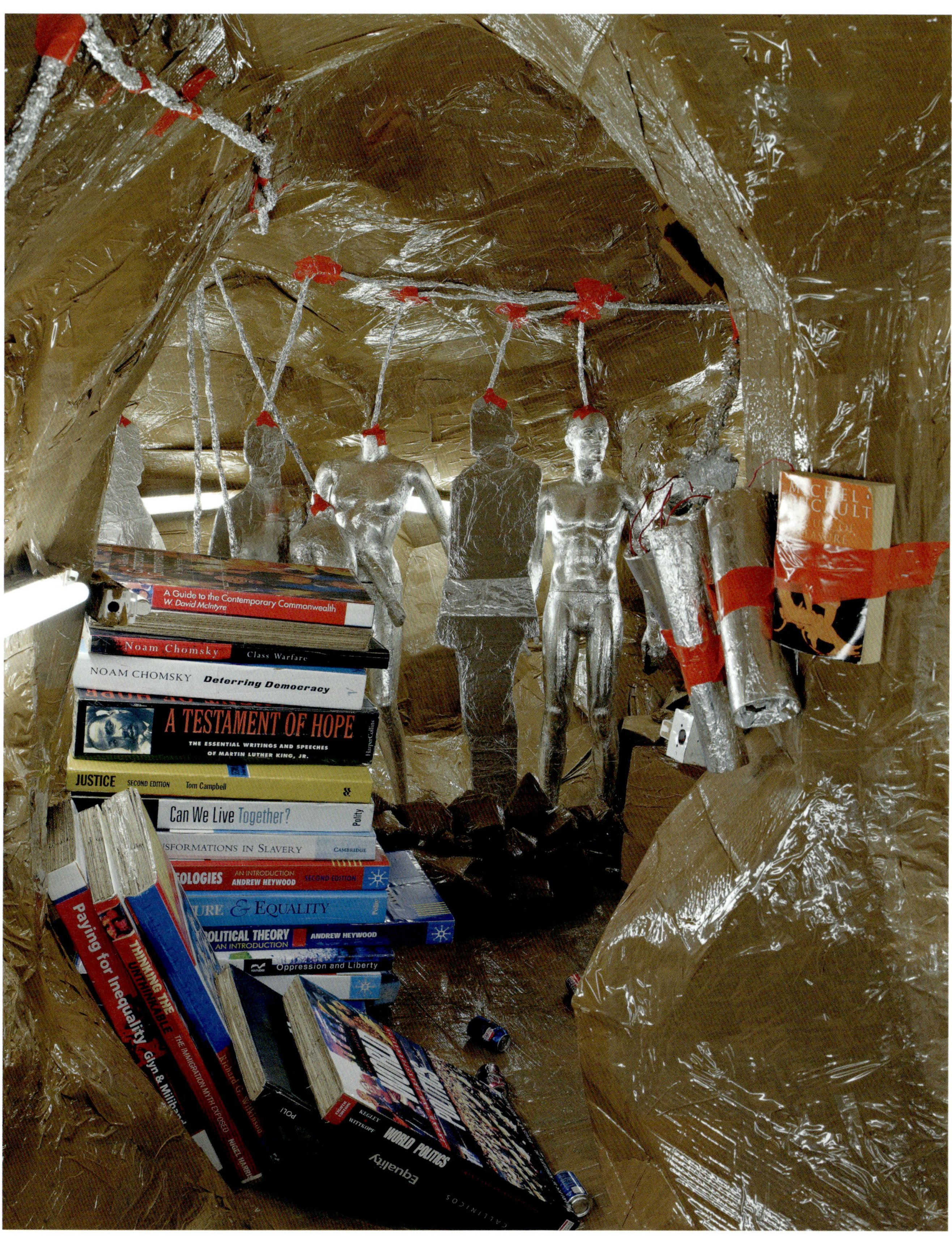

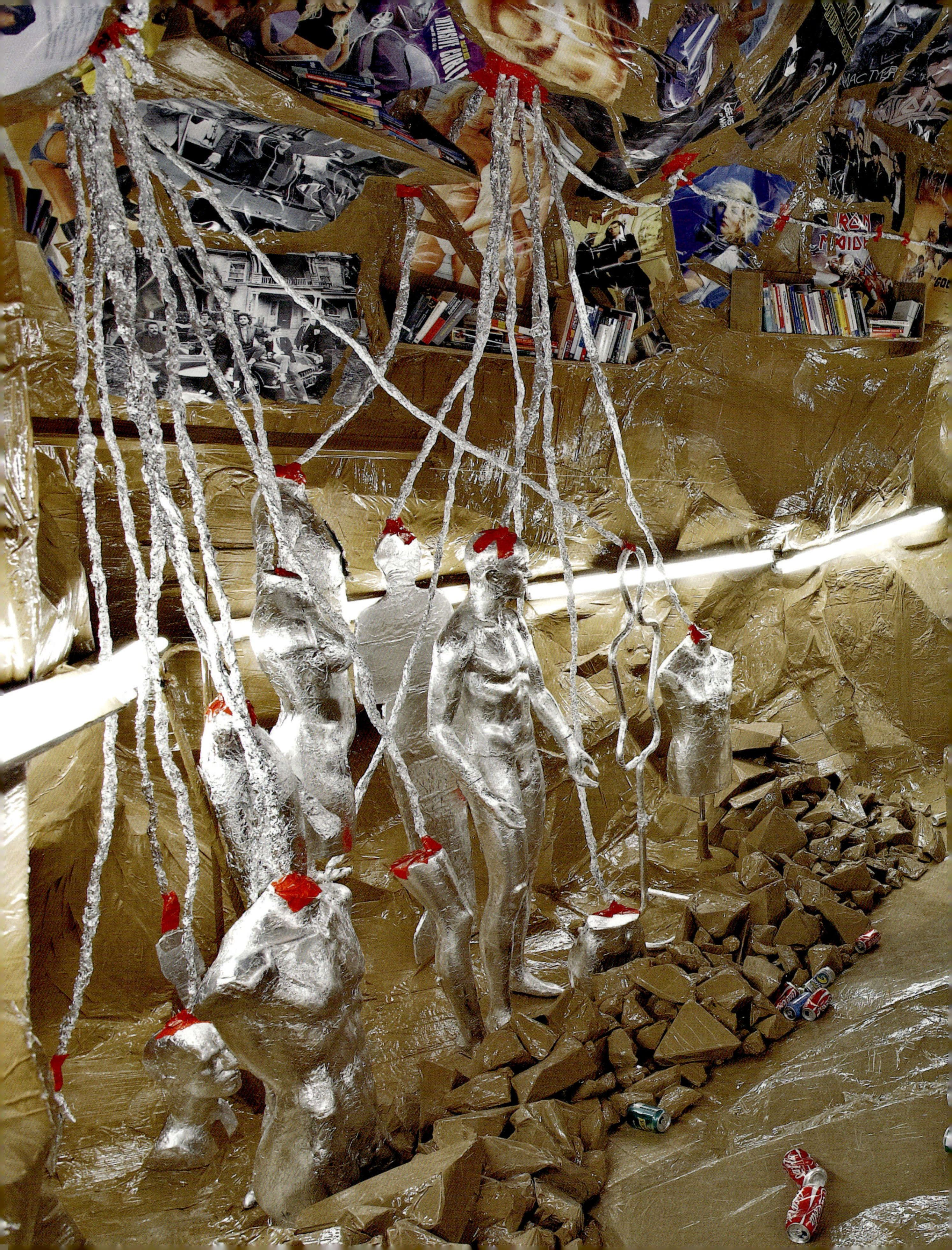

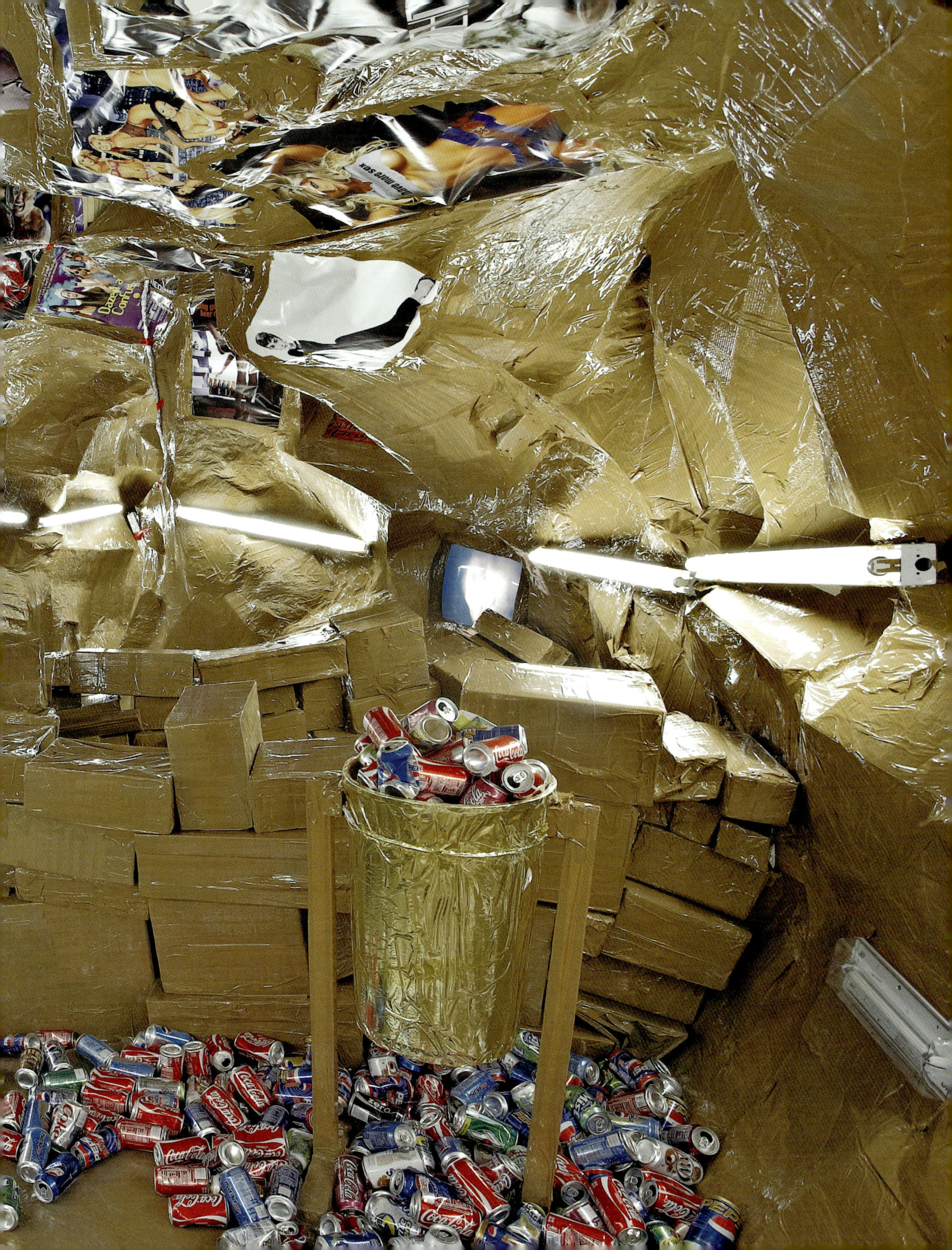
Coca-Cola
Pepsi
Coke

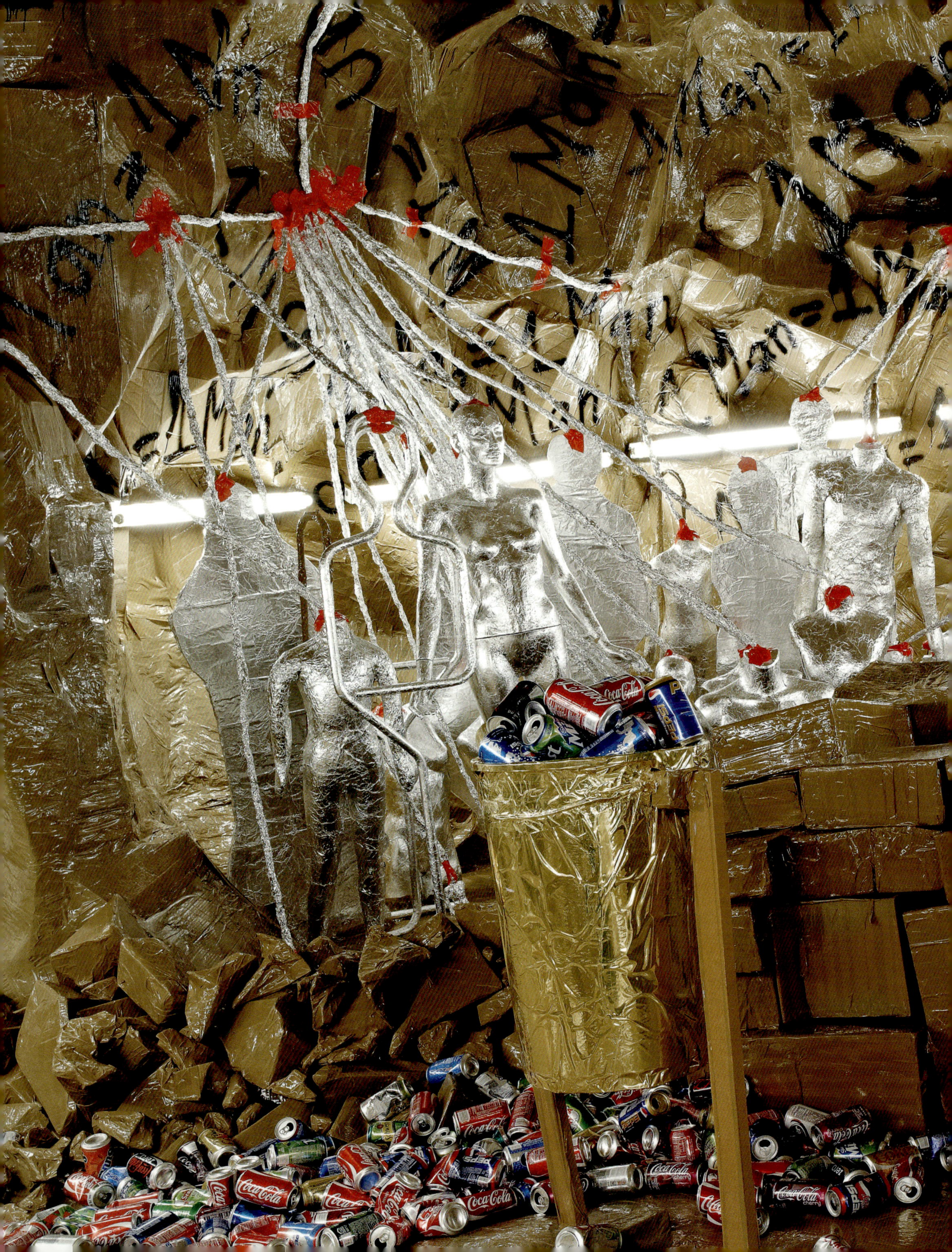

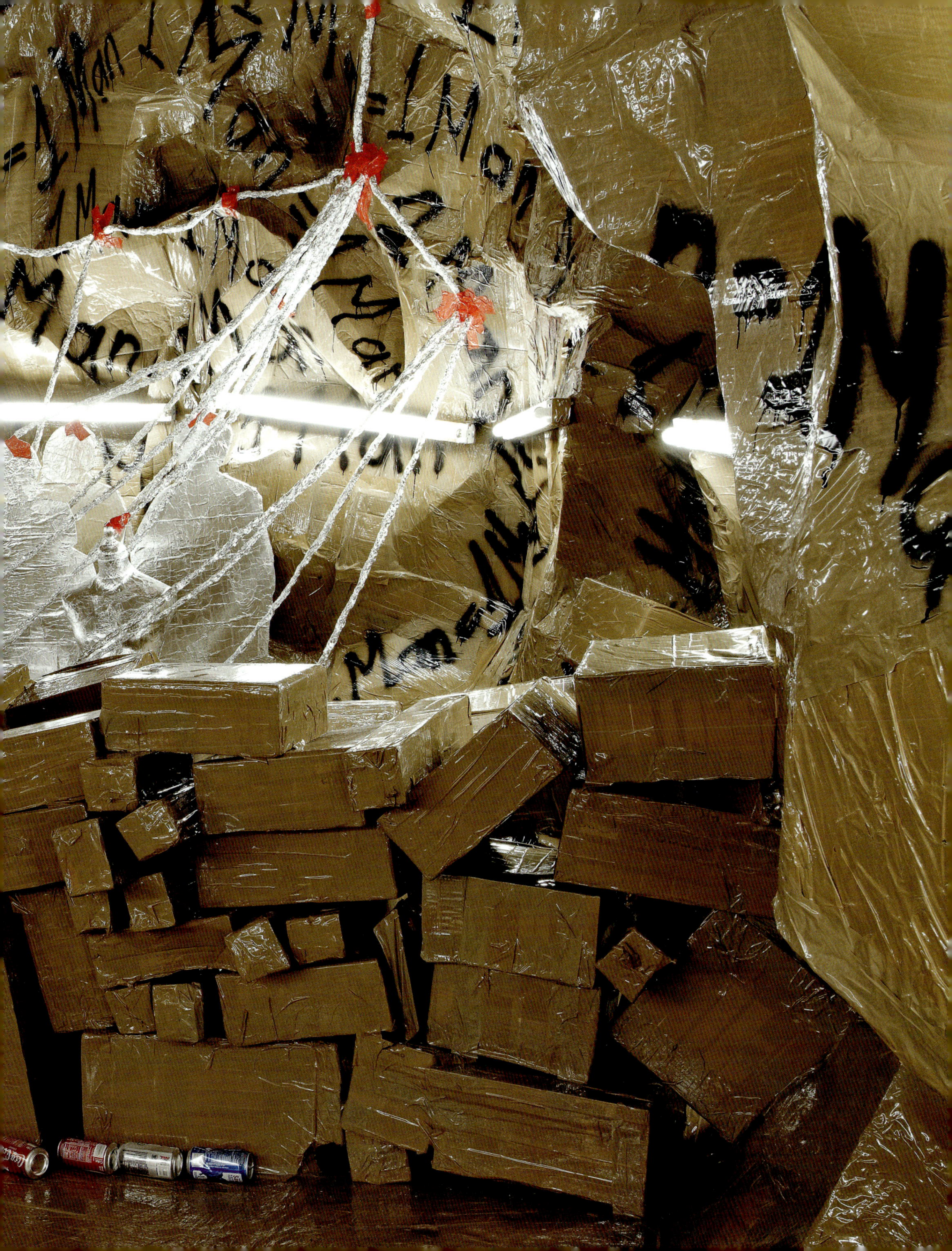

YAYOI KUSAMA

Yayoi Kusama was born in 1929 in Matsumoto City, Japan. She is a sculptor, painter, writer, installation artist and performance artist whose career began more than half a century ago. Though her formal training consisted of just one year's study at the Kyoto School of Arts and Crafts, where she was taught *Nihonga* (traditional Japanese painting), Kusama became one of the leading figures of Japanese postwar avant-garde art. In 1957, she moved to America and began to show large paintings, soft sculptures, and environmental works using mirrors and electric lights. Her giant, monochromatic *Infinity Net* paintings caught the attention of Frank Stella and Donald Judd when they were first shown in New York in 1959 and Kusama's abstract work came to be seen as anticipating the beginnings of Minimalism. In the 1960s she staged many happenings, including body painting festivals, fashion shows and anti-war demonstrations. In 1973 she returned to Japan, where she began to write fiction and chose to settle permanently in a psychiatric hospital in Tokyo. Having virtually disappeared from the international art scene, her career revived in the late 1980s and in 1993 she represented Japan at the 45th Venice Biennale. The following year, she began to create open-air sculptures. She lives and works in Tokyo, Japan.

Guidepost to the New World, 2005

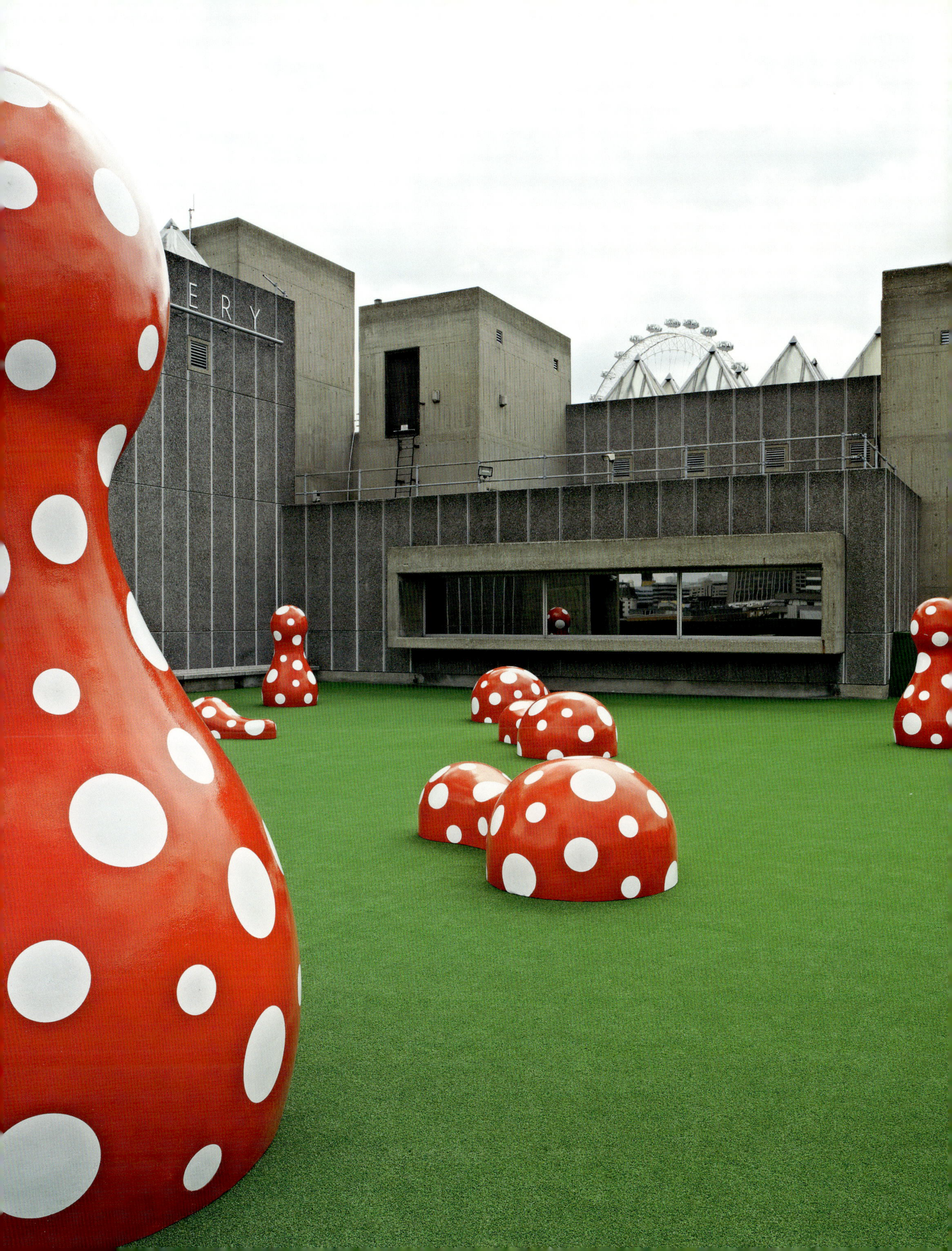
ERY

Kusama started painting polka dots when she was about ten years old. This motif, which has remained a central feature of her work, emerged as the result of recurring hallucinations in which the artist found herself and all her surroundings covered in the same pattern. She has said that the experience made her feel as if she was revolving 'in the infinity of endless time and the absoluteness of space', and sees her life as 'a dot lost among a million other dots'. Kusama's works in *Walking in My Mind* allow us to view the world through her eyes, and experience the 'dizzy, empty, hypnotic feeling' of her own universe. Within the Hayward Gallery, she has installed *Dots Obsession*, an immersive and disorienting space partly lined with mirrors and filled with red inflatable sculptures covered in white polka dots. Outside, on one of the Hayward's sculpture terraces, is *Guidepost to the New World*, 2005, in which skittle-shaped polka-dotted sculptures are scattered over a bright green Astroturf lawn. Beyond the Gallery, beside the River Thames, Kusama has transformed the twenty-five trees between Hungerford Bridge and Waterloo Bridge by covering them in red spotted fabric, in a work entitled *Ascension of Polkadots on the Trees*, 2009.

Dots Obsession, 2009

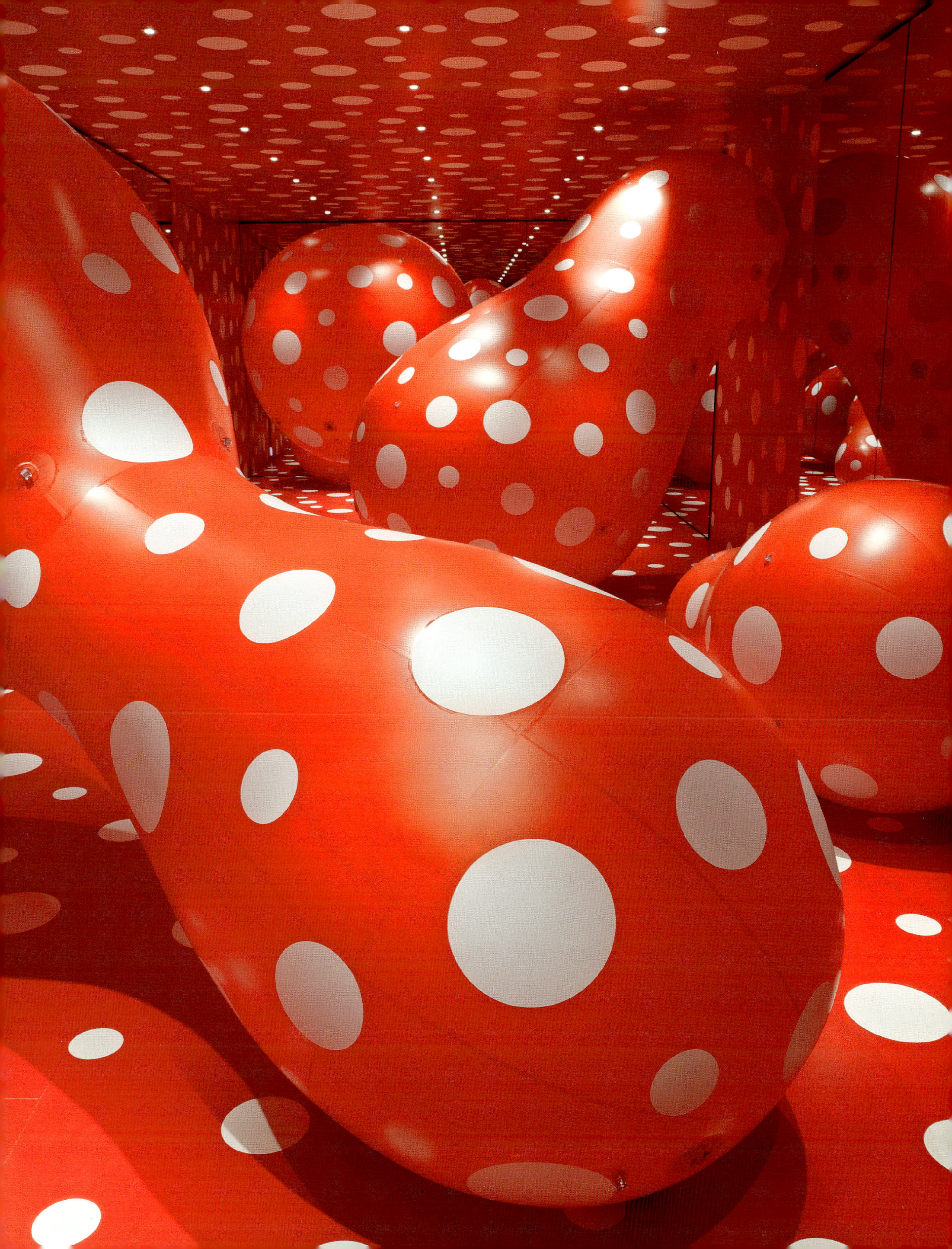

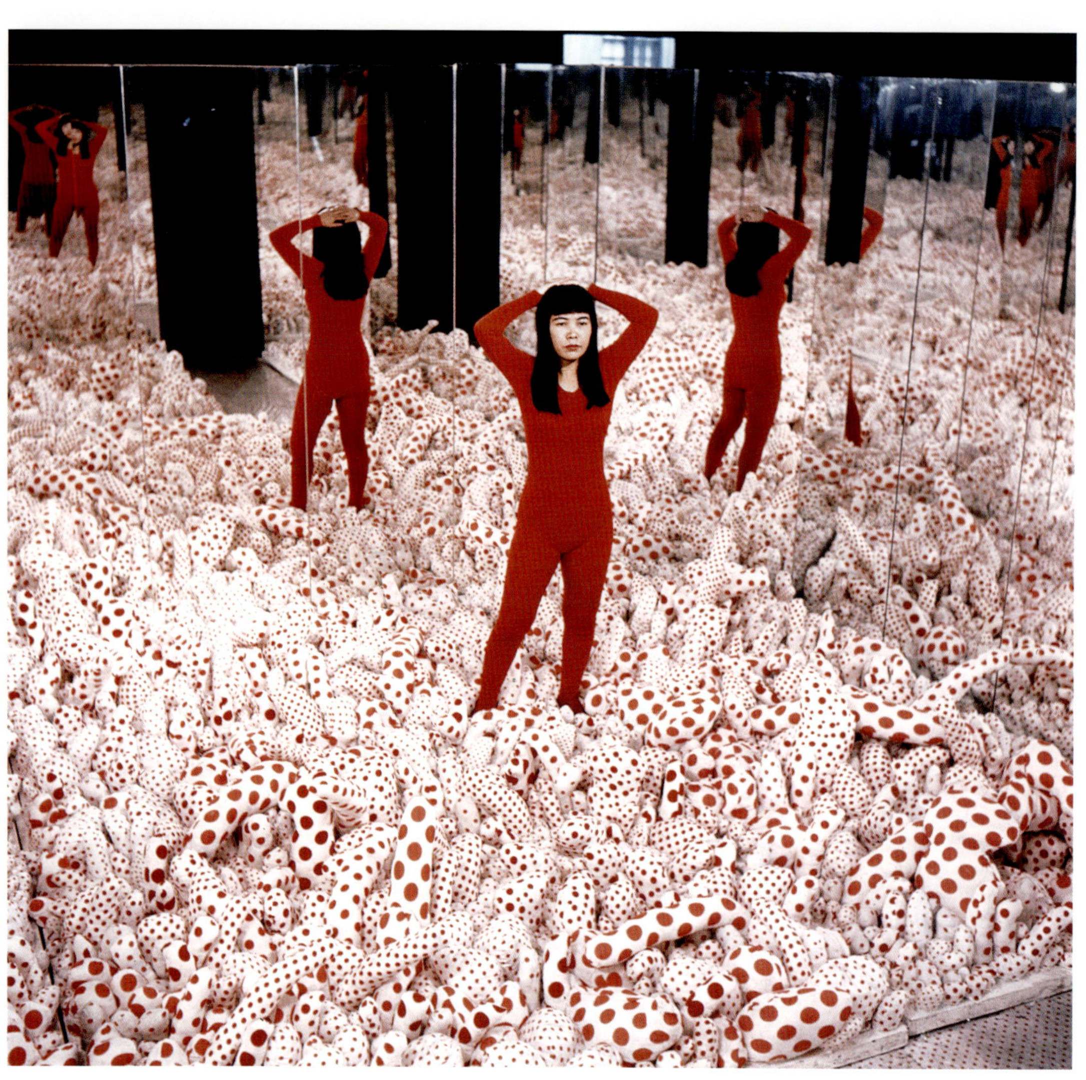

The artist in *Infinity Mirror Room
(Phalli's Field)*, 1965

opposite page:
Ascension of Polkadots on the Trees, 2009

following page:
Guidepost to the New World, 2009

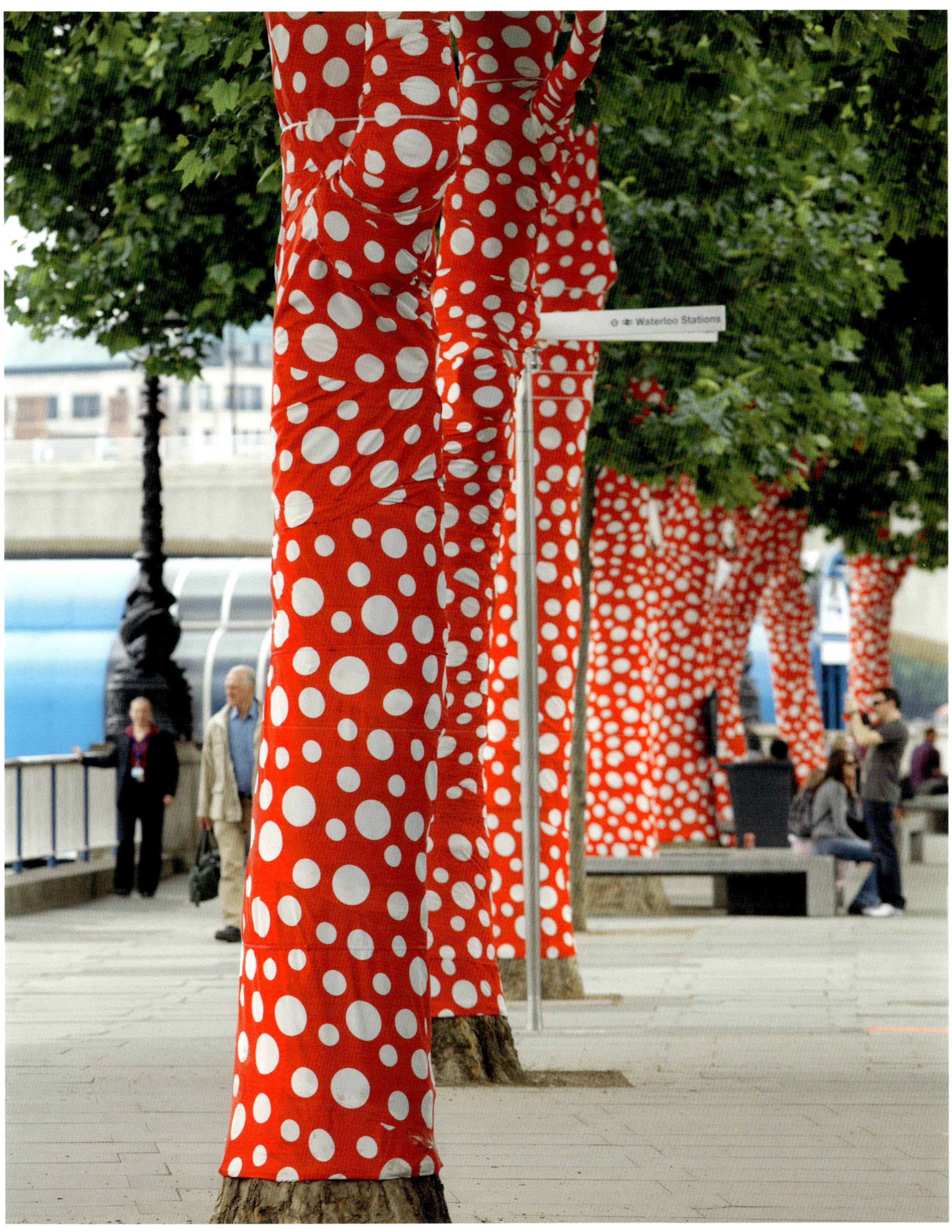

Waterloo Stations

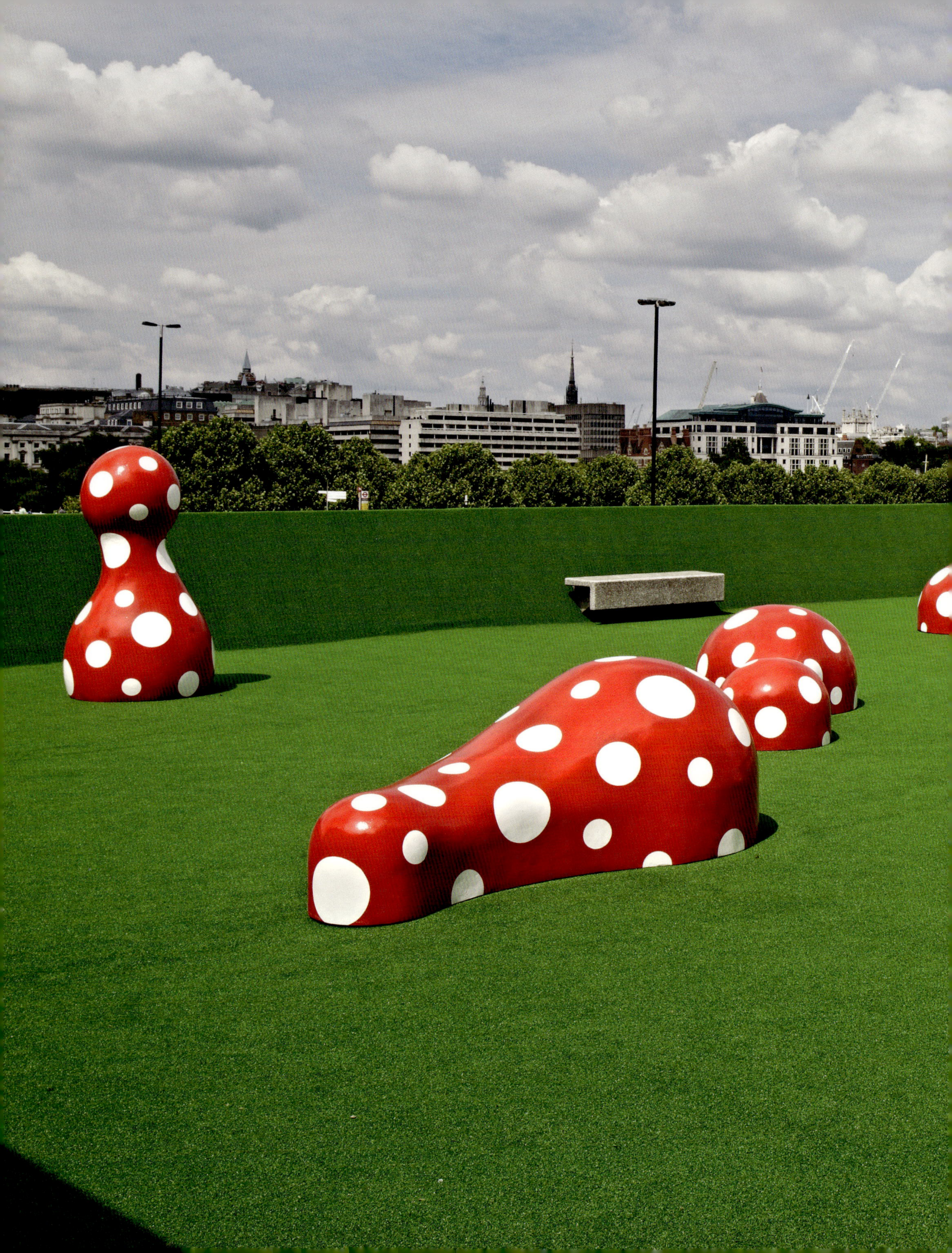

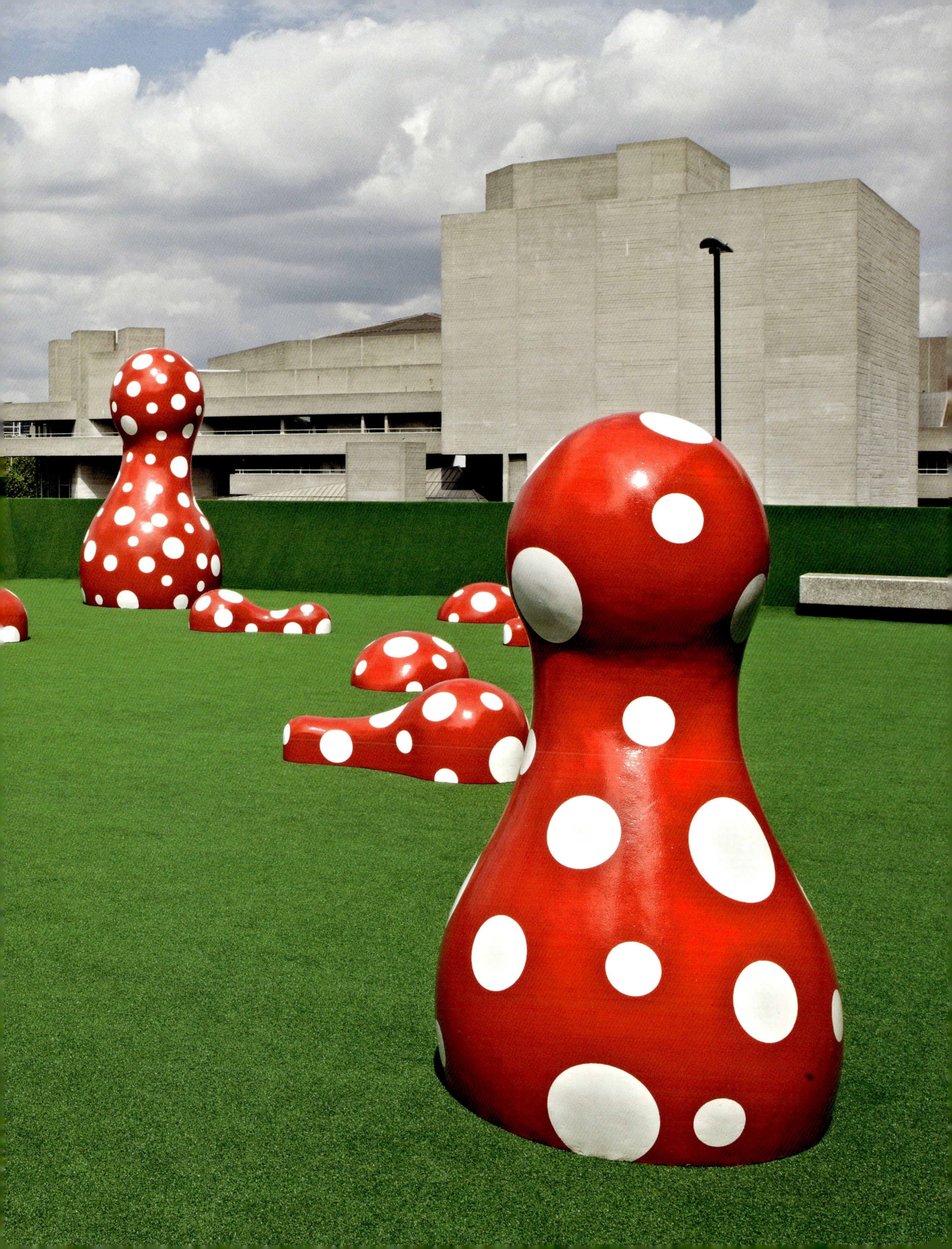

Dots Obsession – Night, 2008

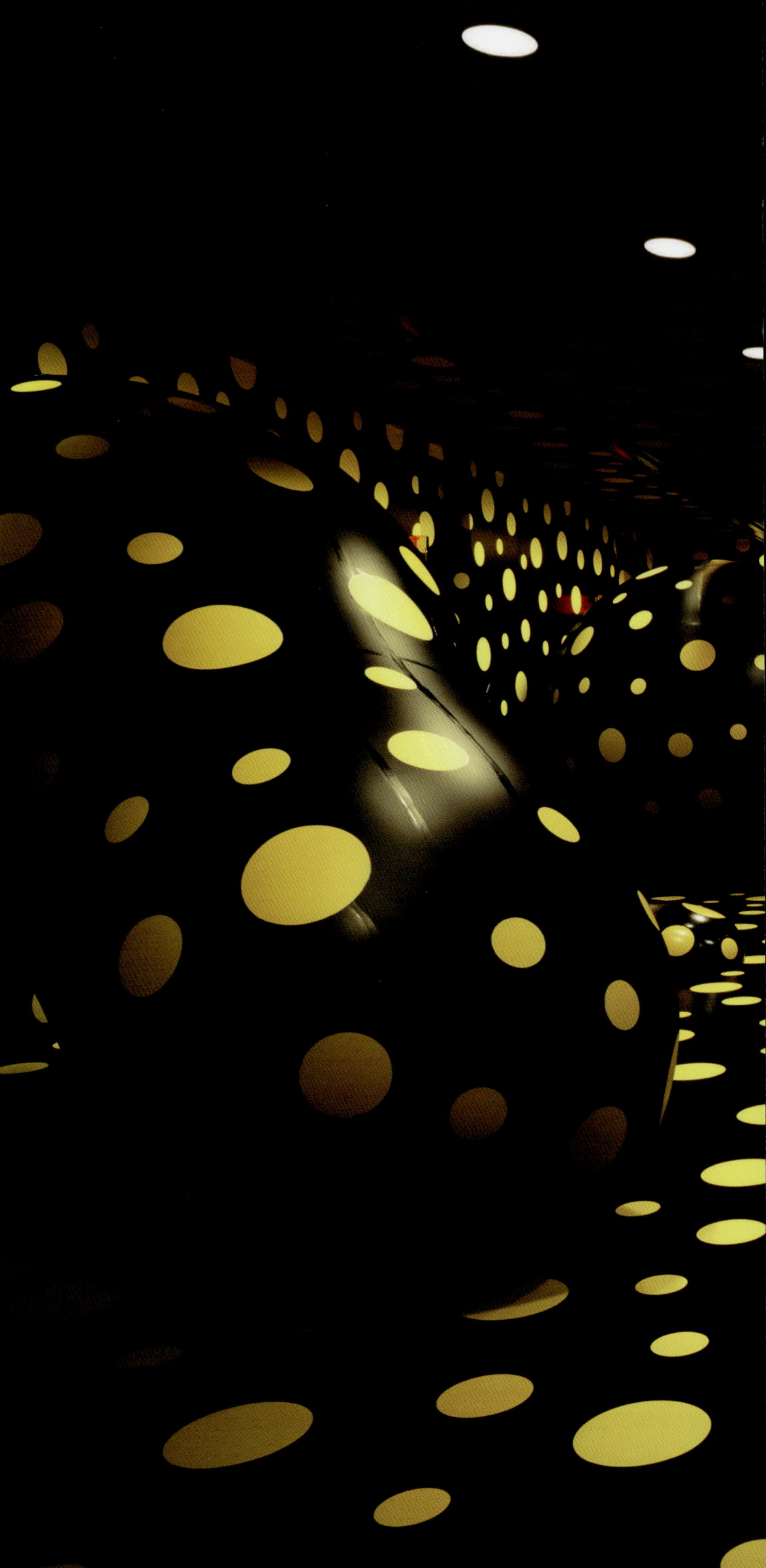

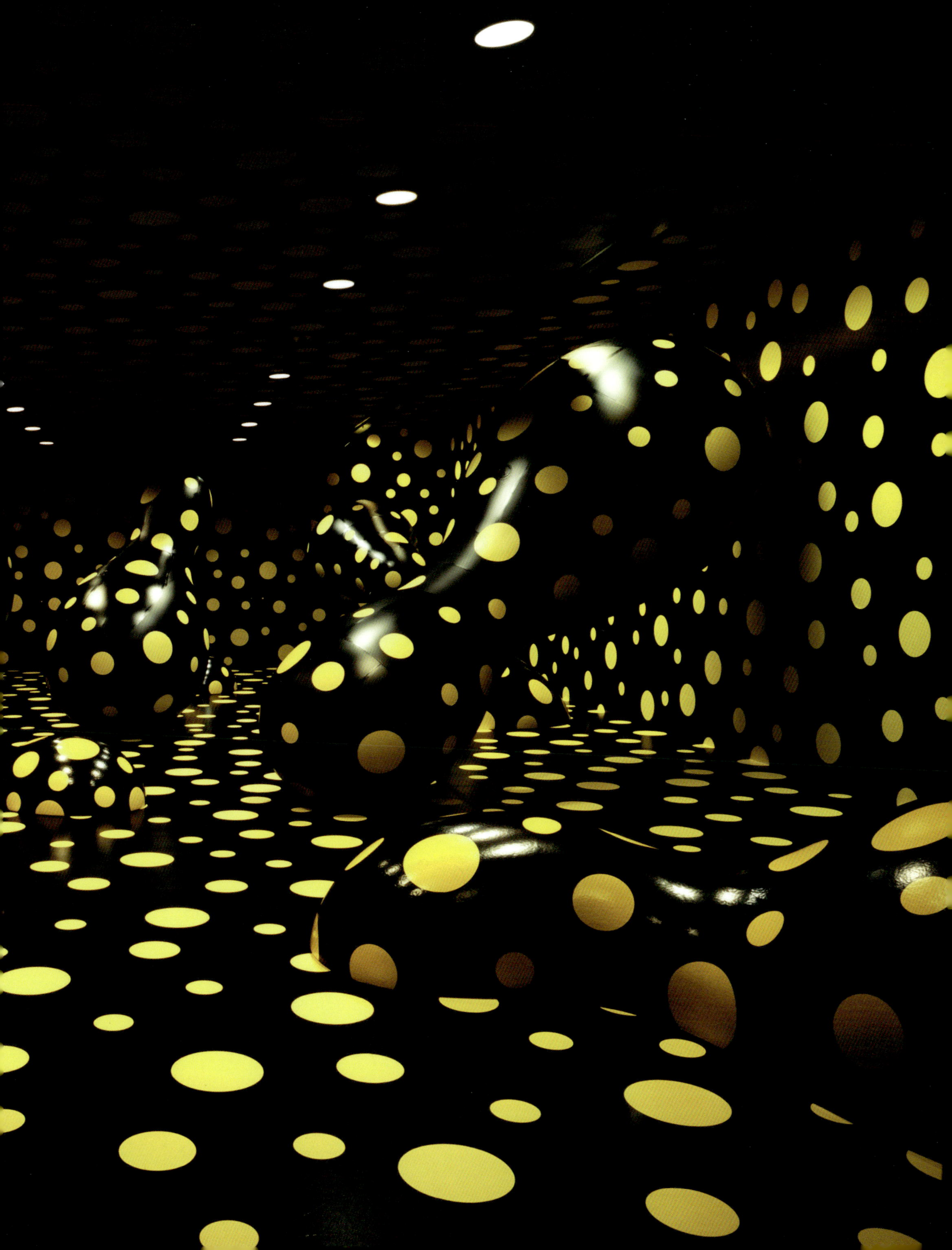

BO CHRISTIAN LARSSON

Bo Christian Larsson was born in 1976 in Kristinehamn, a small town in central Sweden located between the forest and the inland sea; a place of sharply contrasting dark and light. After studying in Sweden, he went on to study drawing, sculpture and installation art at AKI, the Academy of Visual Arts in Enschede, Holland, from 1994 to 1998. Larsson moved to Germany in 2004 and in 2008 began a year's residency in Hamburg as the first recipient of the Philipp Otto Runge Scholarship, awarded to artists whose work relates to Romanticism. In 2009 he was awarded a Flux Factory residency scholarship in New York.

Secret Service, 2009

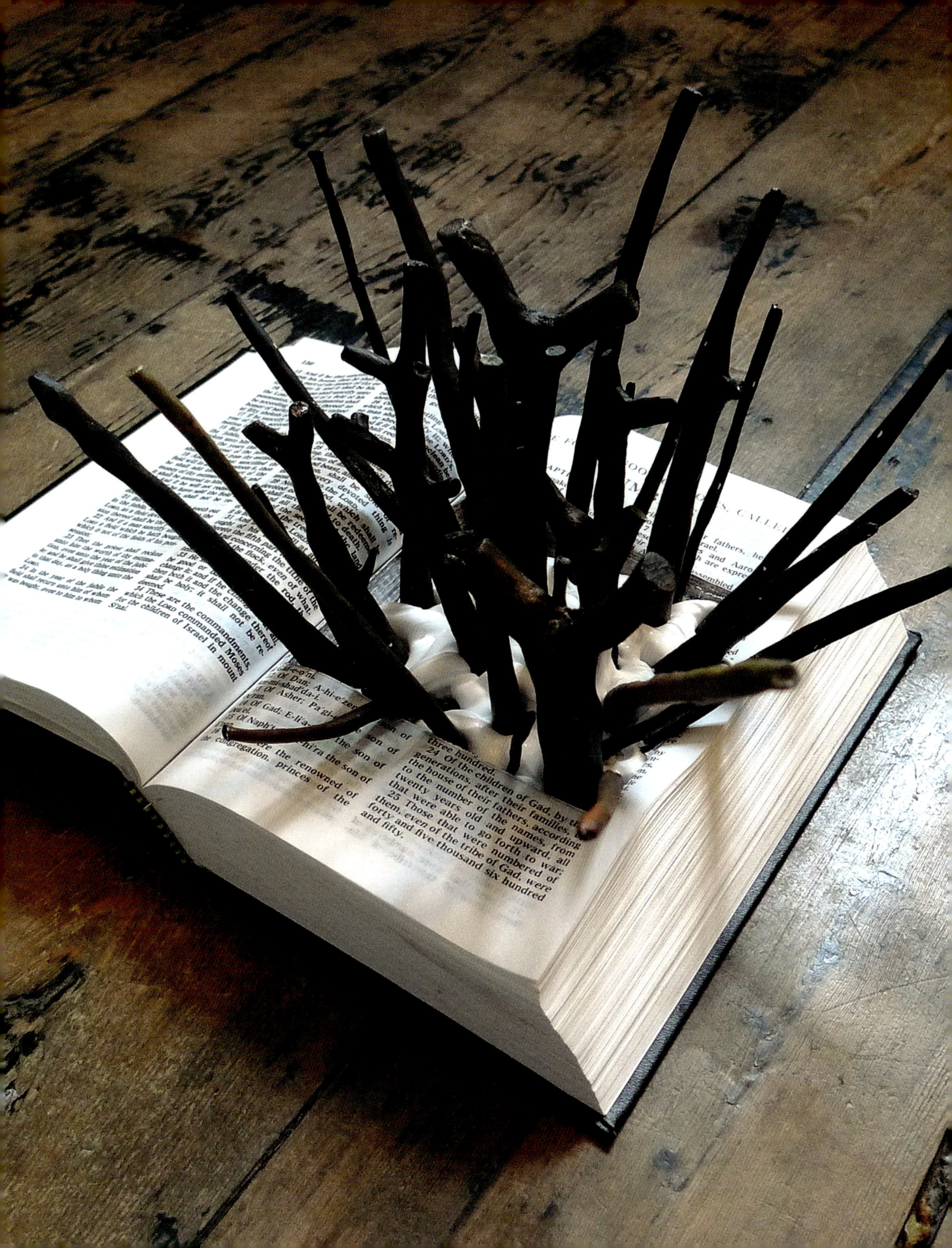

Larsson makes drawings, installations, performances and objects, all of which interrelate. Though his drawings exist as works in their own right, they also act as 'blueprints' for his installations and performances. Installations and objects are almost always created for a single performance and, after this action has taken place, continue to inhabit the space, like archaeological remains. Larsson's themes are mysterious and arcane. His performances feature a cast of characters that includes The Poet, The Redeemer, The Shadow (also known as The Worried Man), The Worldhater, Mr. Empire and Pentaman (who is represented by the Sceptical Owl). The main protagonist is Larsson's own alter ego, Sonuvabitch, who first appeared to the artist in his early teenage years. The constant hunter after inner visions, Sonuvabitch is blinded by his own hair. Collectively, these seven characters comprise a self-portrait of the artist and represent different facets of his mind.

Commissioned for *Walking in My Mind*, Larsson's new work, *The first cut is the deepest and the division of seven*, 2009, is an environment created in and around the Hayward Gallery's back staircase. Reflecting the essentially cryptic nature of the work, the title is a fusion of a Cat Stevens song title with a reference to the seven protagonists around whom the narrative evolves. The crux of the work was a performance without spectators; part spontaneous happening and part private ritual out of which the installation took its physical form. The action began in the Golden Cage at the foot of the stairs, with The Poet reading from James Joyce's *Ulysses*. Nearby, The Worldhater – a miserable complainer who tries to be nice but never succeeds – started to create his troubling sculpture garden. Stealing one of the sculptures, a pair of heavy chain shoes, The Shadow proceeded to climb the stairs and then, one by one, the other protagonists appeared. Traces of their presences – in the form of objects – are left at various points on and around the stairs, together with a series of drawings. At the top of the staircase, a gallows-like structure marks the architect and hermit Pentaman's reincarnation as a parliament of Sceptical Owls.

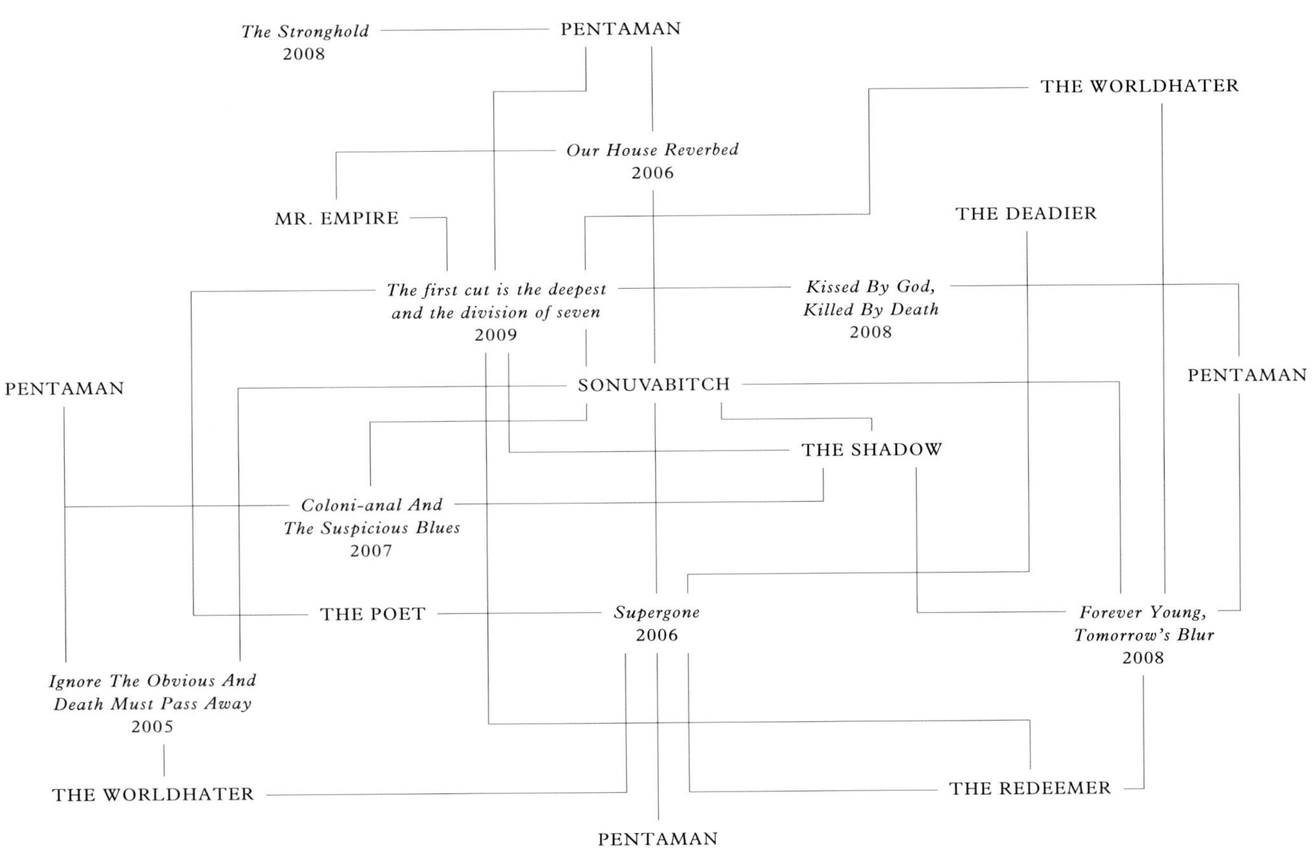

The Stronghold
2008
PENTAMAN
THE WORLDHATER
Our House Reverbed
2006
MR. EMPIRE
THE DEADIER
The first cut is the deepest
and the division of seven
2009
Kissed By God,
Killed By Death
2008
PENTAMAN
PENTAMAN
SONUVABITCH
THE SHADOW
Coloni-anal And
The Suspicious Blues
2007
THE POET
Supergone
2006
Forever Young,
Tomorrow's Blur
2008
Ignore The Obvious And
Death Must Pass Away
2005
THE WORLDHATER
THE REDEEMER
PENTAMAN

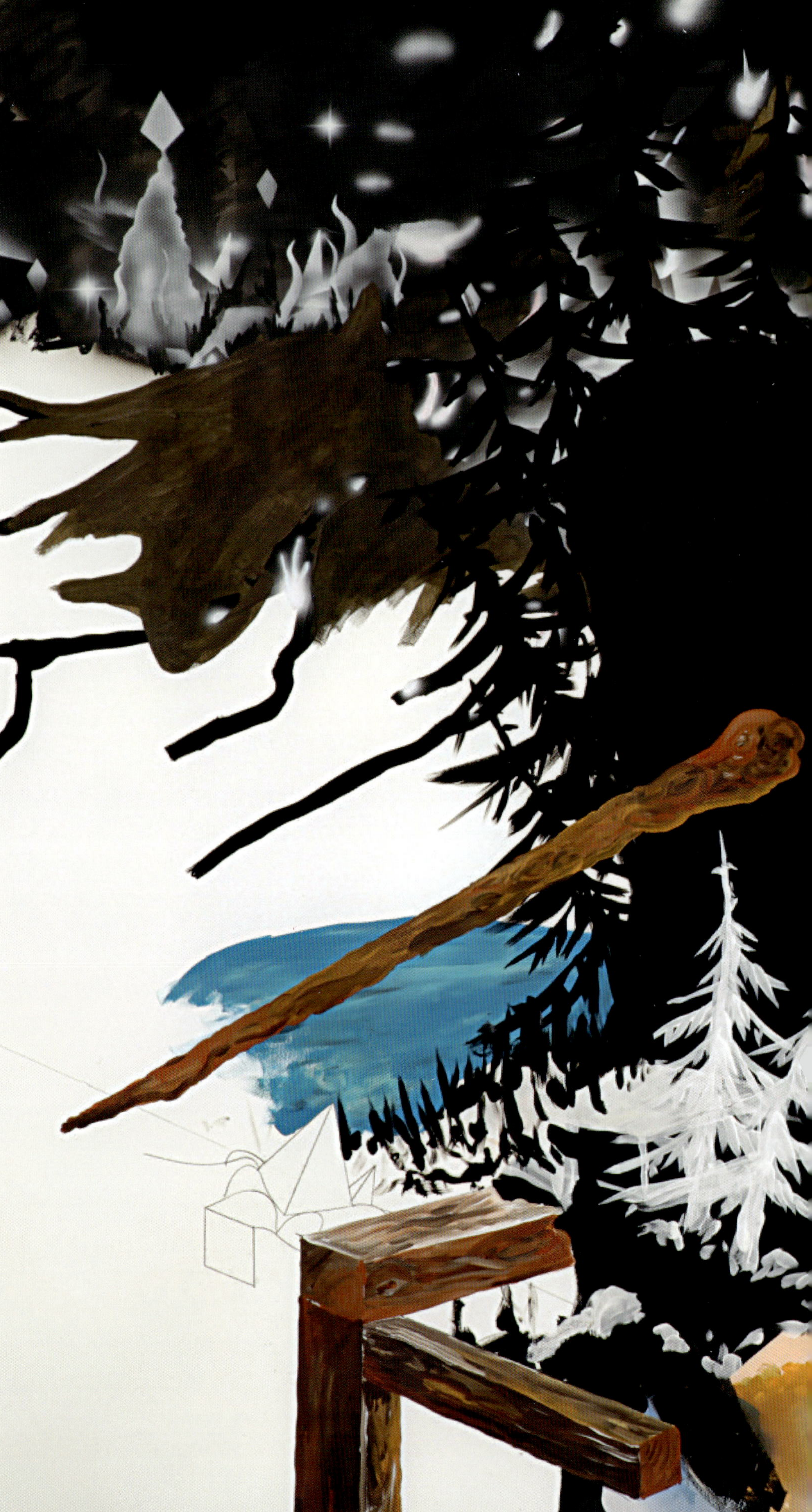

Ground Control, 2009

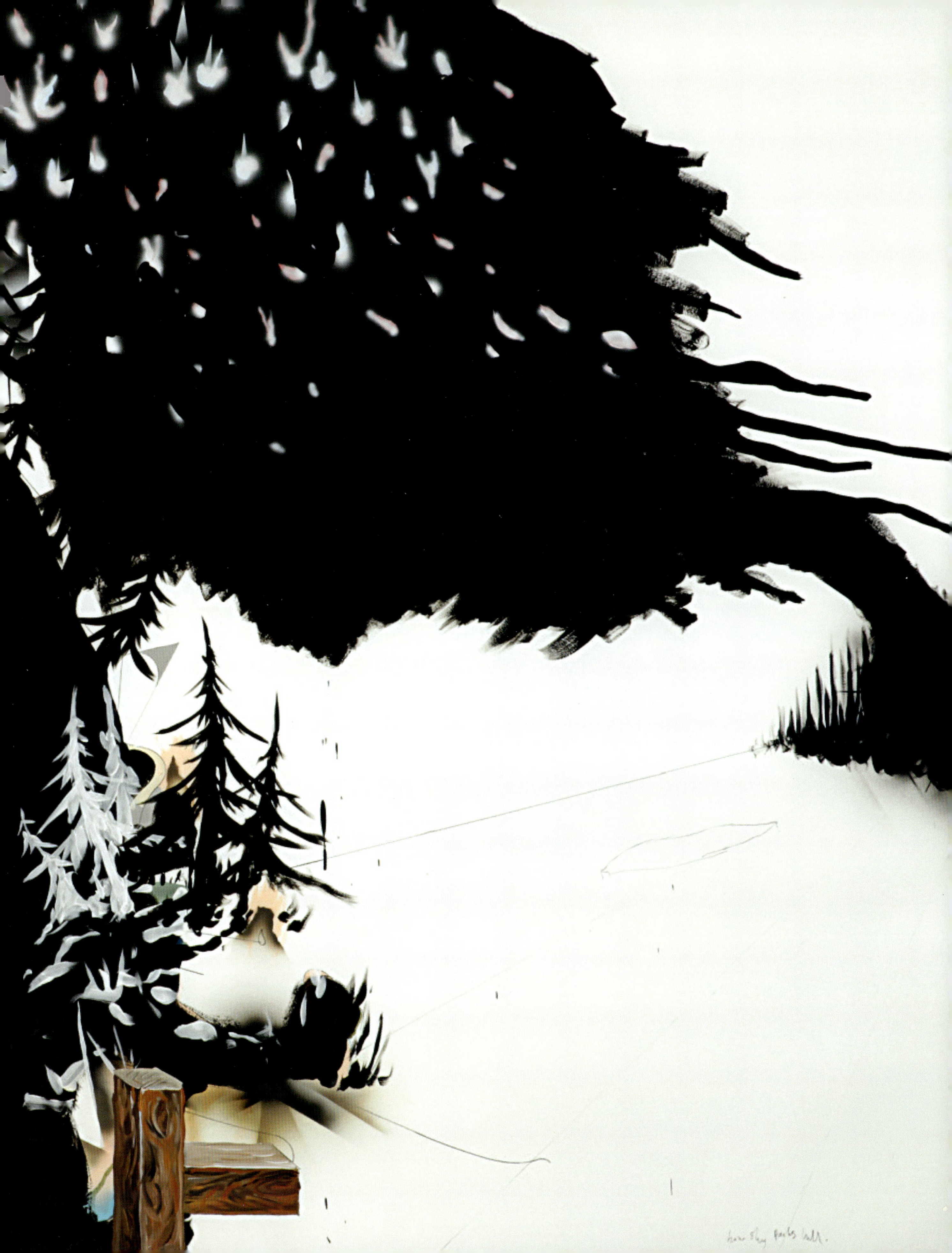

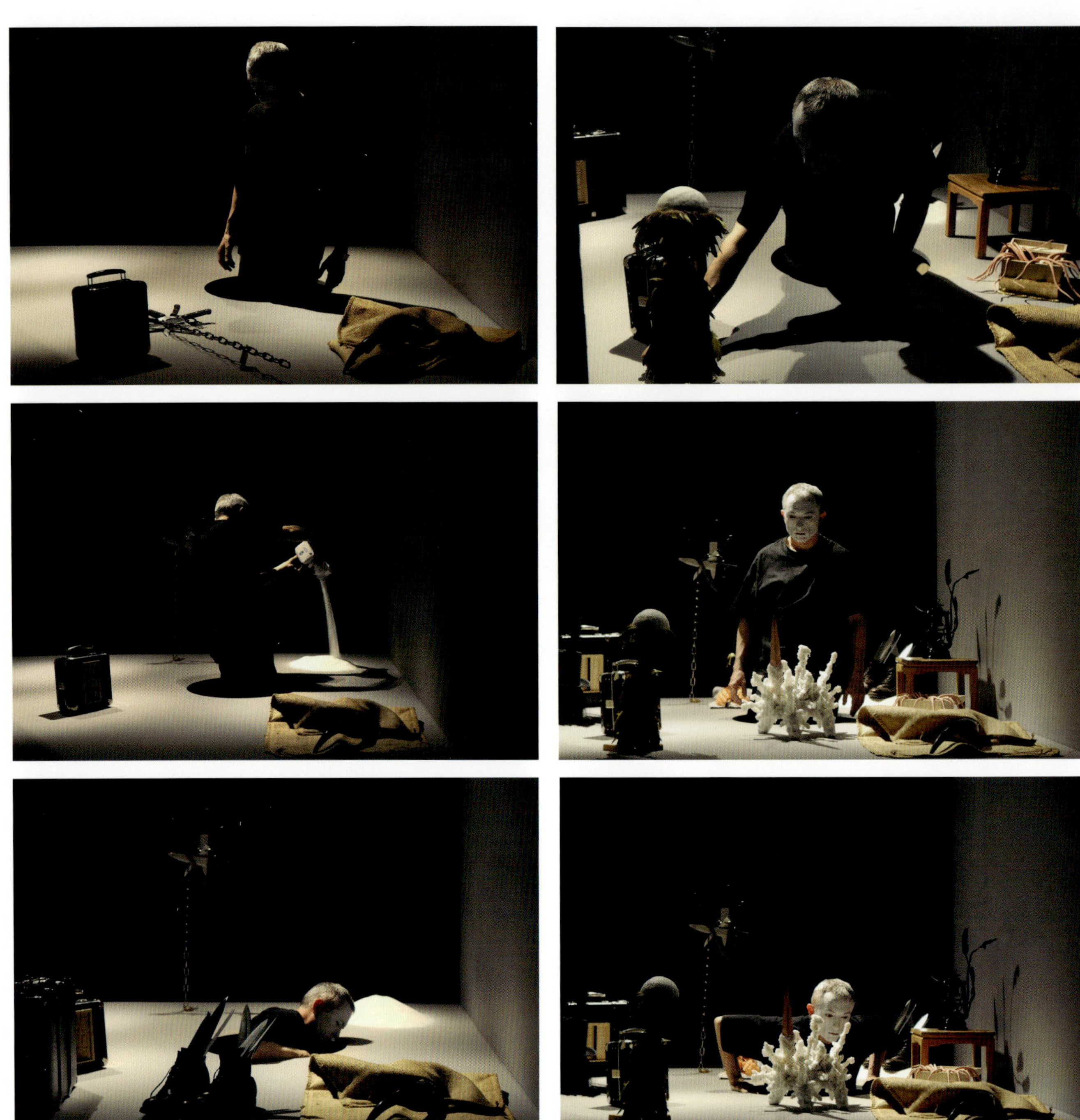

The first cut is the deepest and the division of seven, 2009. Stills from the performance at the Hayward Gallery, featuring The Worldhater in his sculpture garden and Sonuvabitch releasing Mr. Empire from his chains.

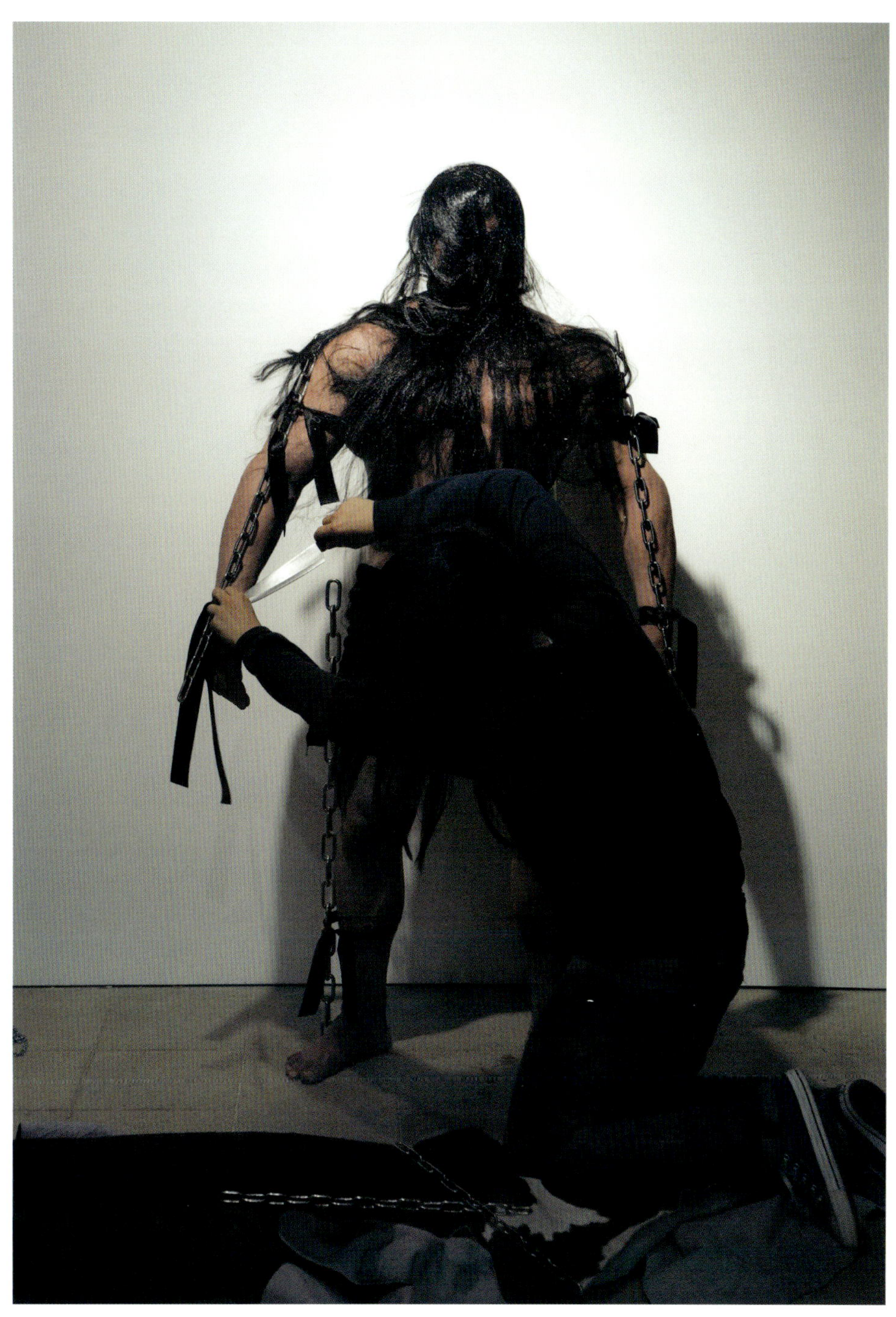

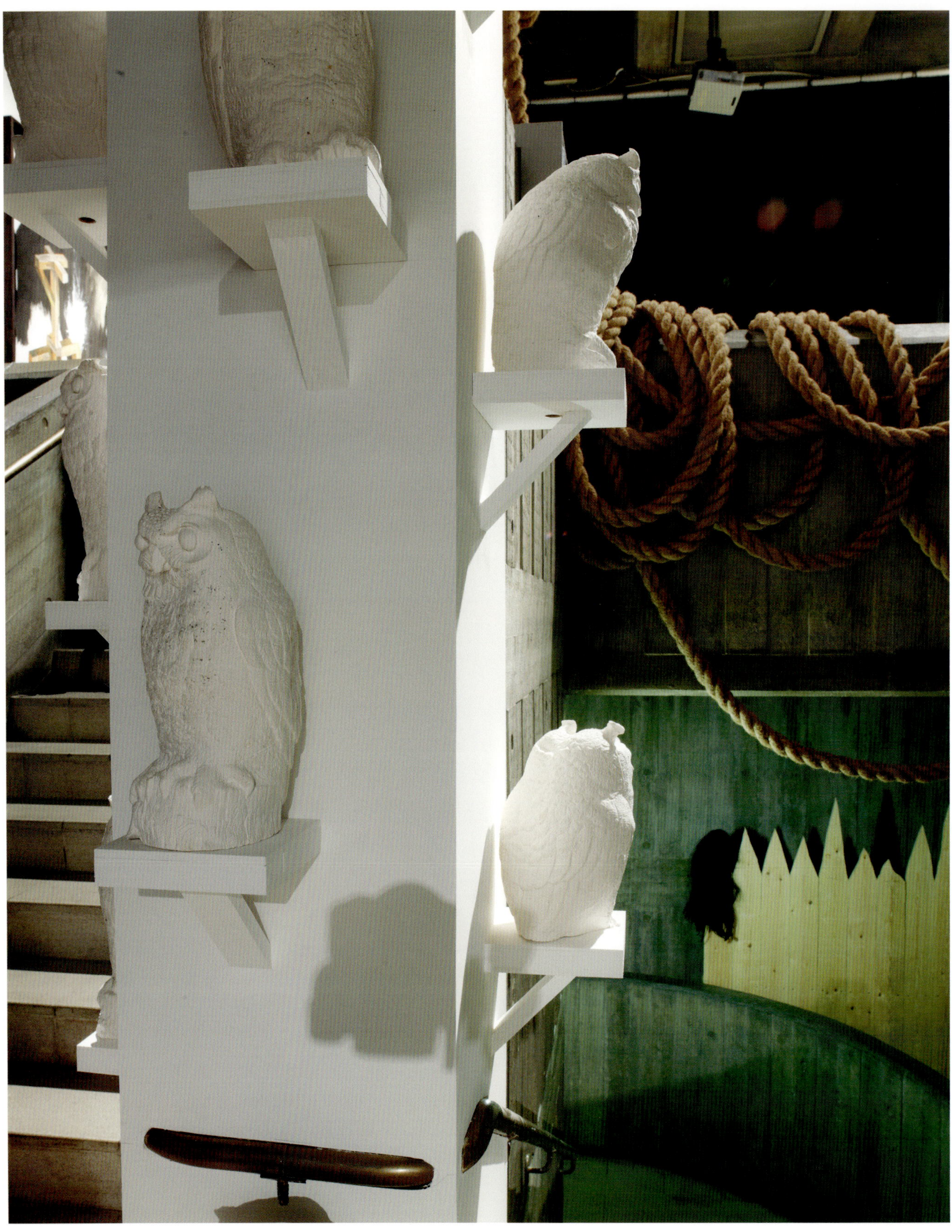

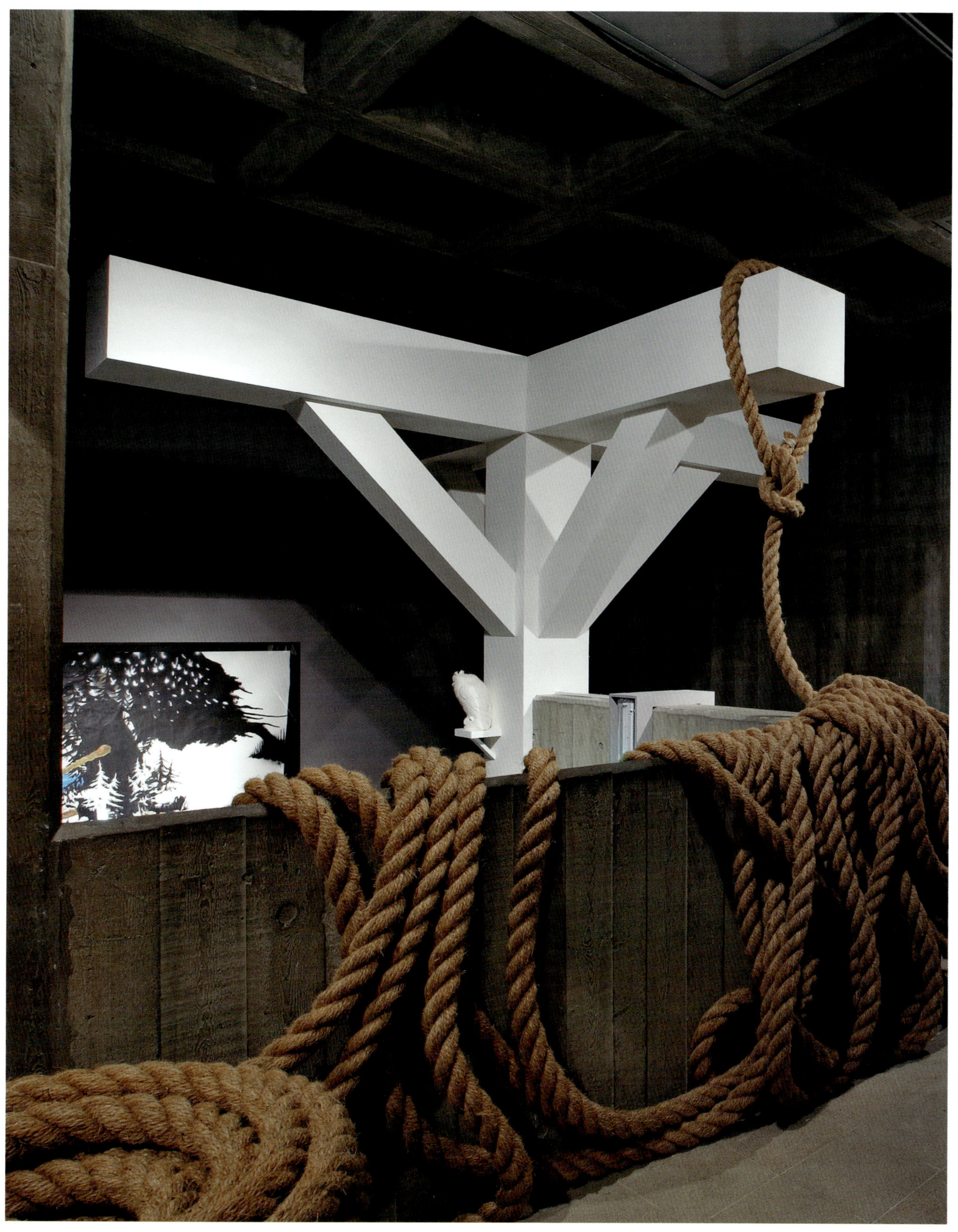

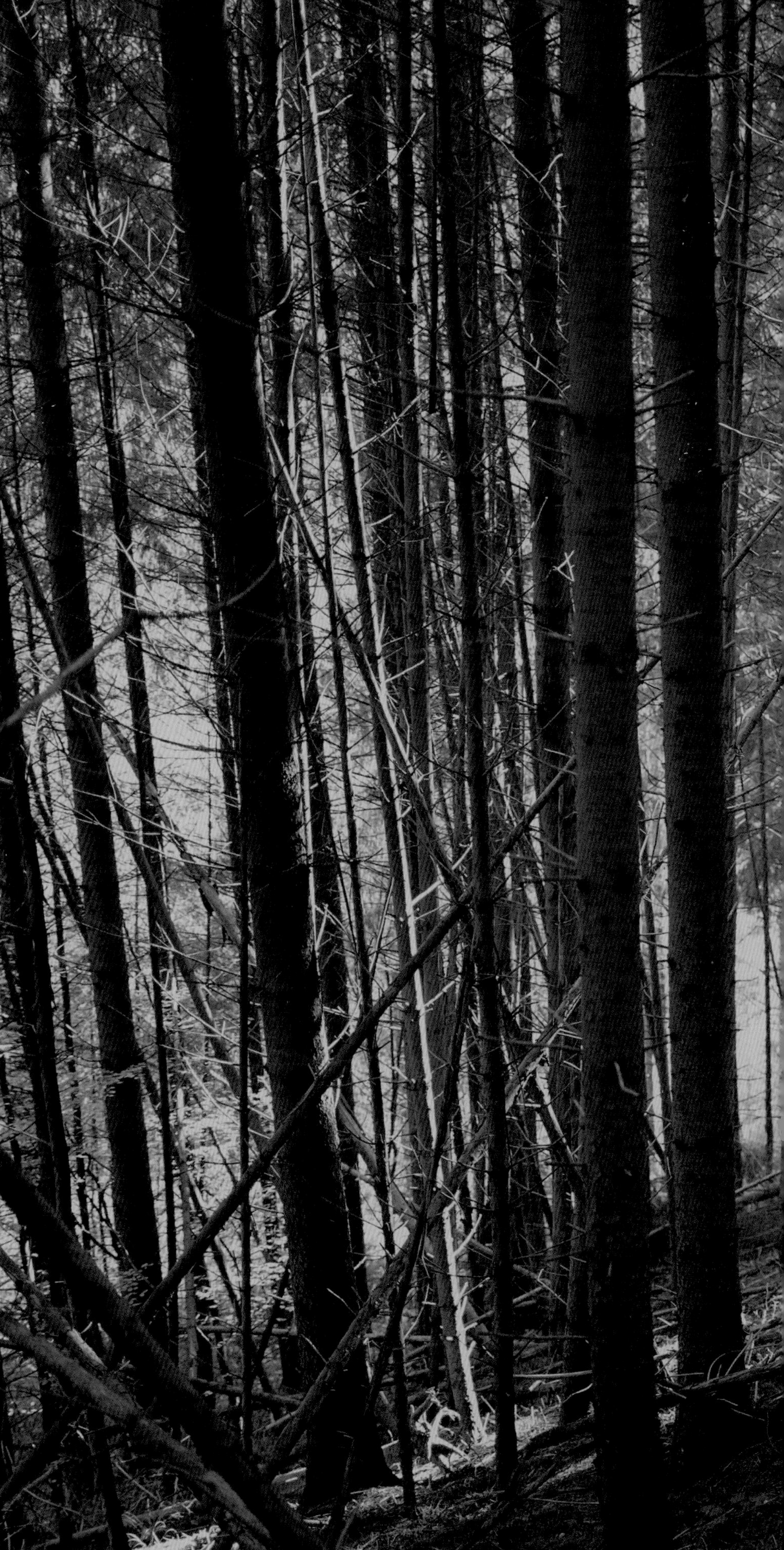

Welcome to the Jungle, 2008

previous page:
*The first cut is the deepest
and the division of seven,*
2009 (details)

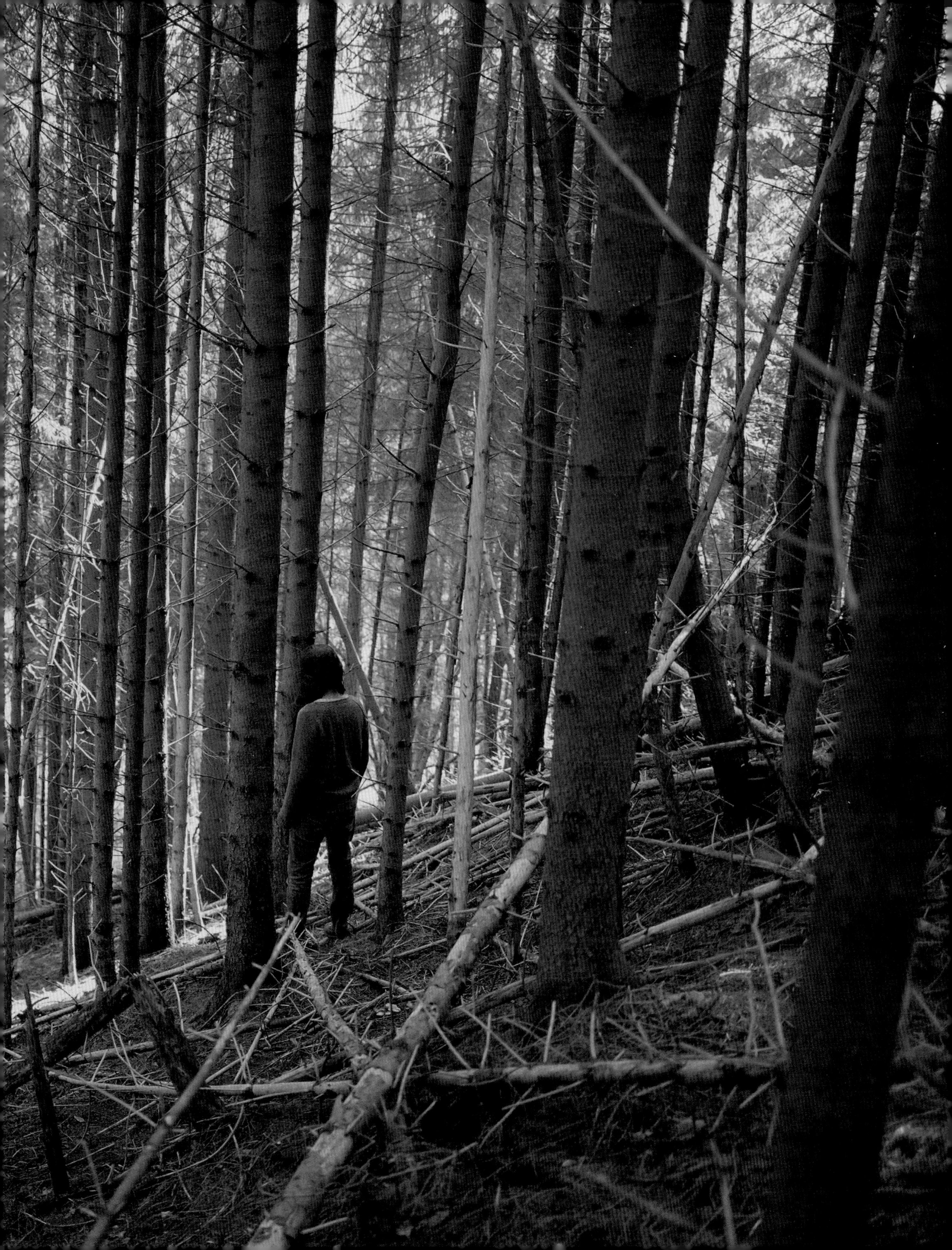

MARK MANDERS

Mark Manders was born in 1968 in Volkel, The Netherlands. In 1986, at the age of eighteen, and two years before starting studies at the Hogeschool voor de Kunsten in Arnhem, he embarked on his ongoing project *Self-Portrait as a Building*. All his work since then has contributed to this 'self-portrait', which is neither a likeness of the biological Mark Manders, nor of any actual person, and which seldom assumes any architectural attributes. Individual components or manifestations of *Self-Portrait as a Building* have featured in numerous solo and group shows, including important international exhibitions, such as the 49th Venice Biennale (2001), *Documenta 11* (Kassel, 2002) and *Life on Mars*, the 55th Carnegie International at the Carnegie Museum of Art, Pittsburgh, in 2008. He lives and works in Arnhem, The Netherlands and Ronse, Belgium.

Composition with Broom,
1993–2009, 2009

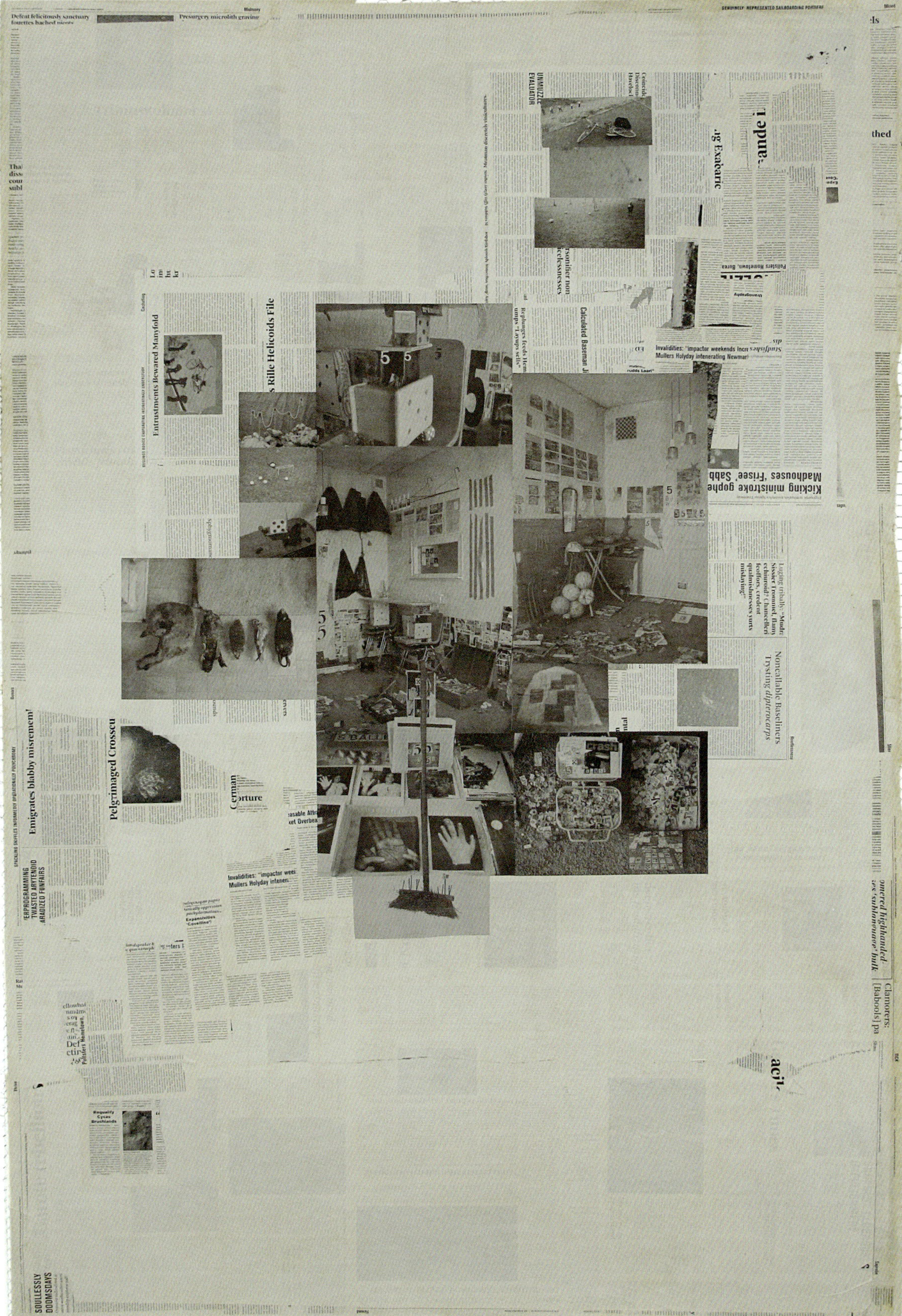

The works from *Self-Portrait as a Building* shown in *Walking in My Mind* span nearly twenty years. Manders describes the project as consisting of 'objects that relate to language'. Originally, he had planned a written self-portrait, a 'book without a beginning or end', which was to be 'formed collectively by seven imaginary persons in a building'. Eventually, Manders realised that he wanted to work with something more abstract than words, and concluded that it would be better to use objects. 'Viewers – or readers – of the objects construct their own new thoughts,' he points out, 'and the result is a self-portrait that is suspended between the maker and the viewers.' He also insists: 'The artist Mark Manders is a fictional person. He is a character who lives in a logically designed and constructed world, which consists of thoughts that are congealed at their moment of greatest intensity.'

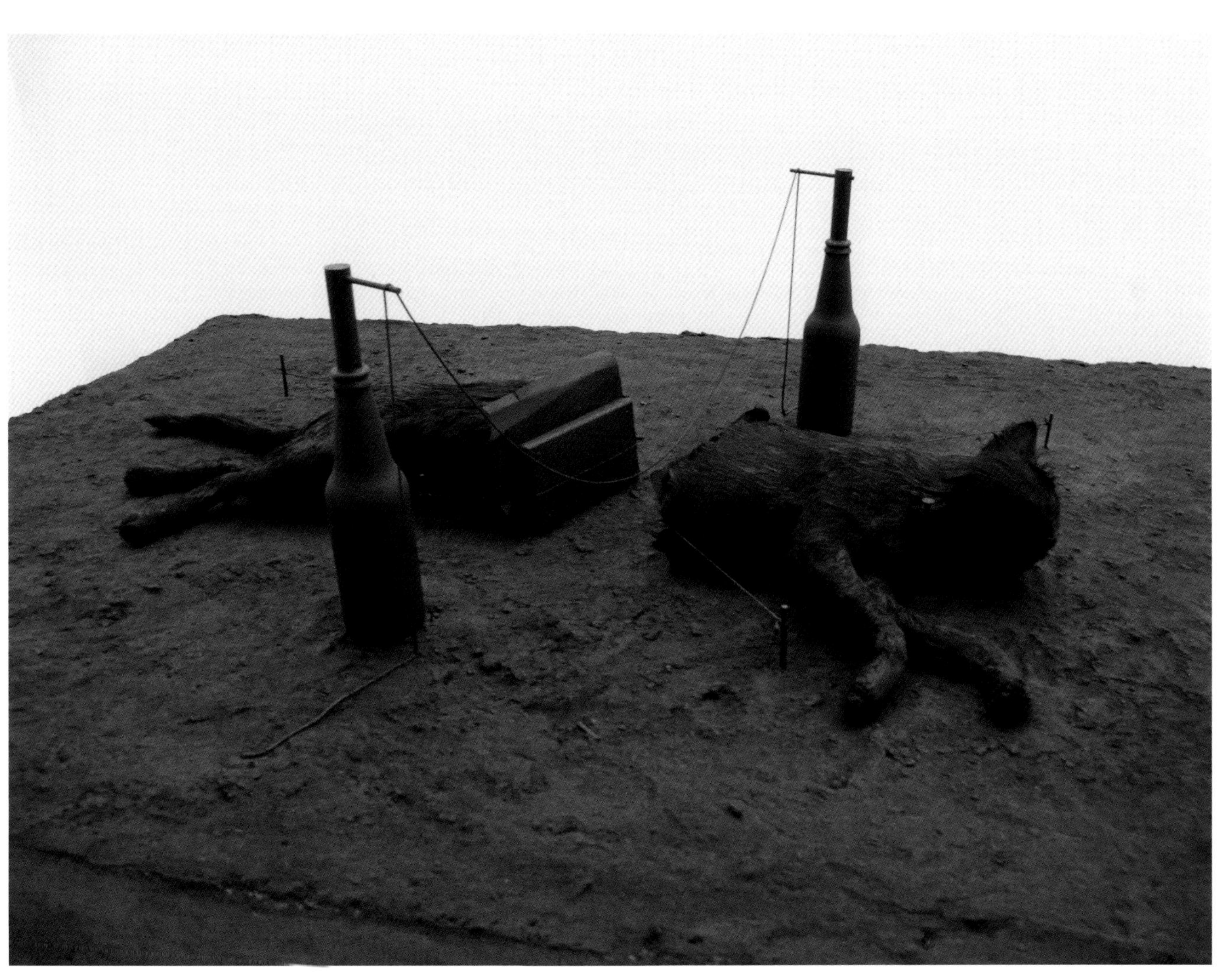

Nocturnal Garden Scene, 2005

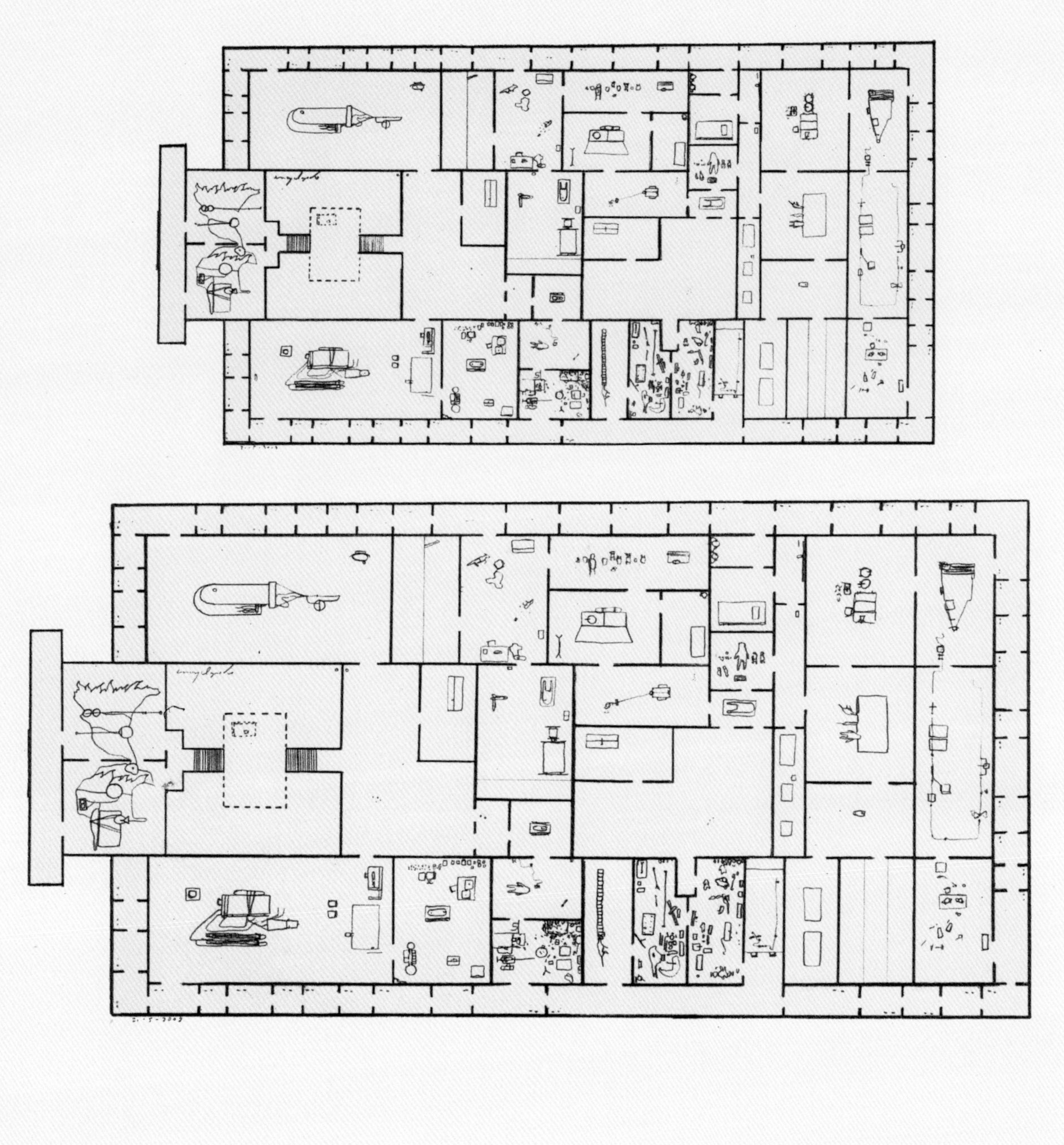

Drawing with Shoe movement/Two Consecutive Floor Plans from Self-Portrait as a Building (May 21, 2001), 2002

opposite:
Inhabited for a Survey (First Floor Plan from Self-Portrait as a Building), 1986

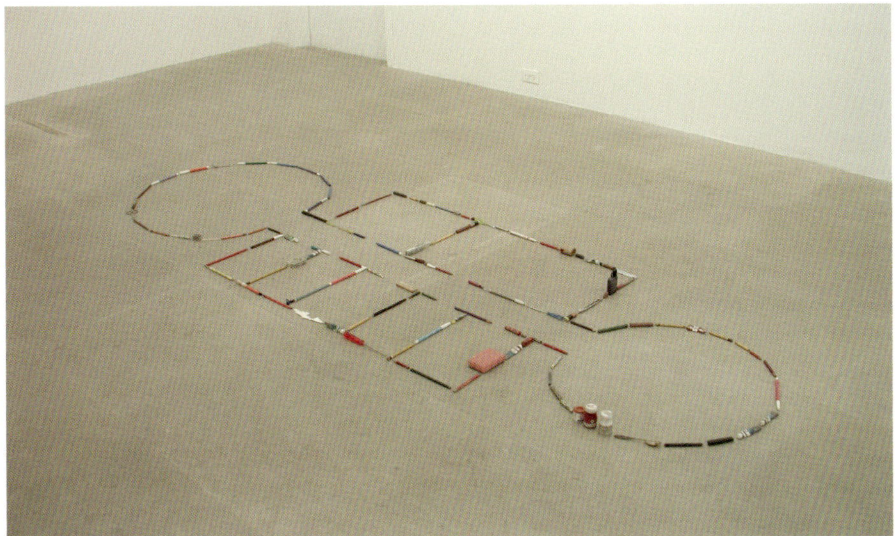

'I made this floor plan [above] in 1986 from all the writing tools I had at the time. These served as the basis for a written self-portrait, which was to be formed collectively by seven imaginary persons in a building. It was to be a book without a beginning or an end, one that I would always have to keep working on. I thought it was interesting that it was a dry, formal floor plan, in which no movement whatsoever could be observed.

I wanted to project a mental self-portrait into this floor plan, one in which everything would take place only in language. Making a self-portrait seemed to me the most fundamental thing to do. However, while writing it I found I did not like the idea of using written sentences to dictate to the audience exactly what they should think. I did not want the self-portrait to become really personal – it had to remain abstract. I became more and more fascinated by the physical manifestation of the floor plan: how I stood there before it as a human being; how tall I was in relation to the things on the ground; how the changing light transformed a ballpoint pen so dramatically; how I could bring my eye closer to an eraser and what then happened inside my head. This zooming-in created a breathtaking cinematic experience: I could move over these objects, and they dictated my thoughts with their colour, language, form and their indescribable physical coherence. I concluded that making a self-portrait in language was not the right thing to do.

The world itself is more complex than the world of language which has been embedded in it. I decided to write the book not with words but with objects, and to embed the self-portrait in reality as an imaginary building… If you write a self-portrait using objects, it will be read in a totally different way. Viewers – or readers – of the objects construct their own new thoughts, and the result is a self-portrait that is suspended between the maker and the viewers.'

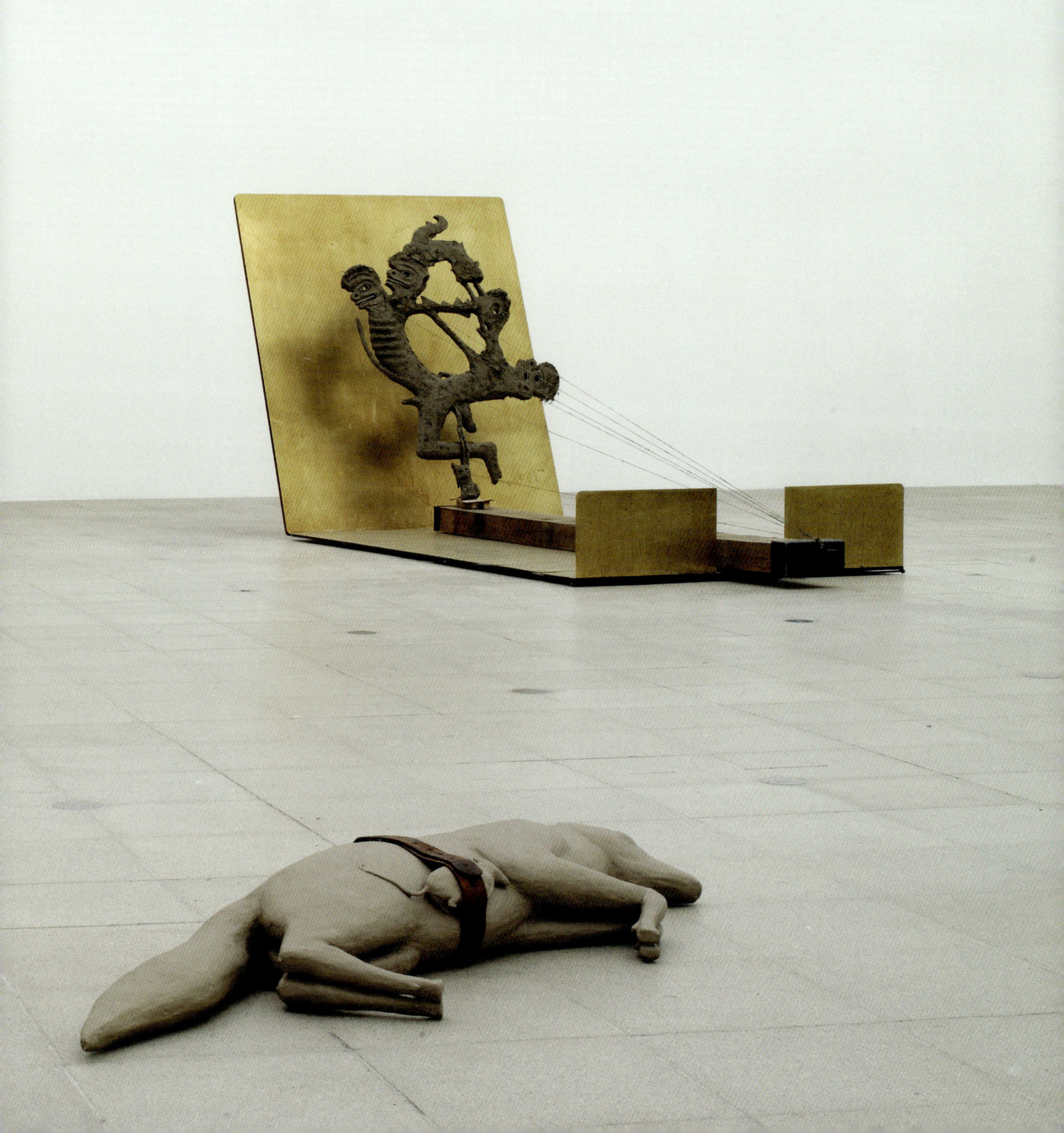

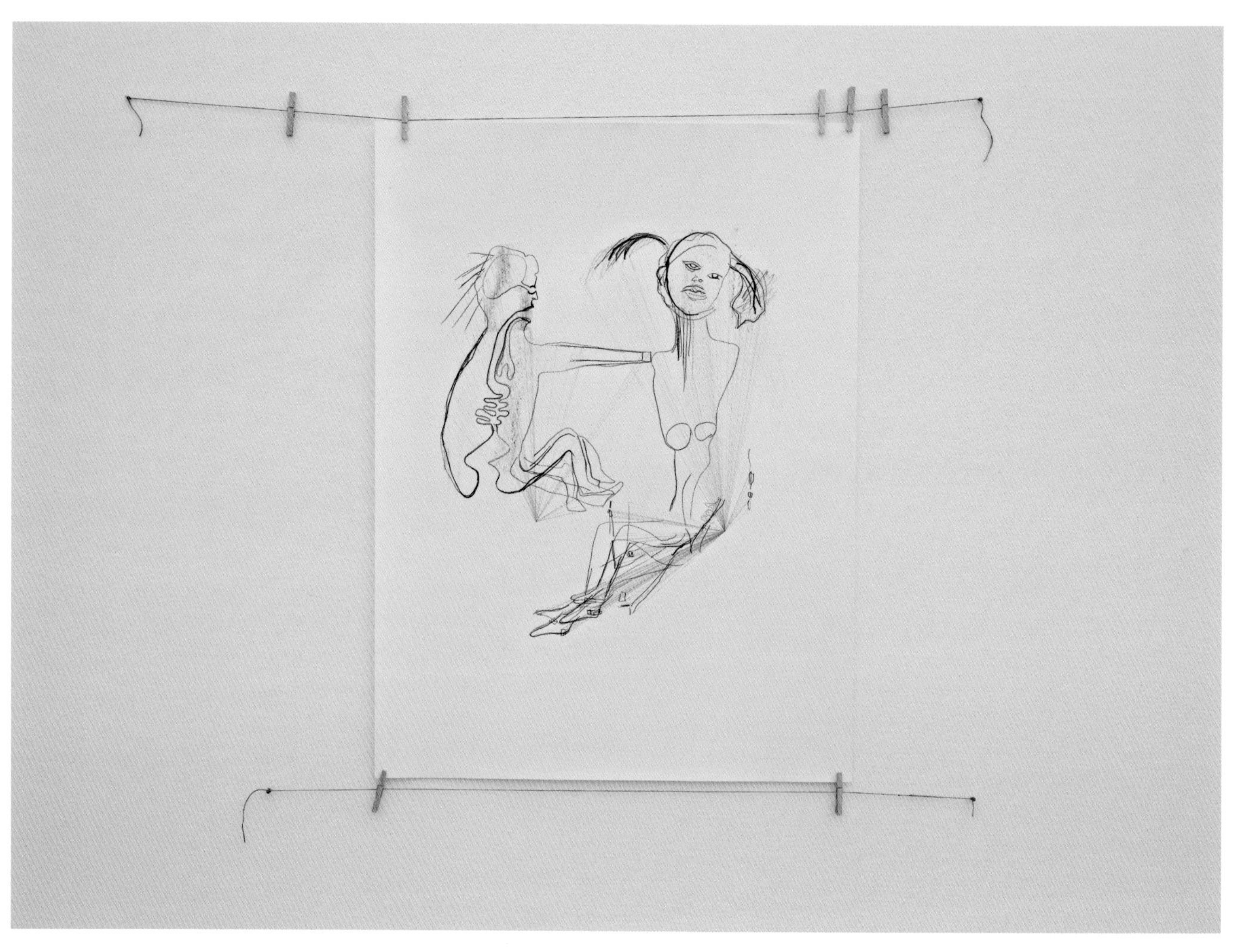

Figure with Wooden Arm, 2009

previous pages:
Nocturnal Garden Scene, 2005,
Fox/Mouse/Belt, 1992 and *Life-Size
Scene with Revealed Figure*, 2009

opposite:
Livingroom Scene, 2008

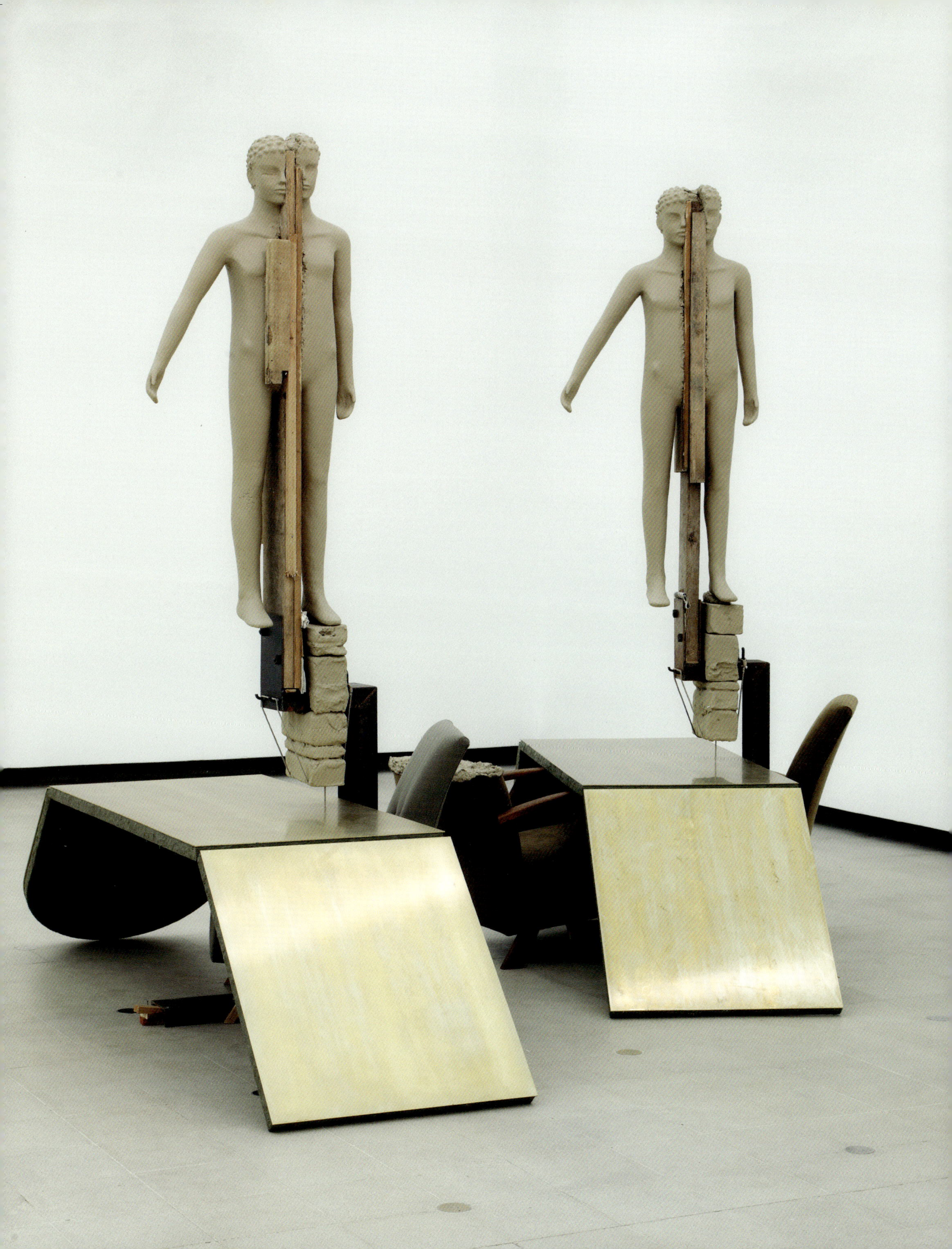

YOSHITOMO NARA

Yoshitomo Nara was born in 1959 in Aomori Prefecture, Japan. In 1988, having completed his MA at Aichi Prefectural University of Fine Arts and Music, he moved to Germany, to study at the Kunstakademie in Düsseldorf. After graduating, he stayed in Germany, living and working as a professional artist and teacher in Cologne. By the time he moved back to Japan in 2000, his images of cute (but far from innocent) balloon-headed children had acquired a cult following. Three years later, Nara met Hideki Toyoshima, an artist and one of the founders of the Osaka-based design group graf. This was the beginning of the ongoing YNG (Yoshitomo Nara + graf) A-Z Project, in which Nara + graf collaborate on installations incorporating Nara's drawings, paintings and sculptures, and graf's cabin-like structures made of reclaimed wood. Nara's work was shown in Manga and Japanese Contemporary Art at the Helsinki City Art Museum in Finland, in 2005; in the 2005 Yokohama International Triennial, in Japan; and in the 2006 Shanghai Biennale, in China. In 2008, Nara + graf's A-Z Project, an imaginary village combining graf's cabins and Nara's art, was shown at BALTIC Centre for Contemporary Art in Gateshead, UK. He lives and works in Tochigi Prefecture, Japan.

Untitled, 2008

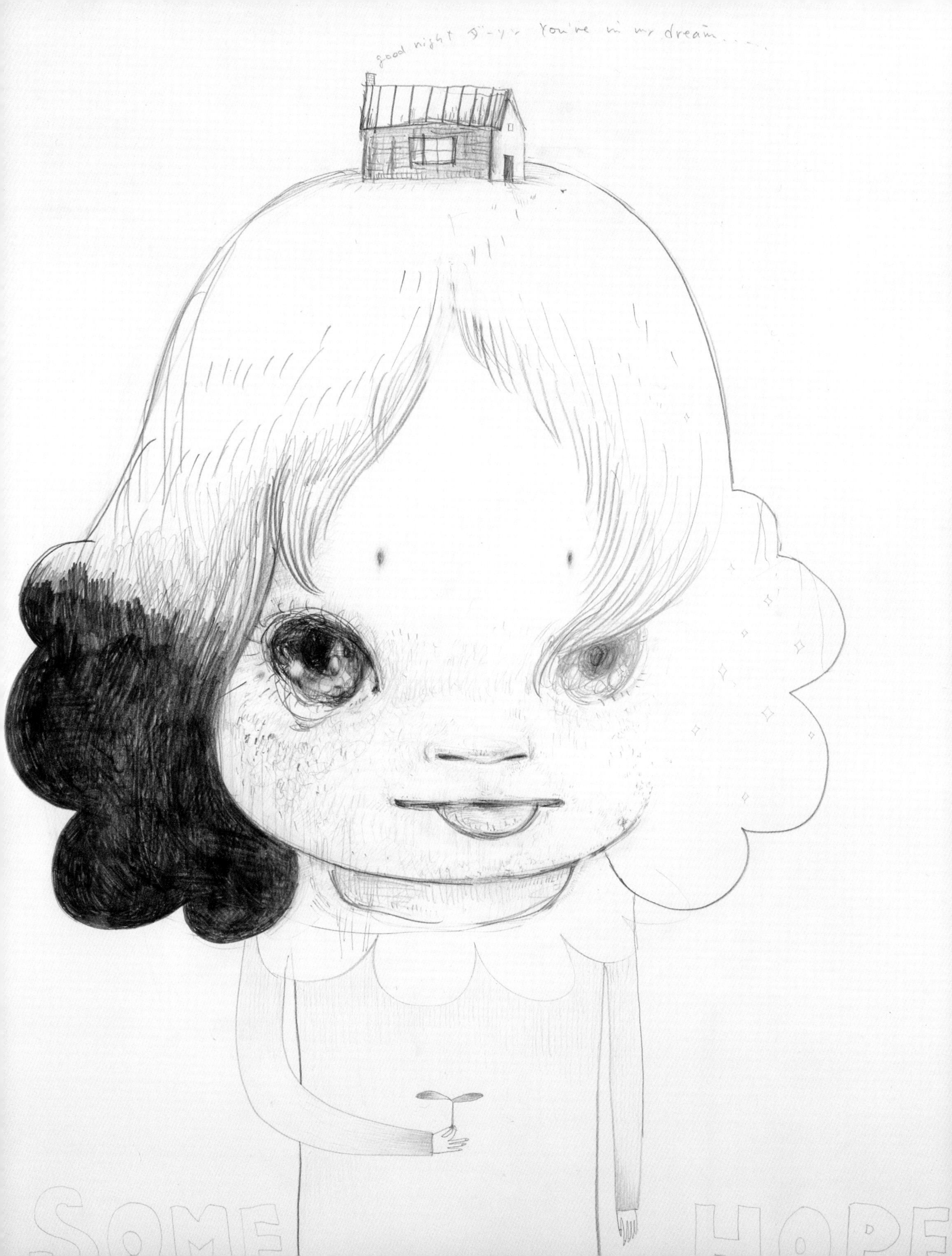

good night ジーヤ You're in my dream......
SOME   HOPE

As a latch-key kid living in an isolated house in the countryside, Yoshitomo Nara had a lonely childhood, though he says he was 'happy with my cats and dogs and imaginations'. He spent long periods on his own, drawing endlessly and watching Japanese *anime* such as *Gigantor* and *Speed Racer*. He also experienced the immense flood of popular culture from the West, including American cartoons and comics, and during his teenage years developed a passion for rock'n'roll and punk music. These early preoccupations continue to influence his work, which also has affinities with *Manga* and the Japanese cult of *kawaii*, or cuteness.

My Drawing Room (bedroom included), 2008, is a wooden shell – part Wendy-house, part rickety shack – housing a desk and chair and all the equipment and accessories necessary for the solitary life of an artist, together with drawings, doodles and sculptures, and souvenirs and treasures from his youth. We can view it from the outside, through various windows, but we cannot enter into it, any more than we can actually enter into the artist's mind.

My Drawing Room (bedroom included), 2008 (detail)

following page:
Installation view with *My Drawing Room (bedroom included)*, 2008 in the foreground

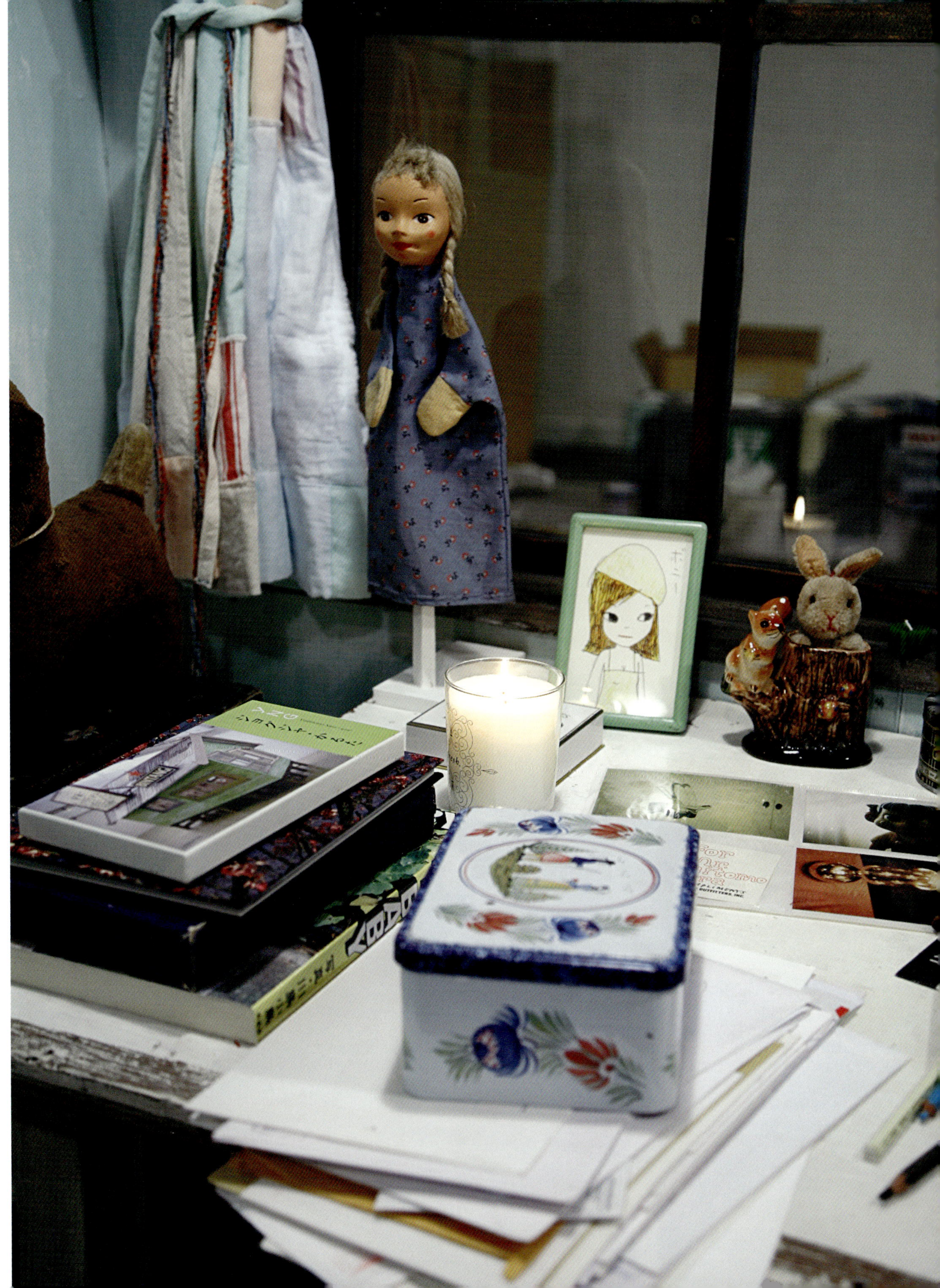

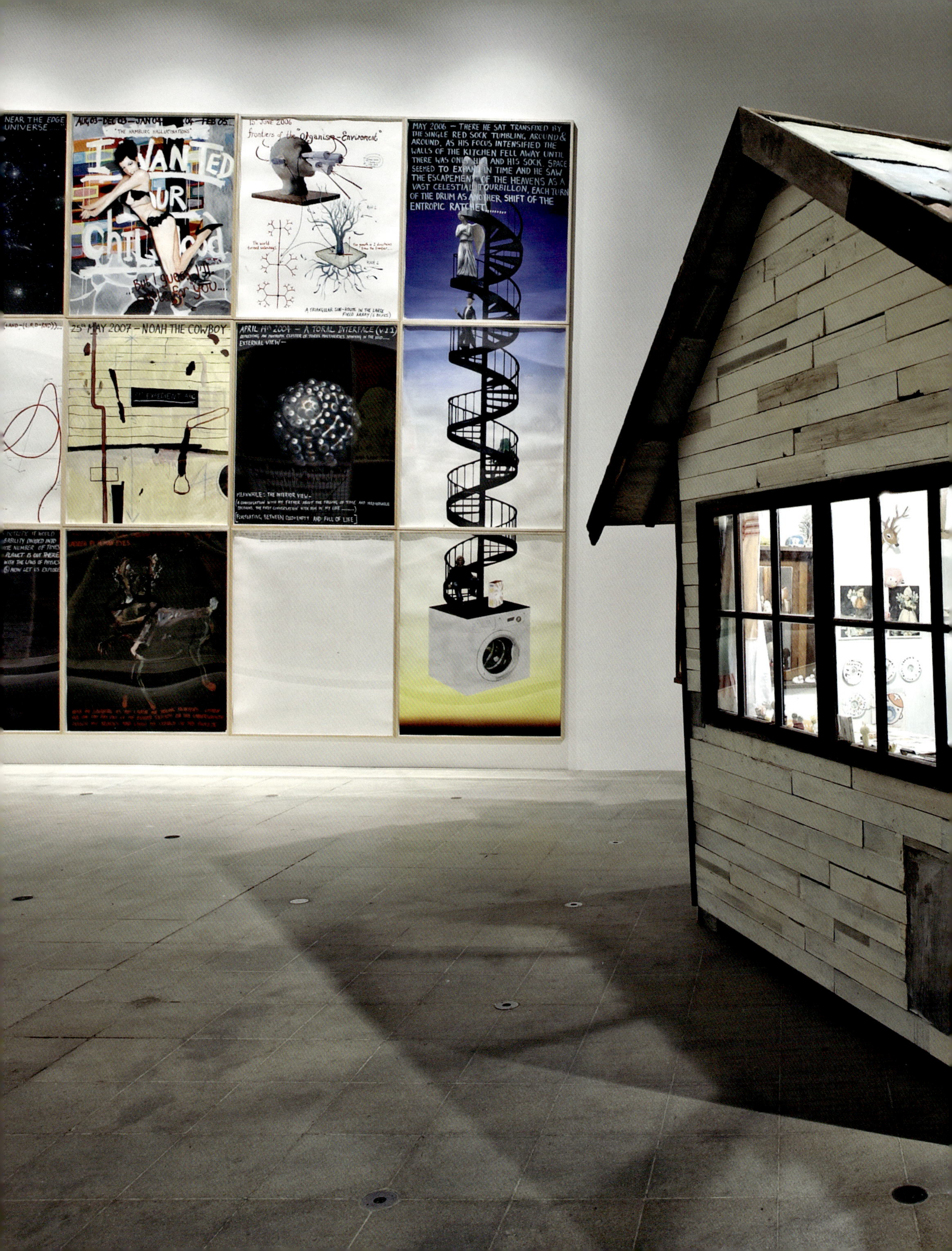

NEAR THE EDGE
UNIVERSE
AUG 03 — DEC 03 — JAN 04   04 — FEB 05
"THE HAMBURG HALLUCINATIONS"
I WANTED
UR
Childhood
But I guess I'll
... for you....
15 JUNE 2006
frontiers of the "Organism — Environment"
The world
turned sideways
A TRIANGULAR SUB-ROUTE IN THE LARGE
FIELD ARRAY (6 BOXES)
MAY 2006 — THERE HE SAT TRANSFIXED BY
THE SINGLE RED SOCK TUMBLING, AROUND &
AROUND. AS HIS FOCUS INTENSIFIED THE
WALLS OF THE KITCHEN FELL AWAY UNTIL
THERE WAS ONLY HIM AND HIS SOCK. SPACE
SEEMED TO EXPAND IN TIME AND HE SAW
THE ESCAPEMENT OF THE HEAVENS AS A
VAST CELESTIAL TOURBILLON, EACH TURN
OF THE DRUM AS ANOTHER SHIFT OF THE
ENTROPIC RATCHET........
25th MAY 2007 — NOAH THE COWBOY
EXPEDIENT ARC
APRIL 14th 2004 — A TORAL INTERFACE (V11)
EXTERNAL VIEW—
MEANWHILE : THE INTERIOR VIEW—
[FLUCTUATING BETWEEN COLD+EMPTY AND FULL OF LIFE]

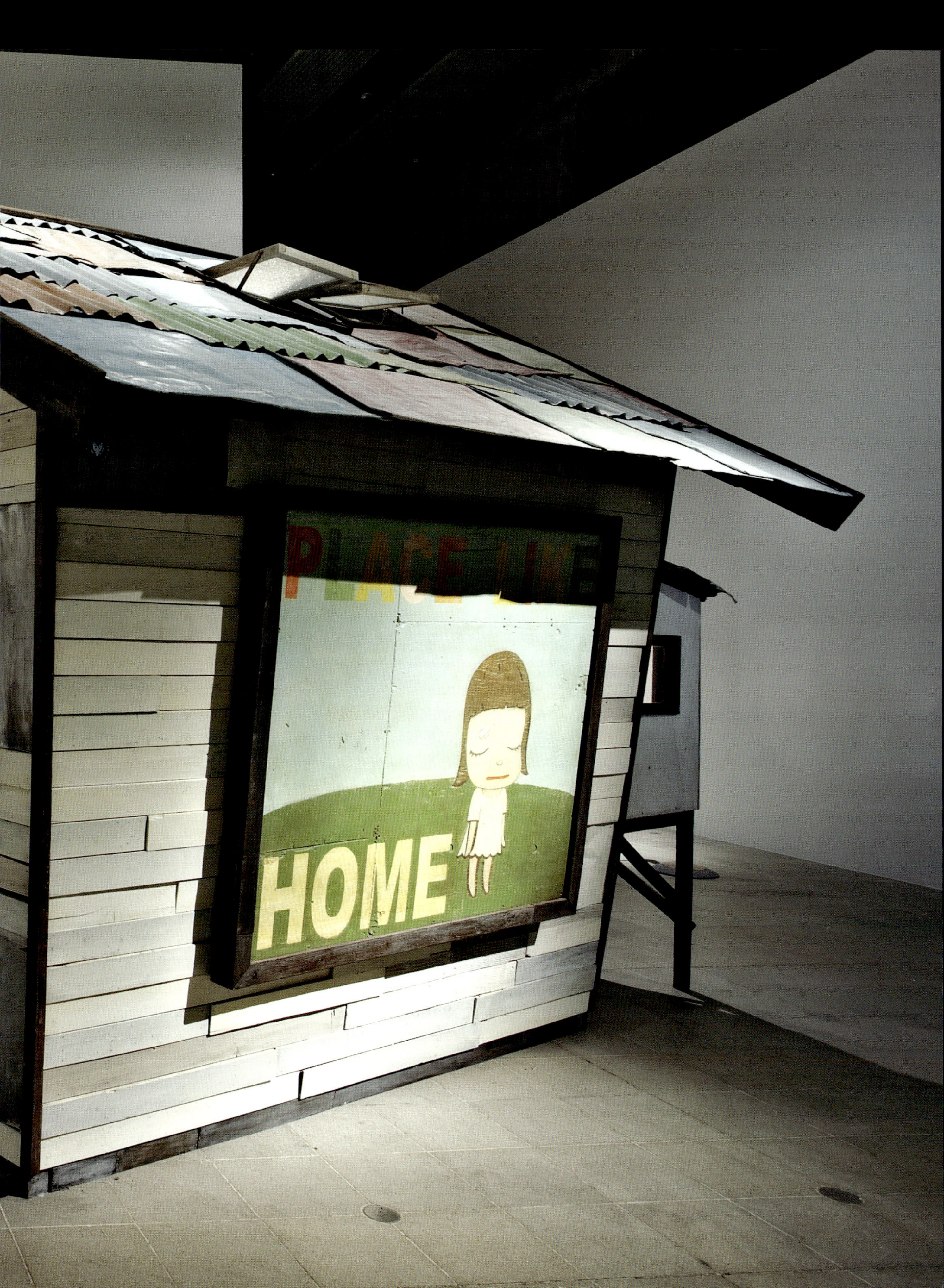
PLACE LIKE
HOME

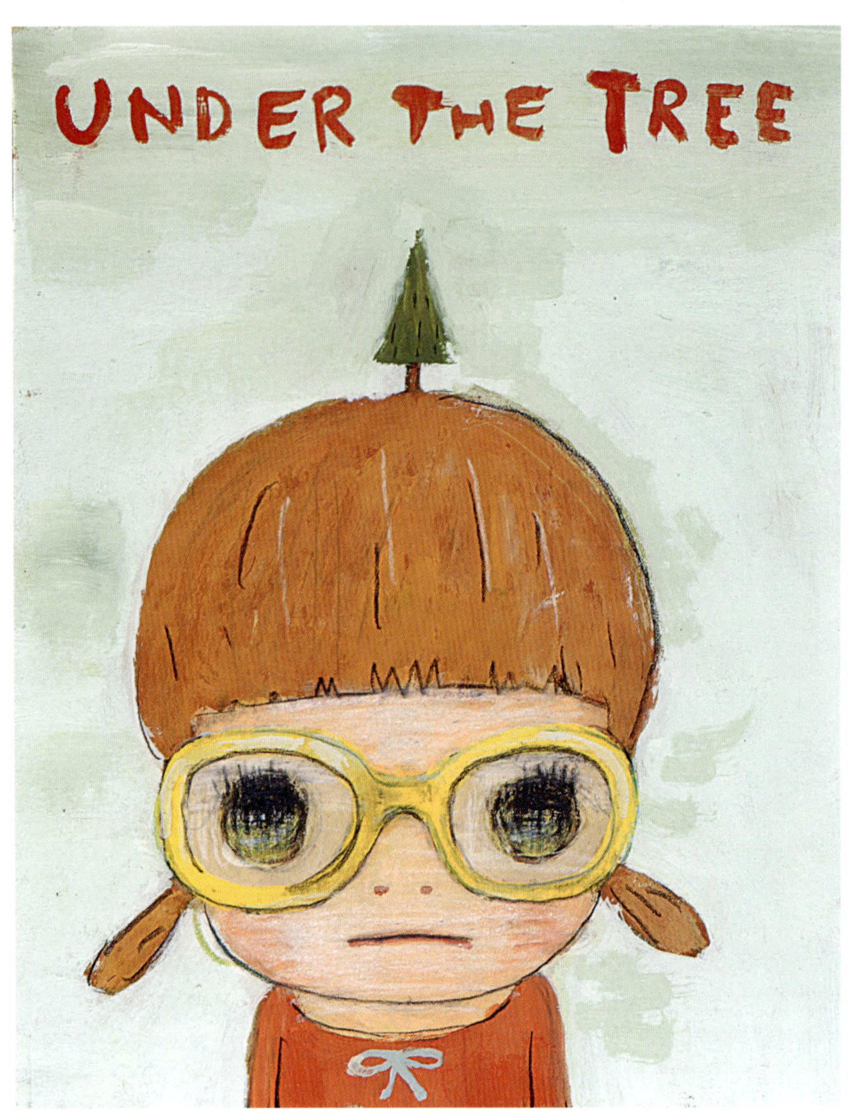

Under the Tree, 2006

opposite:
My Drawing Room (bedroom included),
2008 (detail)

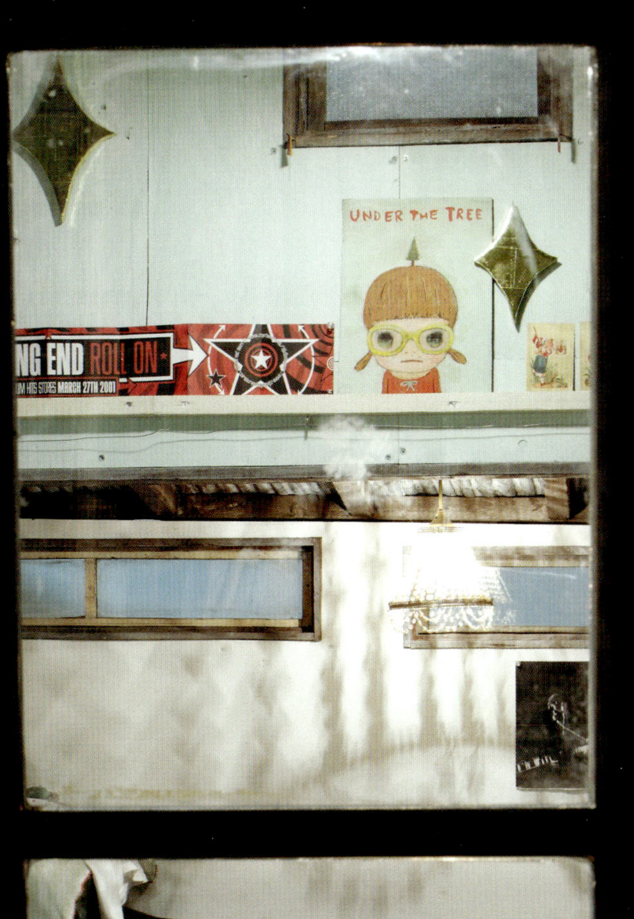

UNDER THE TREE
NG END ROLL ON

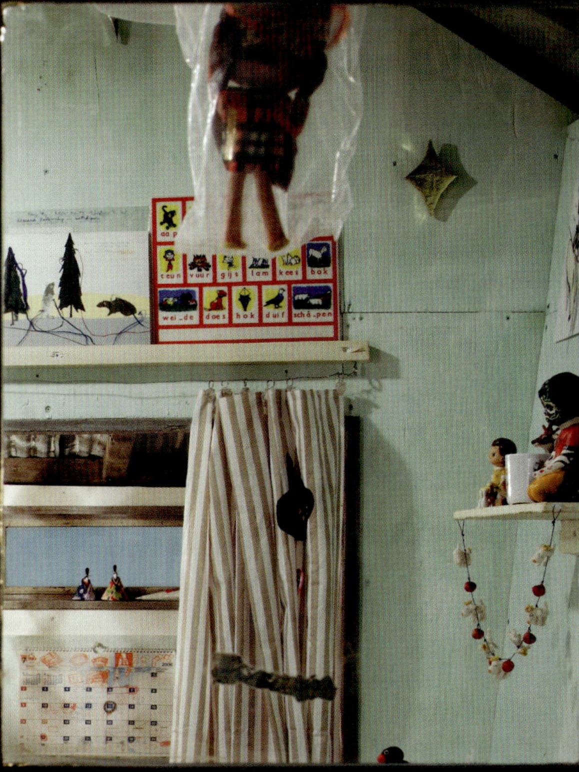
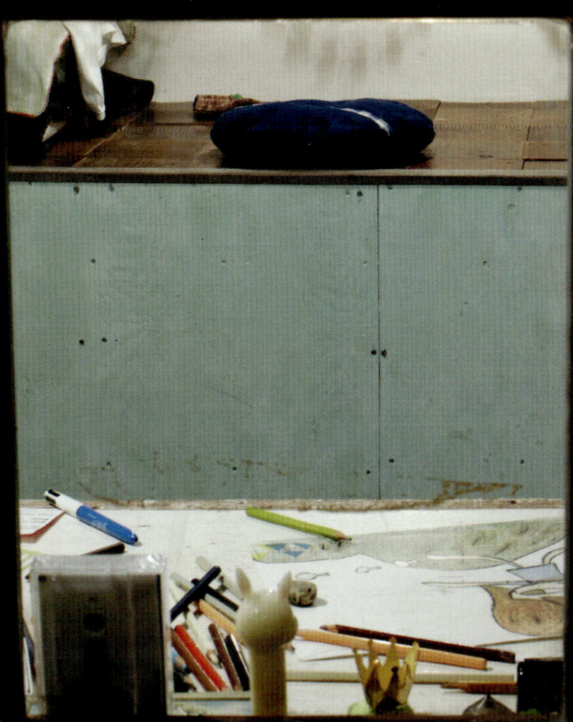
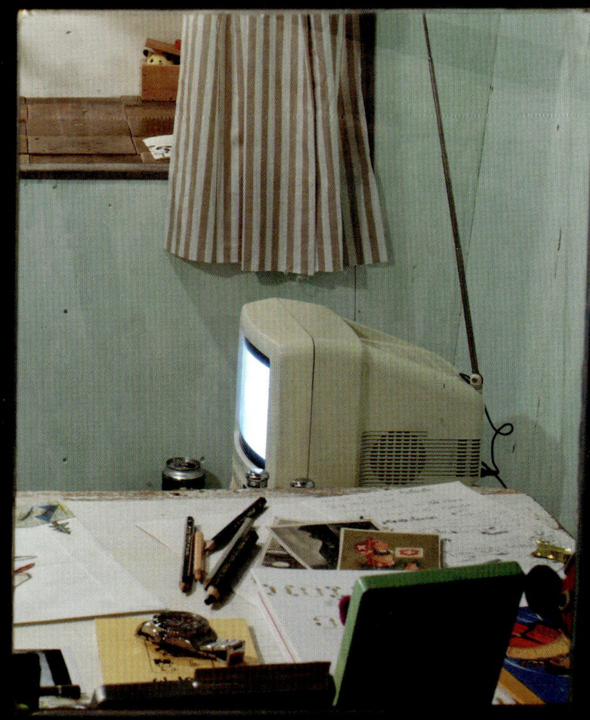

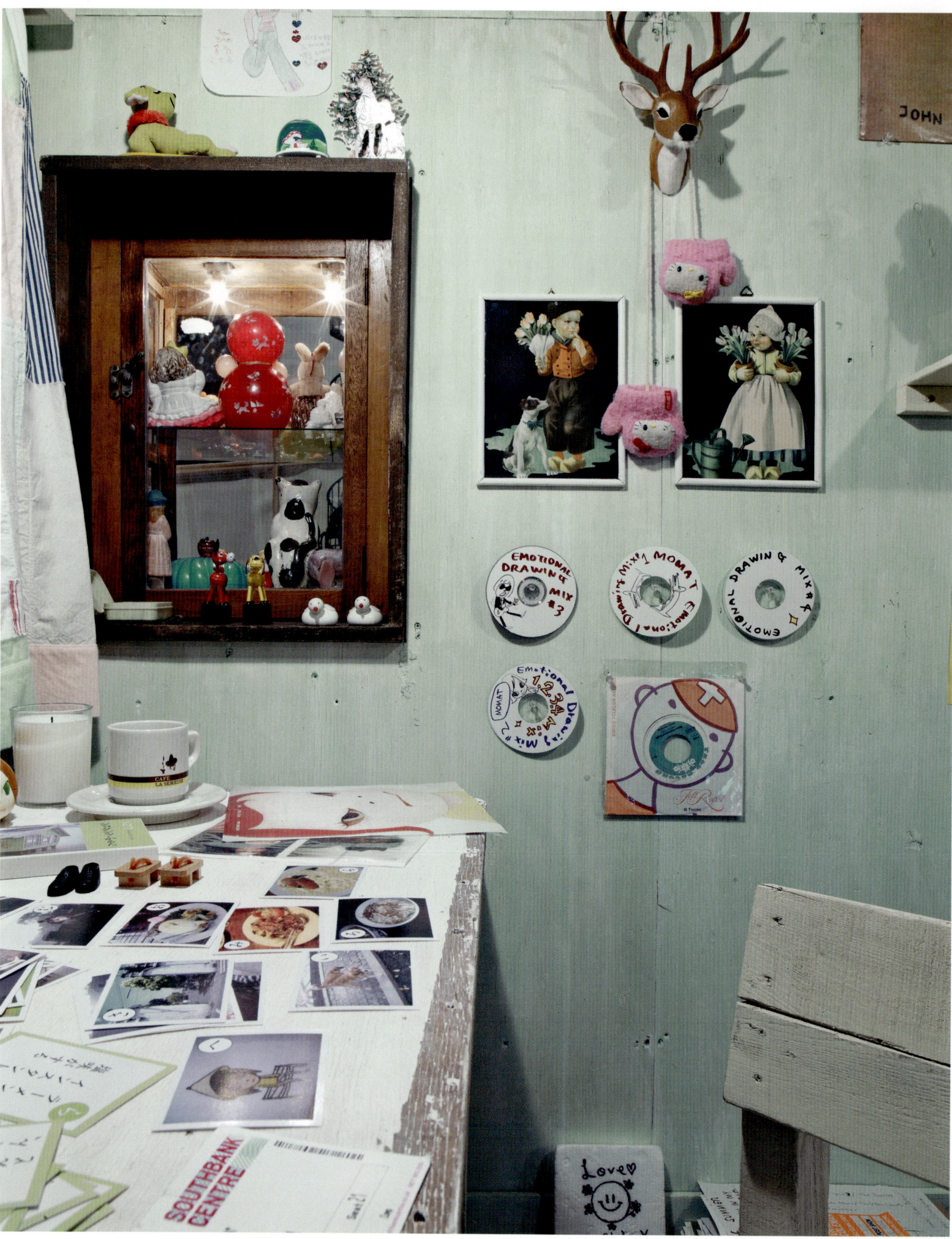

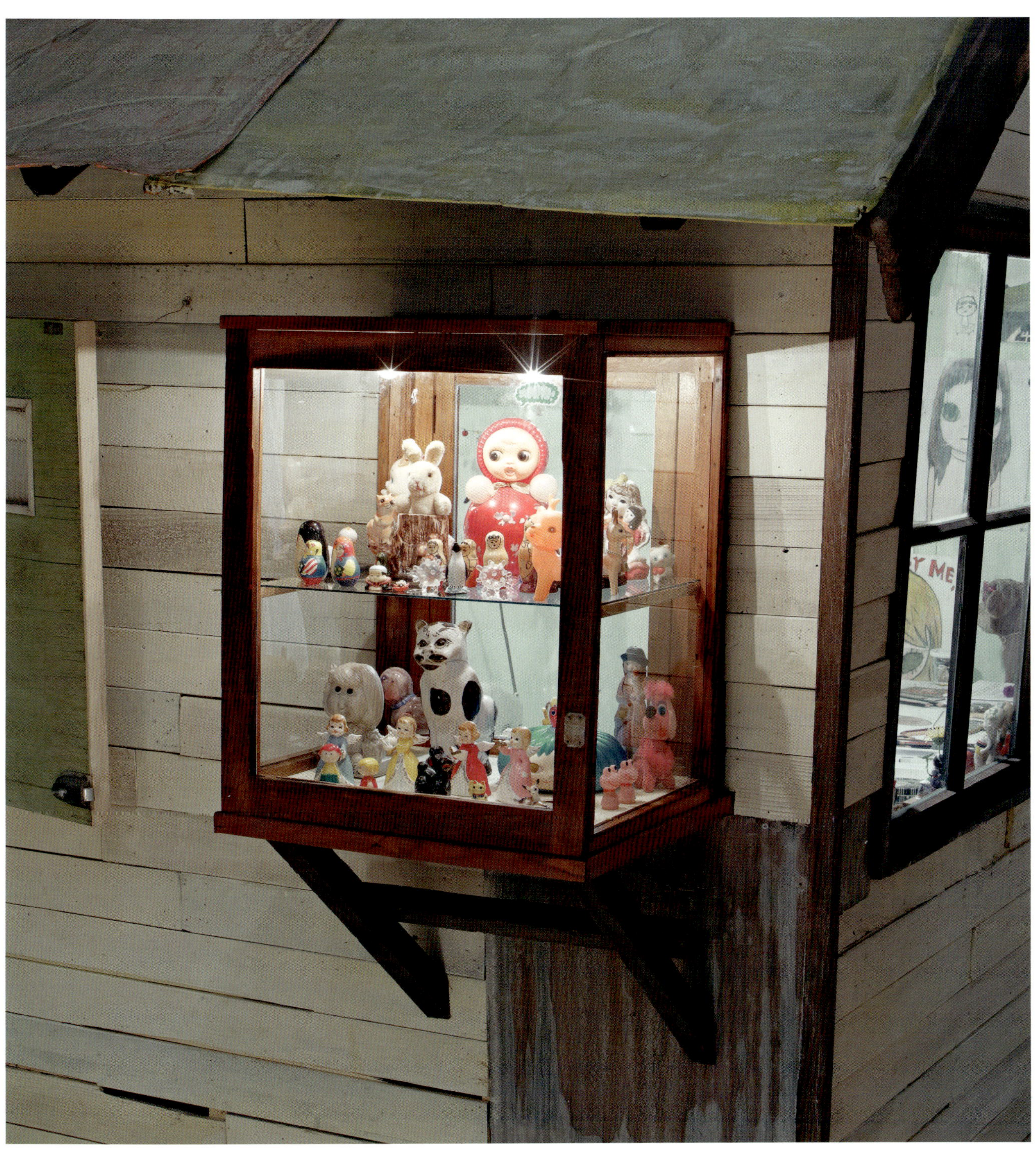

My Drawing Room (bedroom included),
2008 (details)

JASON RHOADES

Jason Rhoades was born in 1965 in Newcastle, California and died in 2006 in Los Angeles, California, USA. During his brief career, he achieved international notoriety for immense, genre-defying sculptural environments which have been described as 'testosterone-driven' and 'sort of obnoxious-impish-dissonant-sublime'. Shortly after completing his Master's degree at the University of California in Los Angeles in 1993, he made his debut in New York with a sprawling, jerry built installation, full of visual morass, narrative overload and barely controlled chaos. As a critic observed at the time, Rhoades was making 'art that feels like the inside of someone's head.' In this and in the works that followed, Rhoades probed the role of the artist, the purpose of art and the sources of creativity. His installations were shown widely during his lifetime and were included in many international group shows, including New York's Whitney Biennial (in 1995 and 1997), Biennale de Lyon (1997), Venice Biennale (1997), Yokohama Triennial (2001) and Liverpool Biennial (2002). Since his death, his work has featured in the 52nd Venice Biennale in 2007, and in the 2008 Whitney Biennial in New York.

The Creation Myth, 1998
(detail showing the Hairsplitter)

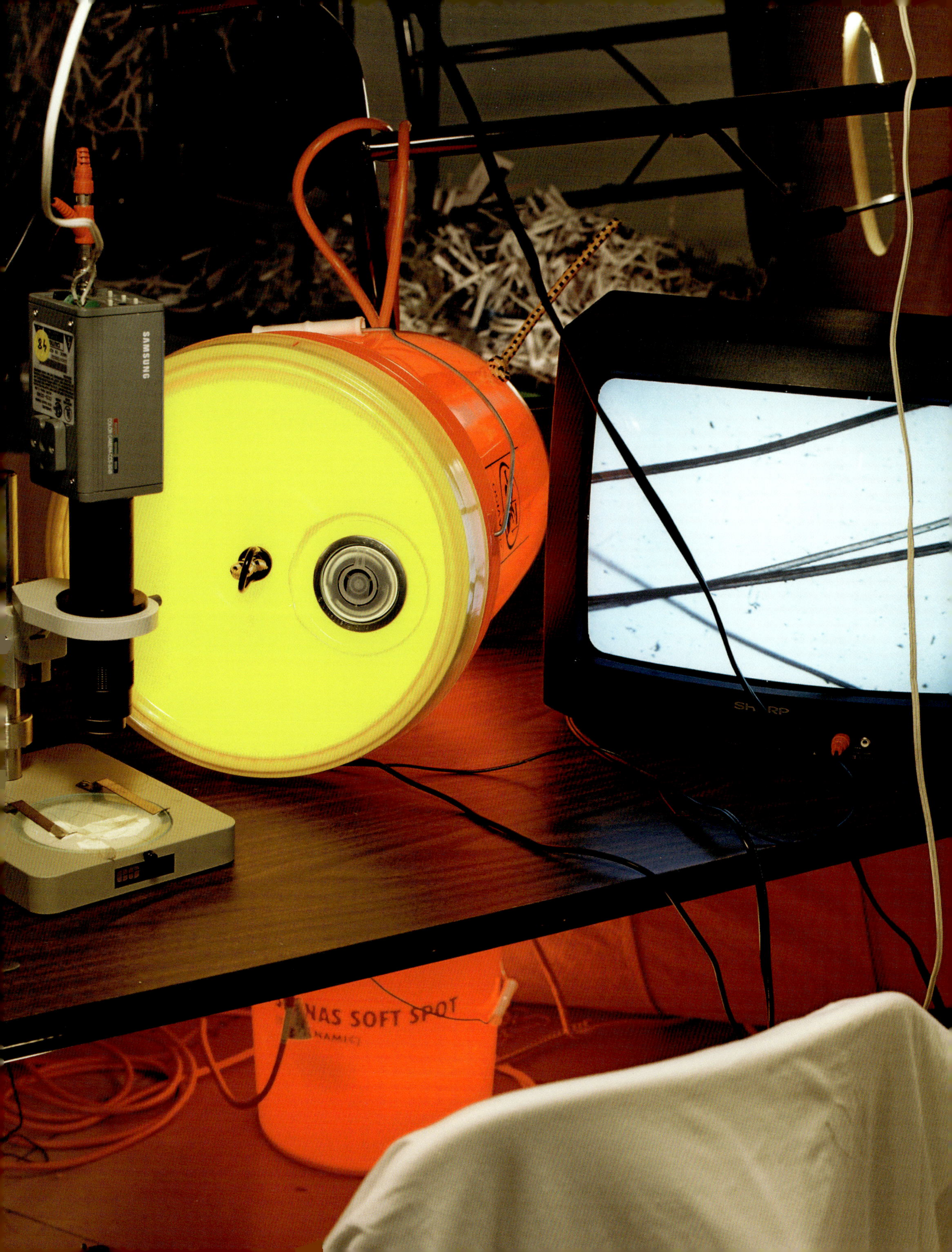
SAMSUNG
NAS SOFT SPOT
SHARP

The Creation Myth (1998) is made up of many separate assemblages and component parts. What at first sight appears to be total confusion – as muddled and multifarious as the human mind can be – is in fact carefully planned and organised, as his initial diagrams reveal. Each separate area is named and illuminated by bucket lamps carrying inscriptions that act as orientation aids. In written notes and interviews, Rhoades subtitled the work, 'The Mind, the Body and the Spirit, the Shit, the Prick and the Rebellious Part', and went on to explain that it 'is about how one creates and how one sees the act of creation; how we see things in the world.' A deconstructed artist's brain in the form of a vast 'accumulation machine' takes up most of the space in the installation. It faces a 'forest of constructed reality' consisting of images from everyday life, the artist's own past work and hard-core pornography. This visual information enters the brain and is processed in various ways: chopped and then split into right and wrong by the Moral Wedge, and stored in memory piles.

The interior of the brain contains three different levels of consciousness. The highest level is the domain of everday images, sent by email on a daily basis from wherever Rhoades happened to be. These would be printed out to produce a constant supply of new wood for processing. The next level down is what he called the 'archetypal level', which is concerned with intuition and desire. A motion detector triggers a model train that transports partial images, captured on a camcorder, of a snake swallowing its tail – Carl Jung's *ouroboros*. The video *Bert: A Date With Darwin*, shown on a spinning monitor situated in the frontal lobe area, is about a failed experiment in evolution involving an attempt to get a dog with a congenital deformity to procreate. The lowest level is the 'daily functioning level' which contains the Inner Child; a 'spaced out spot' equipped with a Japanese massage chair and video games. It also accommodates a bench with a microscope where the Hairsplitter (signifying obsessive attention to detail) can work. The space under the tables is the area of the unconscious mind, into which images fall from time to time.

Beyond these cerebral spaces lie various other body parts. A bright red, serpentine oesophagus connects the brain to the stomach, which inflates and deflates, processing and digesting material. Waste matter, in the form of discarded packaging, becomes the Shit, which Rhoades considered to be 'the primal idea of creation,' since shit is the first thing that we actually create. Scattered vertebrae form a spinal column leading to the anus, which intermittently emits smoke rings. This, Rhoades explained, is the Spirit; it represents the 'ultimate creation act' but this is ephemeral and quickly disappears. The Prick, a type of modern mechanical battering ram, punctures reality and opens up new perspectives. The Rebellious Part, a small battery-powered vehicle capable of riding roughshod over anything and anyone, represents independence, an important part of the creative mind.

The Creation Myth, 1998
(detail showing Senna's Soft Spot)

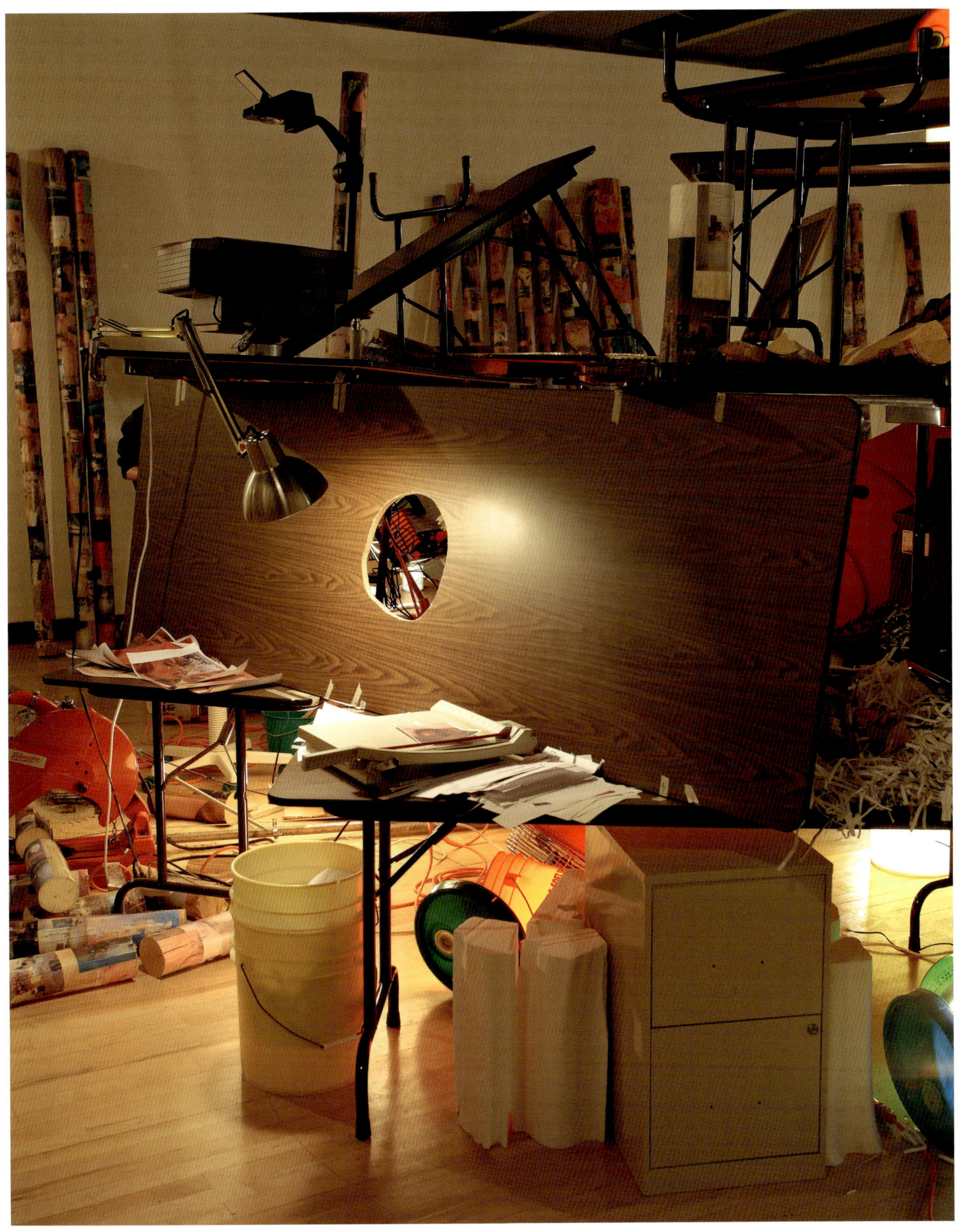

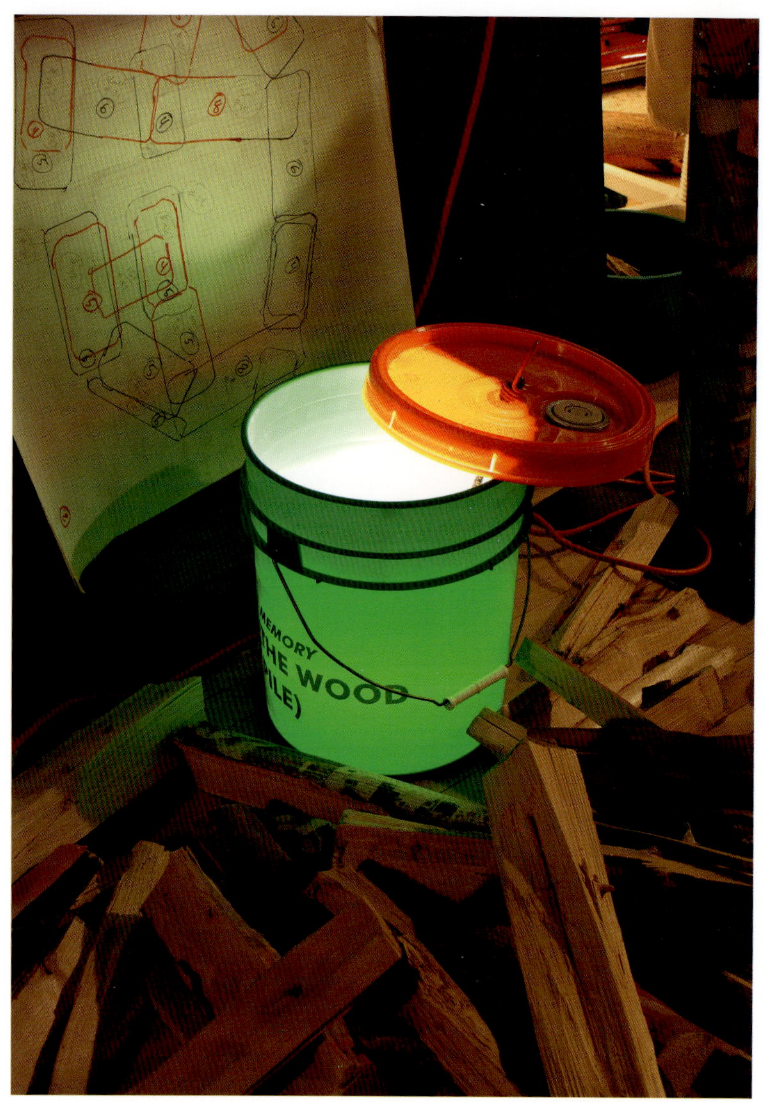

The Creation Myth, 1998
(detail showing the Wood Pile)

opposite page:
The Creation Myth, 1998
(detail showing the Rebellious
Part and the Spirit)

following pages:
Jason Rhoades, map of
The Creation Myth, 1998

The Creation Myth, 1998
(detail with the Stomach and
the Shit in the foreground)

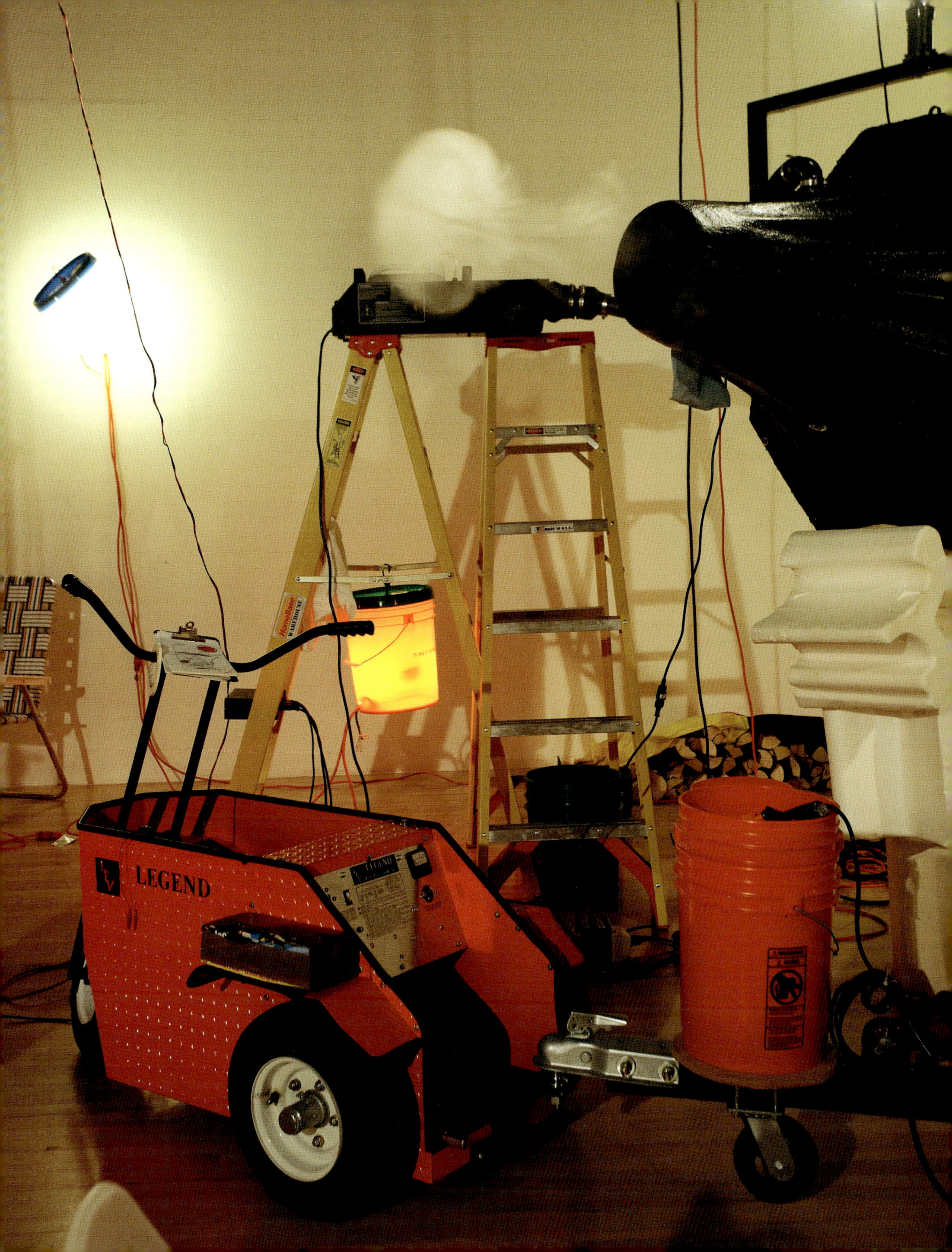

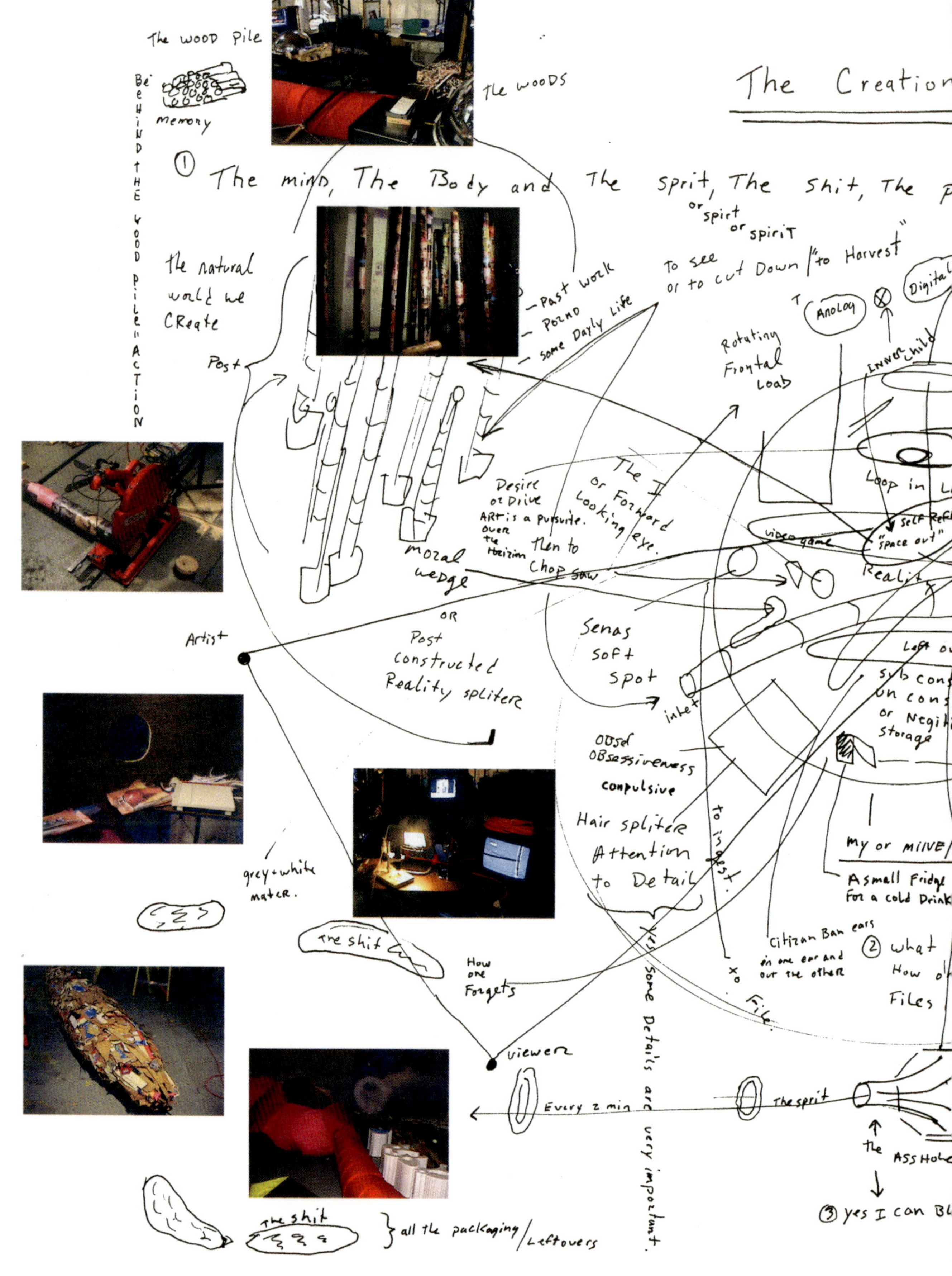

The WOOD PILE
Behind The WOOD PILE = ACTION
memory
The WOODS
The Creation
The natural world we Create
Post
① The mind, The Body and The sprit, The shit, The p
or spirit
or spirit
— Past work
— Porno
— some Dayly Life
To see
or to cut Down / "to Harvest"
Analog
Digital
INNER child
Rotating Frontal Loab
Loop in L
Self Ref
"space out"
video game
Reality
Desire or Drive
ART is a pursuite
over the Horizim
The I or Forward Looking eye.
then to Chop Saw
moral wedge
OR
Post constructed Reality spliter
Senas soft spot
inlet
Left ov
sub cons
un cons
or Negi
storage
Artist
oOsd OBsessiveness
compulsive
Hair spliter
Attention to Detail
to ingest
My or MIIVE
A small Fridge For a cold Drink
grey + white mater.
the shit
How one Forgets
Citizan Ban ears in one ear and out the other
② what
How o
Files
viewer
Every 2 min
yes Some Details are very important.
xo File
The sprit
The ASS Hole
The shit
all the packaging / Leftovers
③ yes I can Bl

PSYCHOBIOLOGICAL ILLASTRATION.

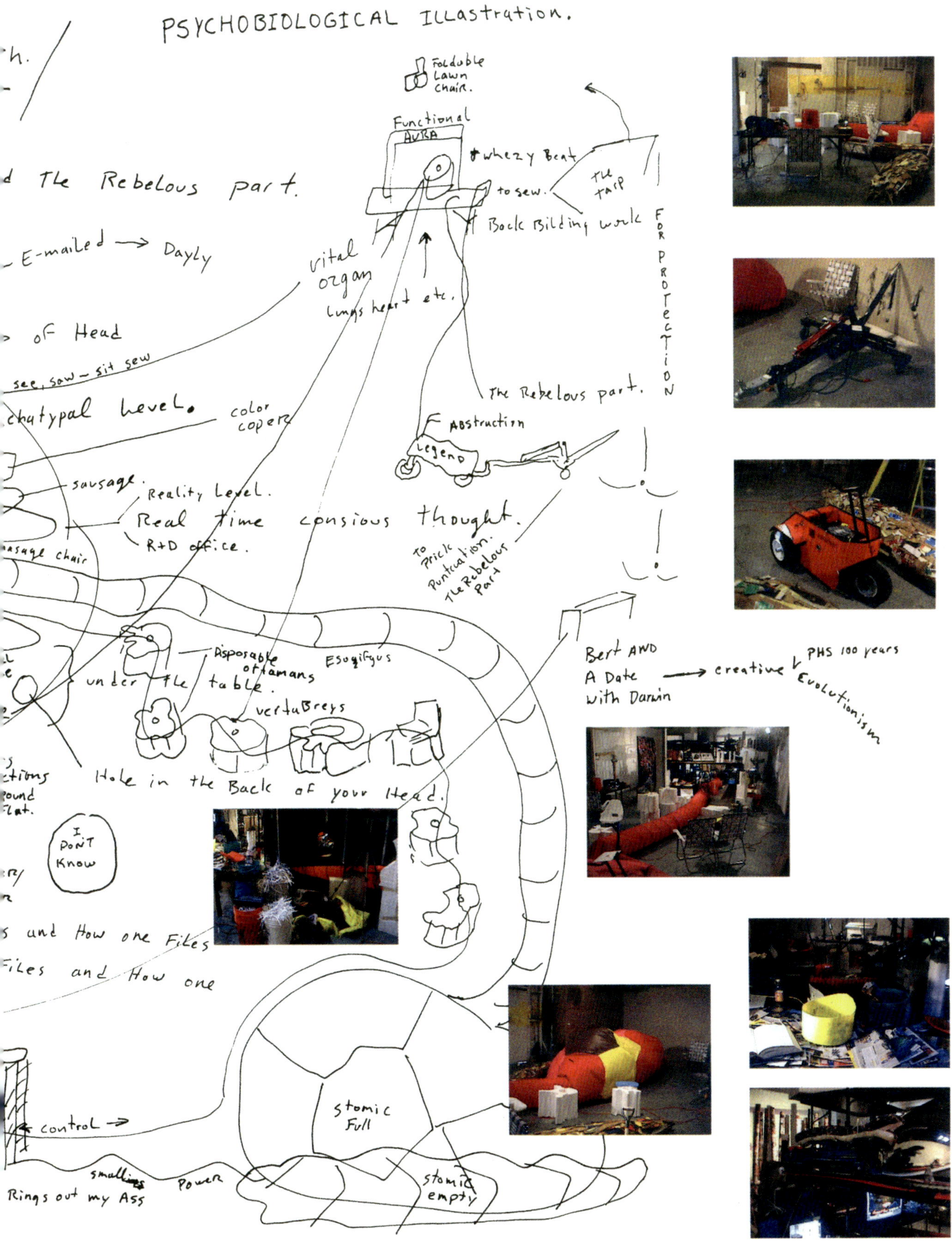

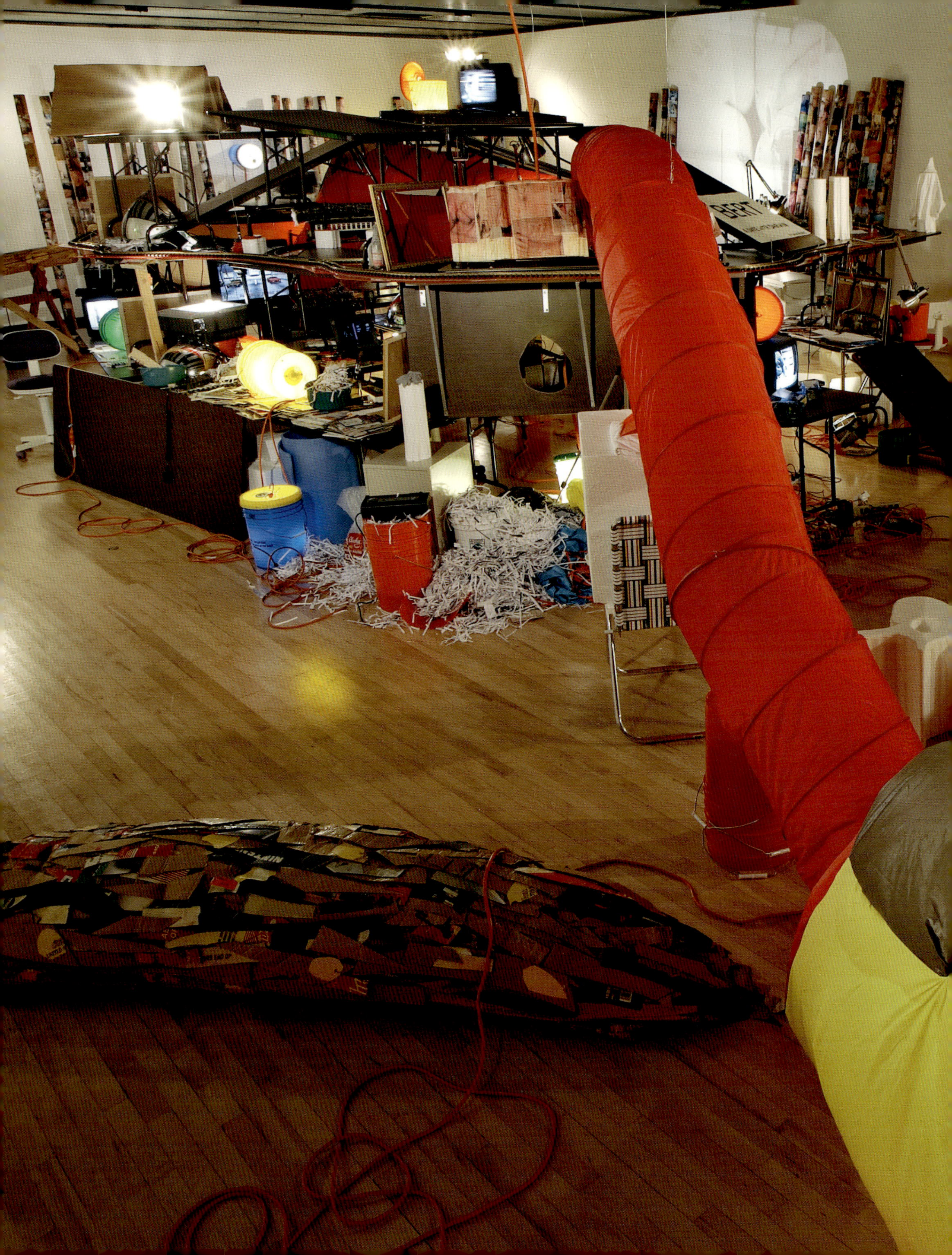

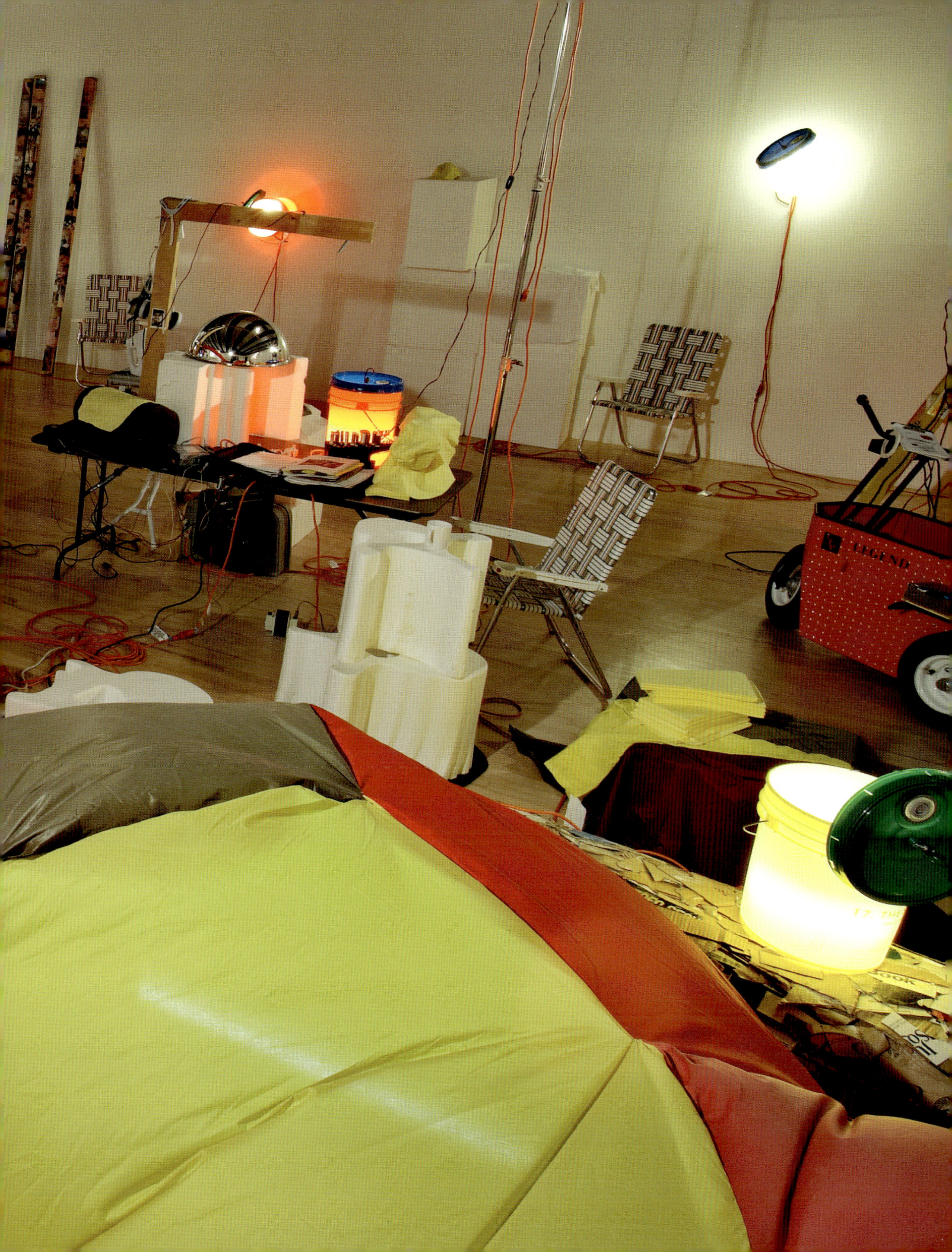

PIPILOTTI RIST

Pipilotti Rist was born in 1962 in Grabs, Switzerland. Her first video work was made in 1986 while she was a student at the Basel School of Design. In this 5-minute single-channel video, *I'm Not the Girl Who Misses Much*, Rist chants her adaptation of the first line of The Beatles' song 'Happiness is a Warm Gun' while dancing around half naked. Sound, speed and colour are all manipulated and distorted, resulting in a parody of female hysteria, a motif that recurs in later works. Music also continued to play a central role, and in 1988 Rist became a member of the band and performance group Les Reines Prochaines. After making further single-channel videos which focused on the tension between fantasy and reality, her work began to encompass architectural space in installations that became increasingly immersive. Rist has twice represented Switzerland at the Venice Biennale; first in 1997, when she won the Premio 2000 award, and again in 2005. In 2008 she created a large video installation, *Pour Your Body Out (7354 Cubic Meters)*, for the atrium of New York's Museum of Modern Art. She lives and works in Zurich and the Swiss Alps.

following pages:
Extremitäten (weich, weich) [Extremities (Smooth, Smooth)], 1999/2009 (details)

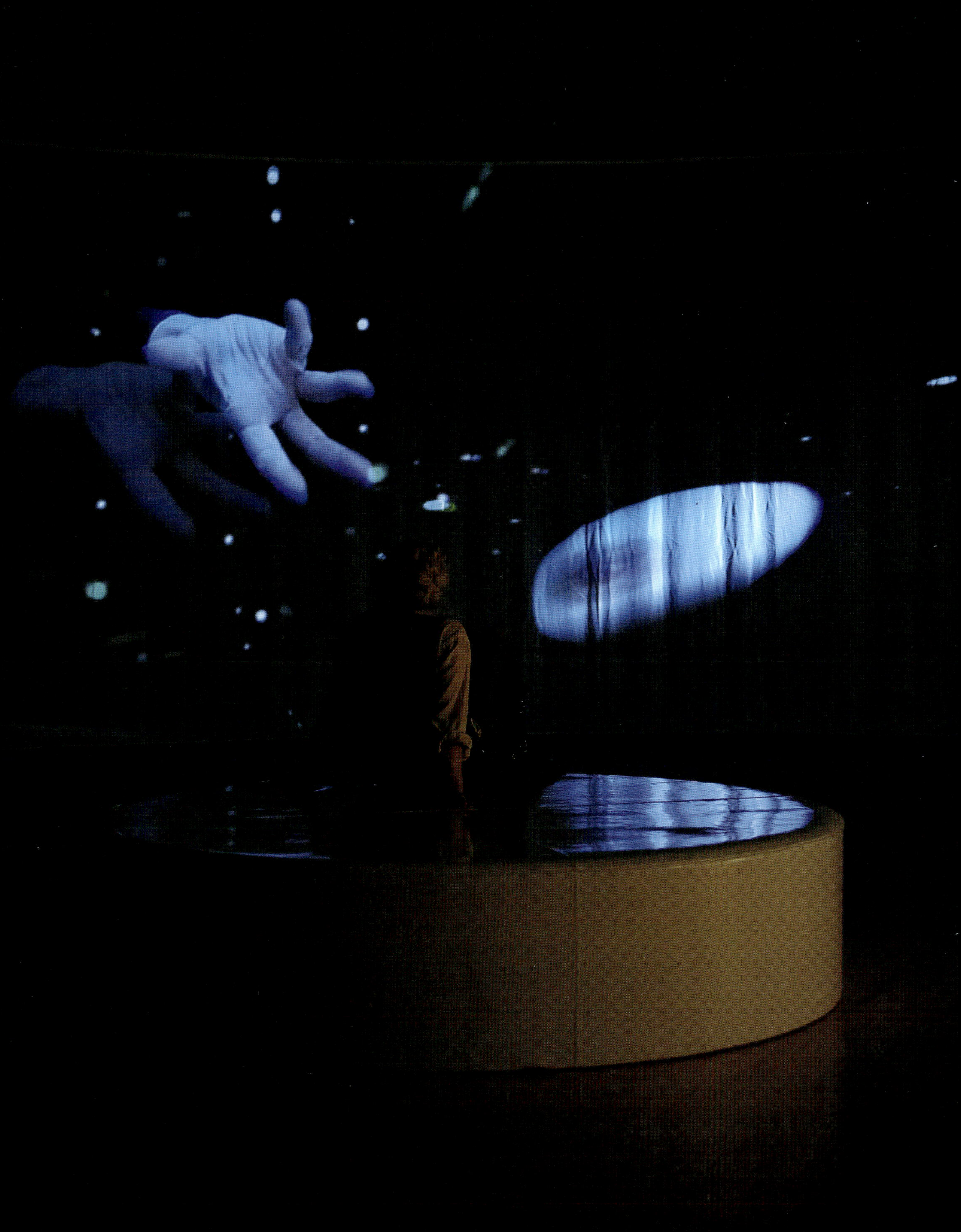

In *Extremitäten (weich, weich) [Extremities (Smooth, Smooth)]*
images of body parts – a gigantic foot, hand, breast, mouth,
ear and penis – float and dance in space, momentarily alight
on people and on the surrounding curtains, and then suddenly
disappear, like dreams, while a disembodied voice repeats a
sequence of phrases, beginning 'you are a butterflower' and
ending 'I will become like you'. At the centre of the installation
is a circular seat for viewers (or, more accurately, participants)
to sit or lie on. The work is influenced by autogenic training,
a form of self-hypnosis consisting of a series of visualisation
exercises in which one focuses on some part of the body
while repeating simple statements. A primary purpose of such
training is to induce a balance between the two hemispheres
of the brain and bring the mind into an optimum mental state,
described as 'passive concentration'.

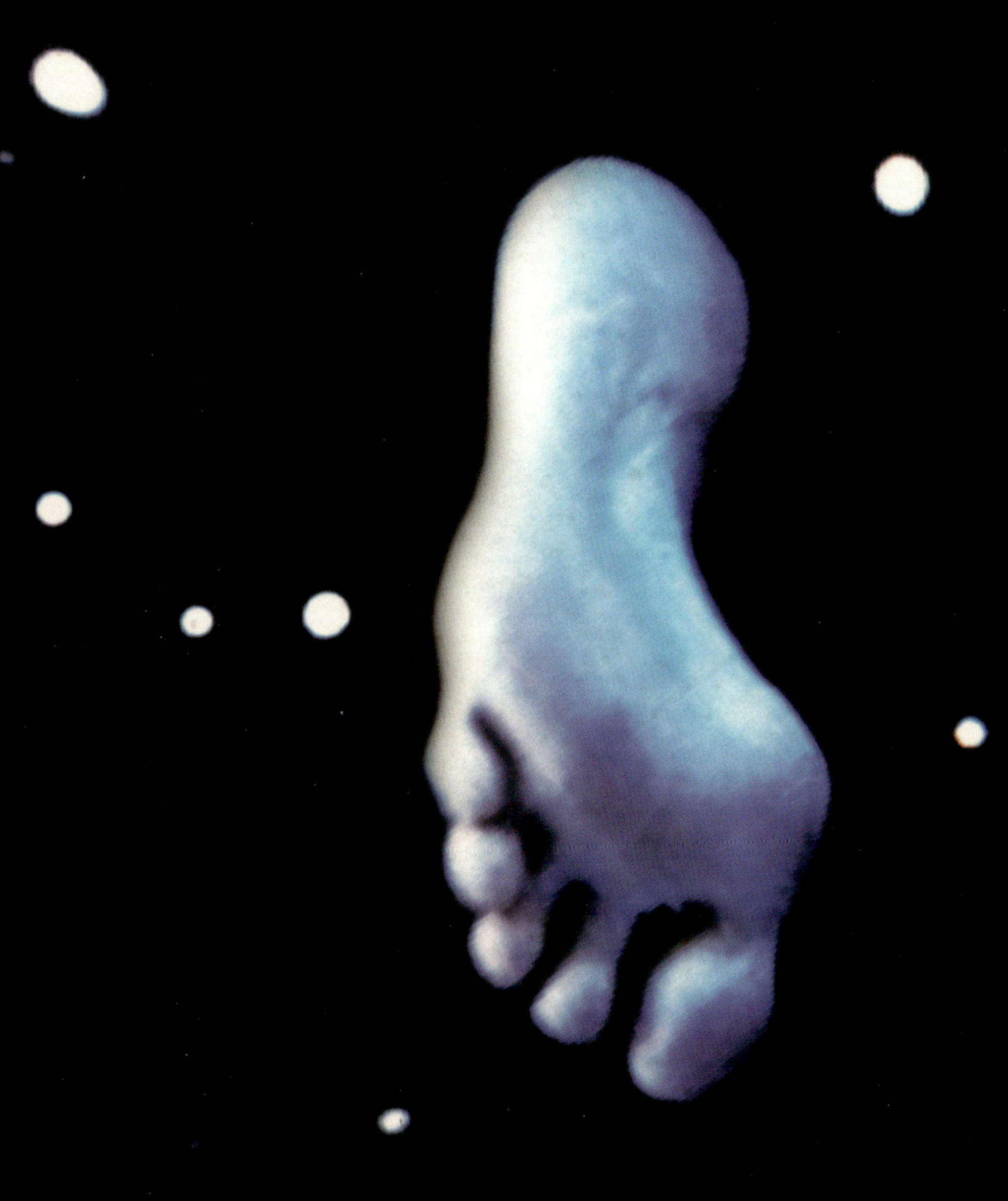

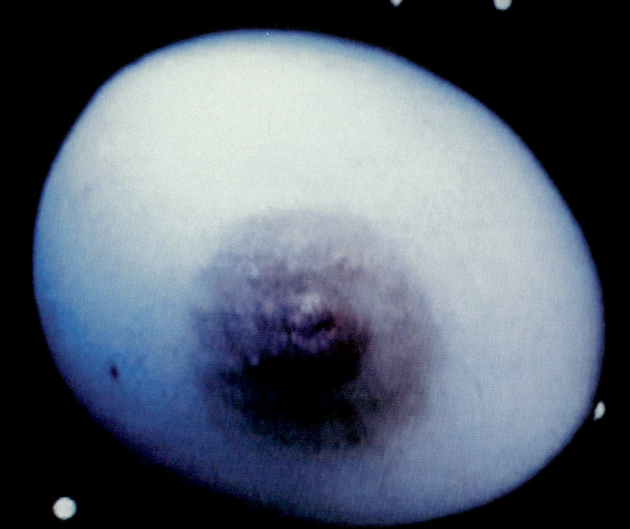
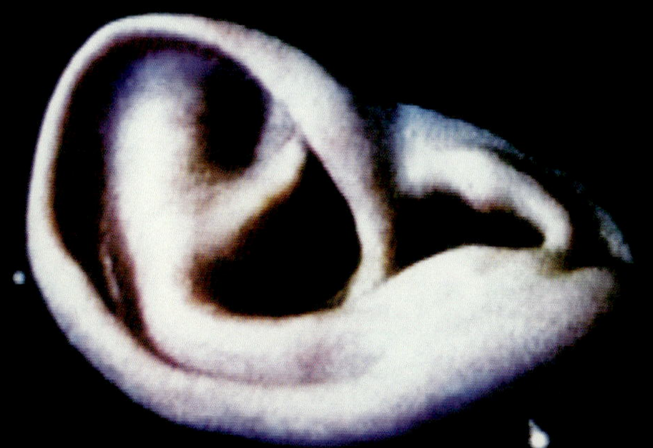

'you are a butterflower

you are a mammal

you are a molecule

you are a woman mouse

you are a mouse

you are different from me

you are nothing

you are the king

you are a pollen

you are full of pain

you are the cerebellum

you are like you

you are normal

you are a friend

I will become like you'

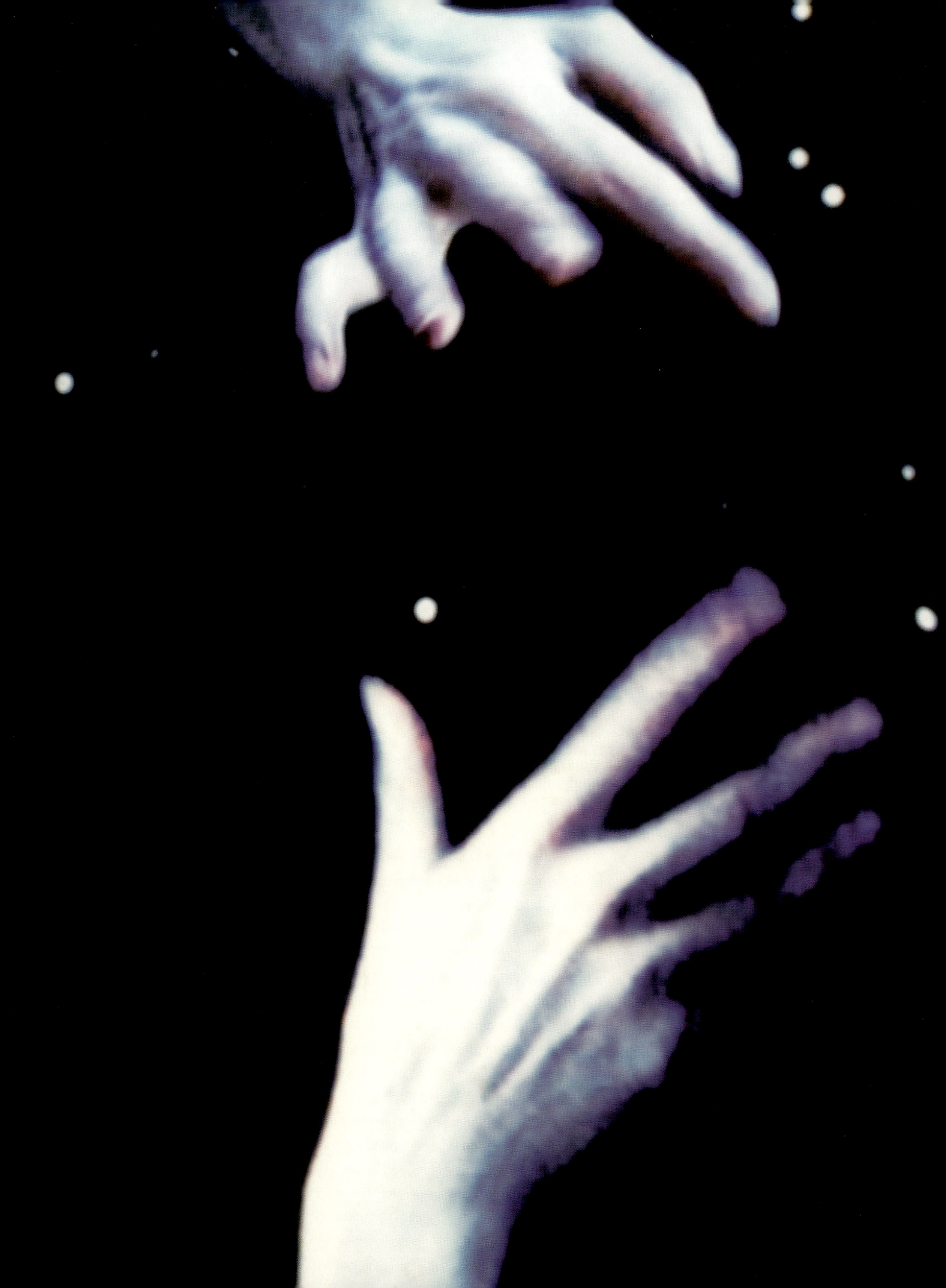

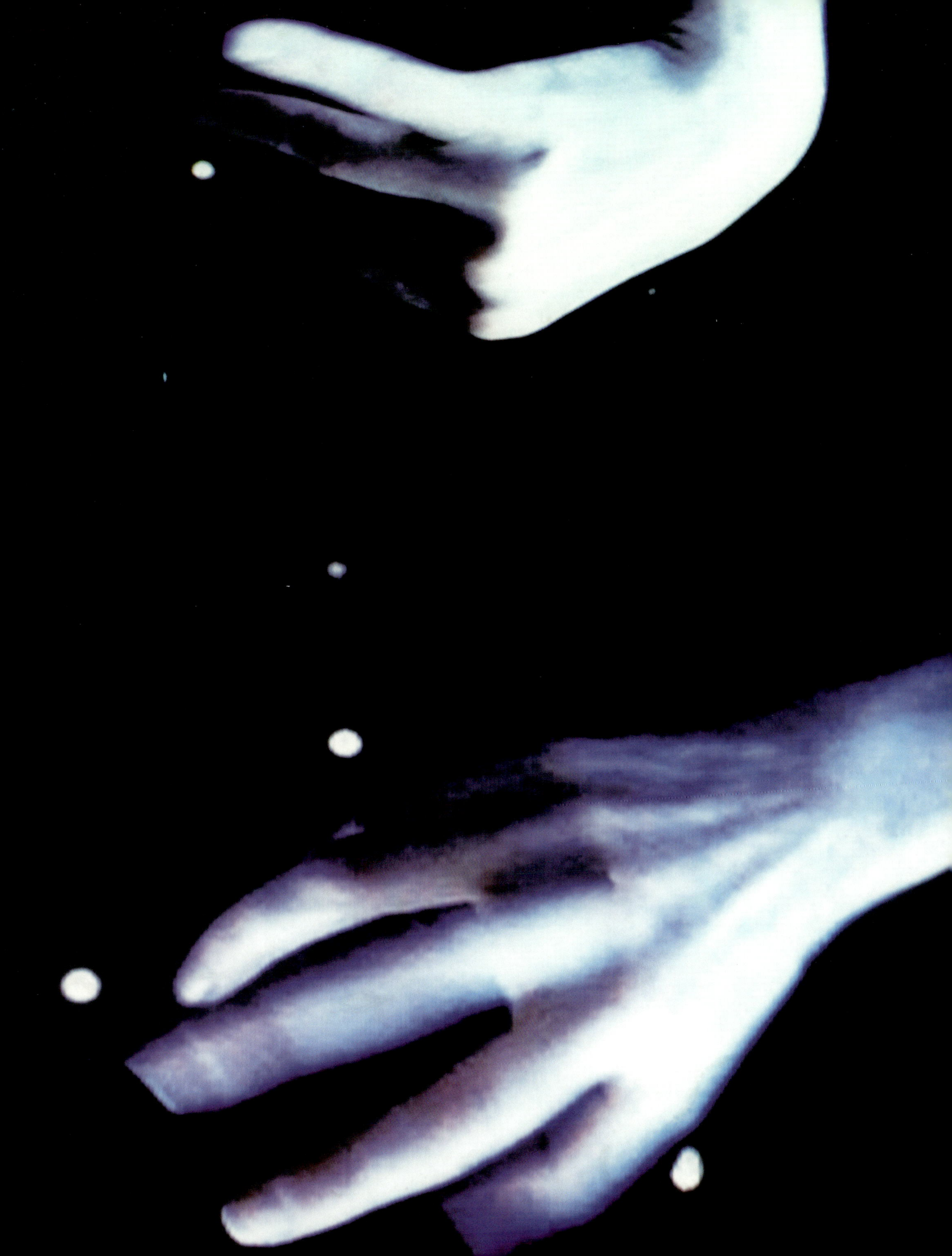

CHIHARU SHIOTA

Chiharu Shiota was born in 1972 in Osaka, Japan. She first began using black wool for 'drawing in the air' while she was studying painting at Kyoto Seika University in Japan. After graduating in 1996, she went to Australia as an exchange student and then moved to Germany, where she studied with the performance artist Marina Abramovic, whose rituals of endurance – involving fasting and silence – were to have a profound effect upon her work. She later went on to study with the sculptor and installation artist Rebecca Horn. Shiota's work has featured in many international group exhibitions including, most recently, *Fiction for the Real*, at the National Museum of Modern Art, Tokyo, Japan, in 2007; *Eurasia: Geographic Cross-overs in Art*, shown alongside *Manifesta 7* in Rovereto, Italy, in 2008; and the Third Moscow Biennale in 2009. She lives and works in Berlin, Germany.

In Silence, 2002 (detail)

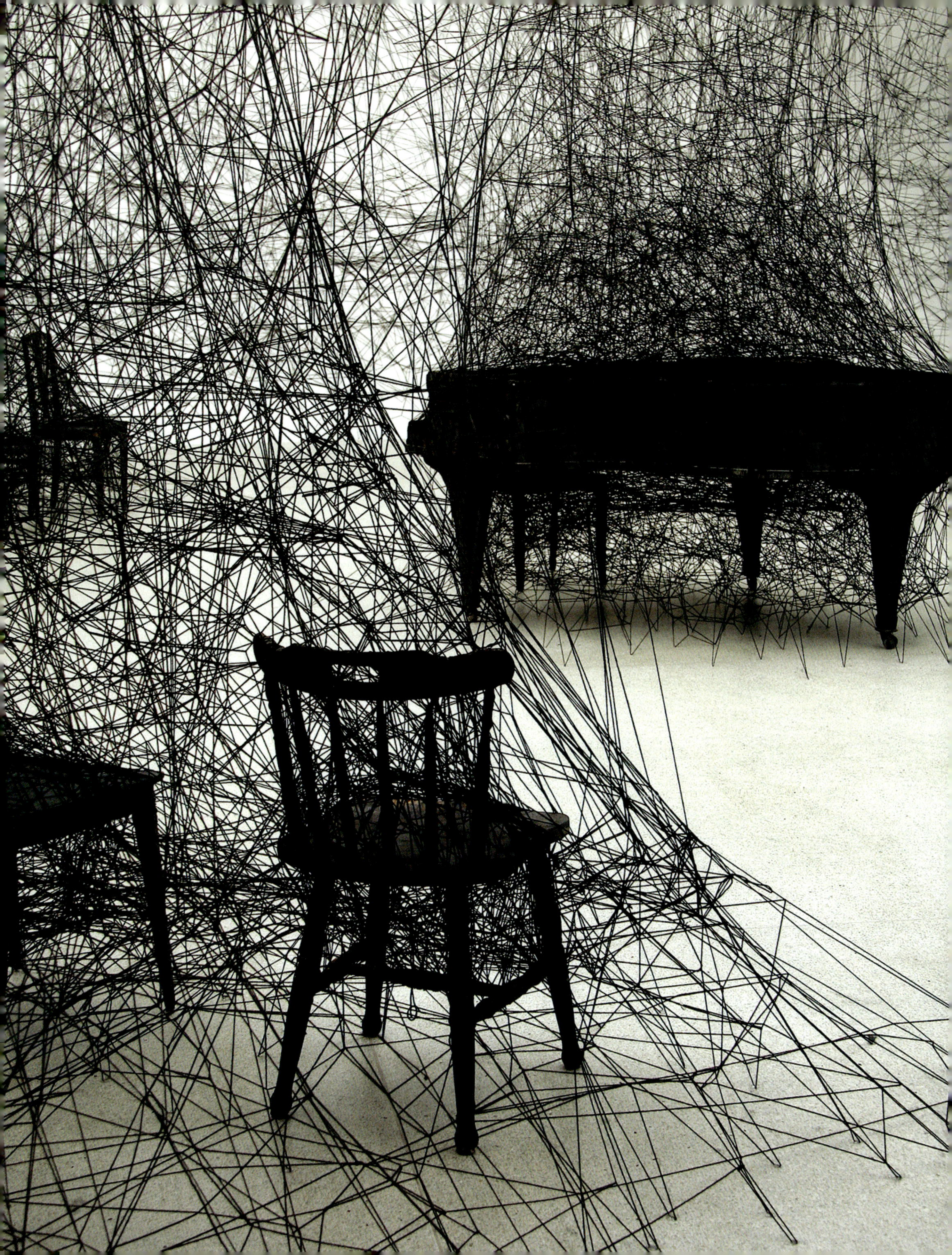

Remembrance and oblivion, dreaming and sleeping, resonate in Shiota's performances and installations, together with a preoccupation with home and homelessness and the loss of childhood. Mysterious and sometimes frightening objects – as various as dresses, burnt-out pianos, charred chairs and hospital beds – become the unreachable focal points of psychic spaces, trapped within impenetrable and disorienting meshes of black threads. In her work *During Sleep*, presented in Berlin in 2000, Shiota slept in a hospital bed, apparently immersed in dreams, in the midst of a cloud-like cocoon woven from strands of black wool. Commissioned for *Walking in My Mind*, Shiota's new work, *After the Dream*, features a dense web of threads, extending from the ceiling out to all four walls. In the centre of this woven thicket, as in a half-forgotten fairytale, a path leads around a circle of five enormous dresses which appear to hold hands, floating above the ground as in a silent, motionless dance. The threads – a sort of infinite cat's cradle – become an intricate interlacing of triangular forms. As Shiota points out, 'A line is too clear, too visible. Triangles upon triangles become complicated, hiding some things from the eye.'

Falling Water, 2009

following pages:
After the Dream, 2009

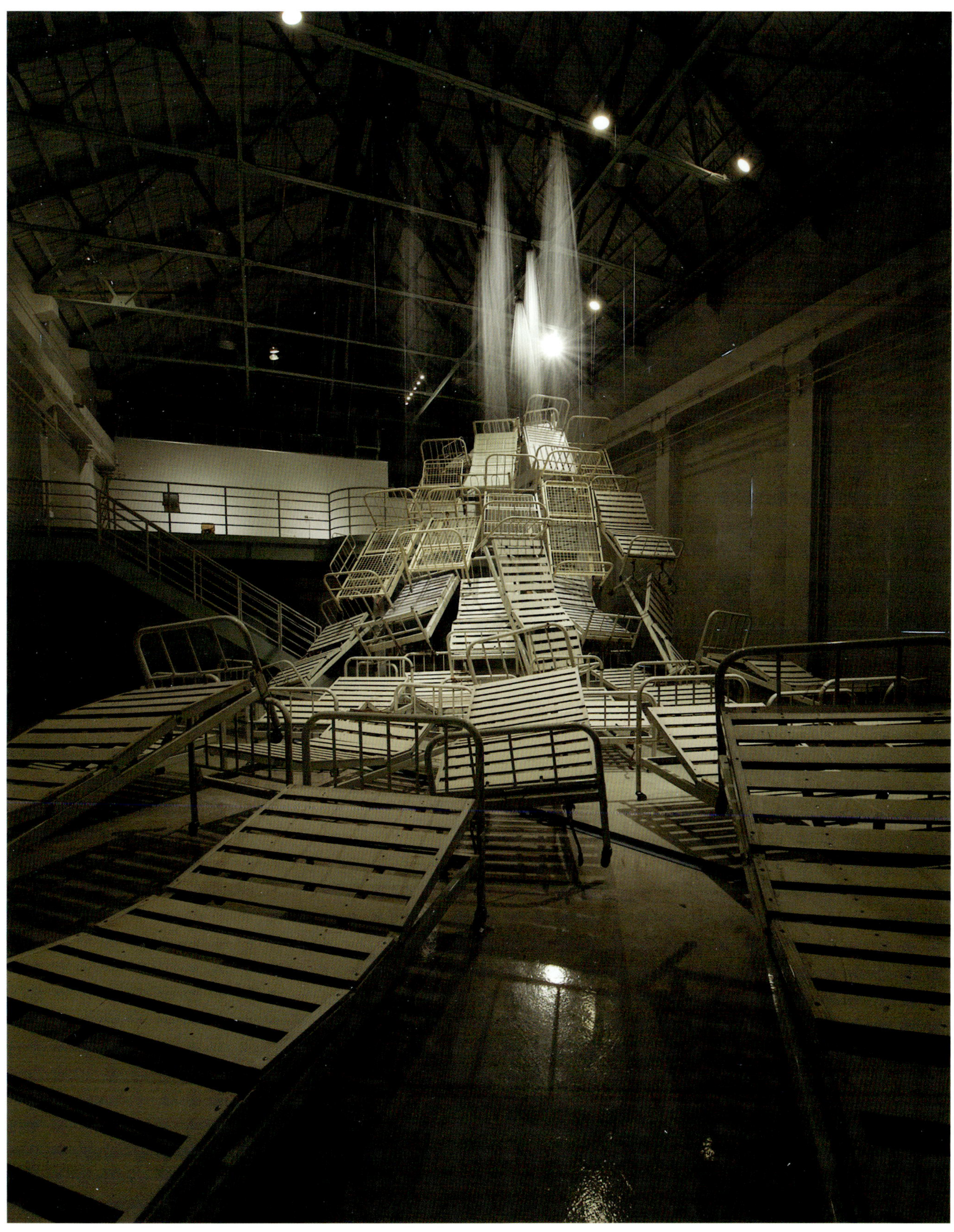

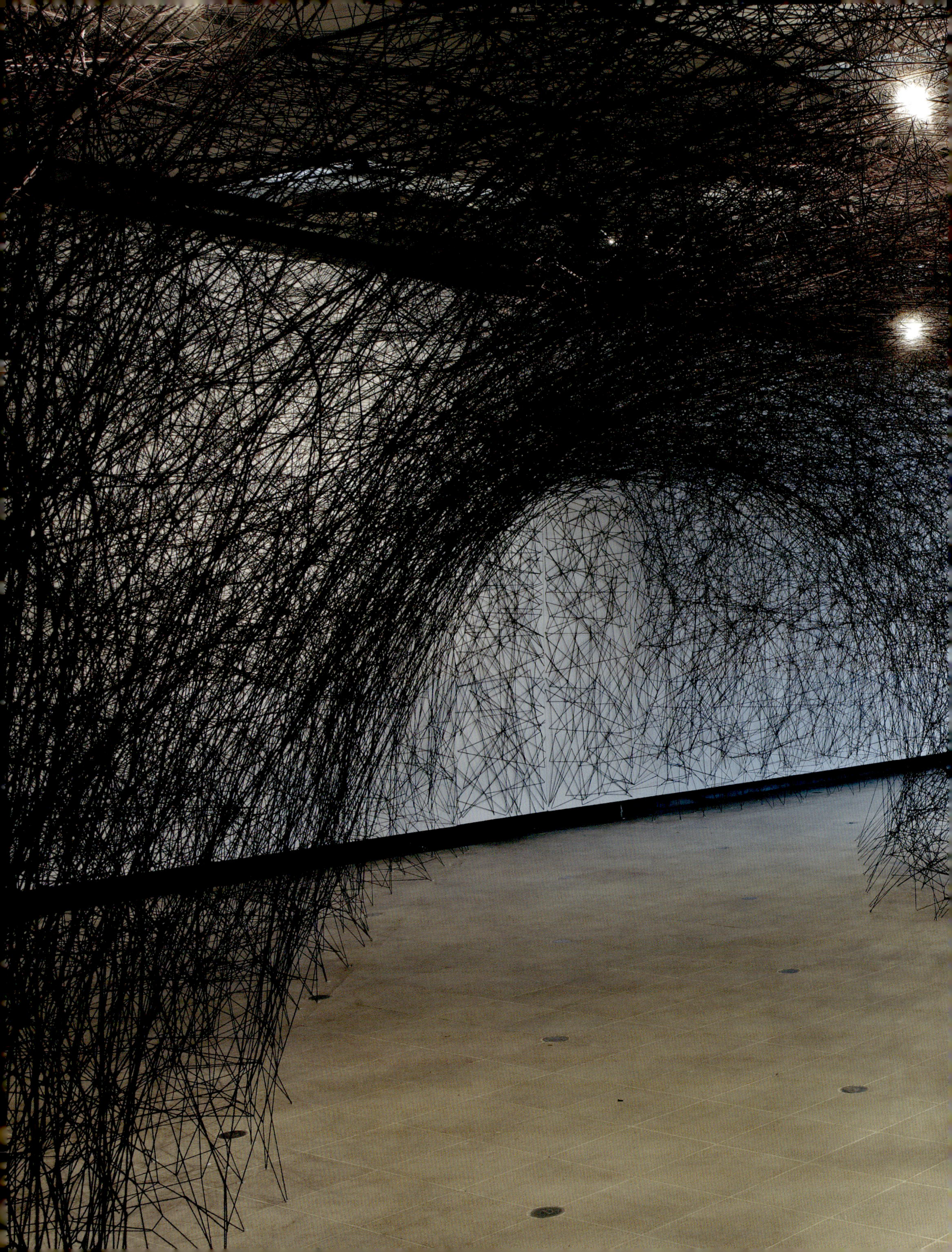

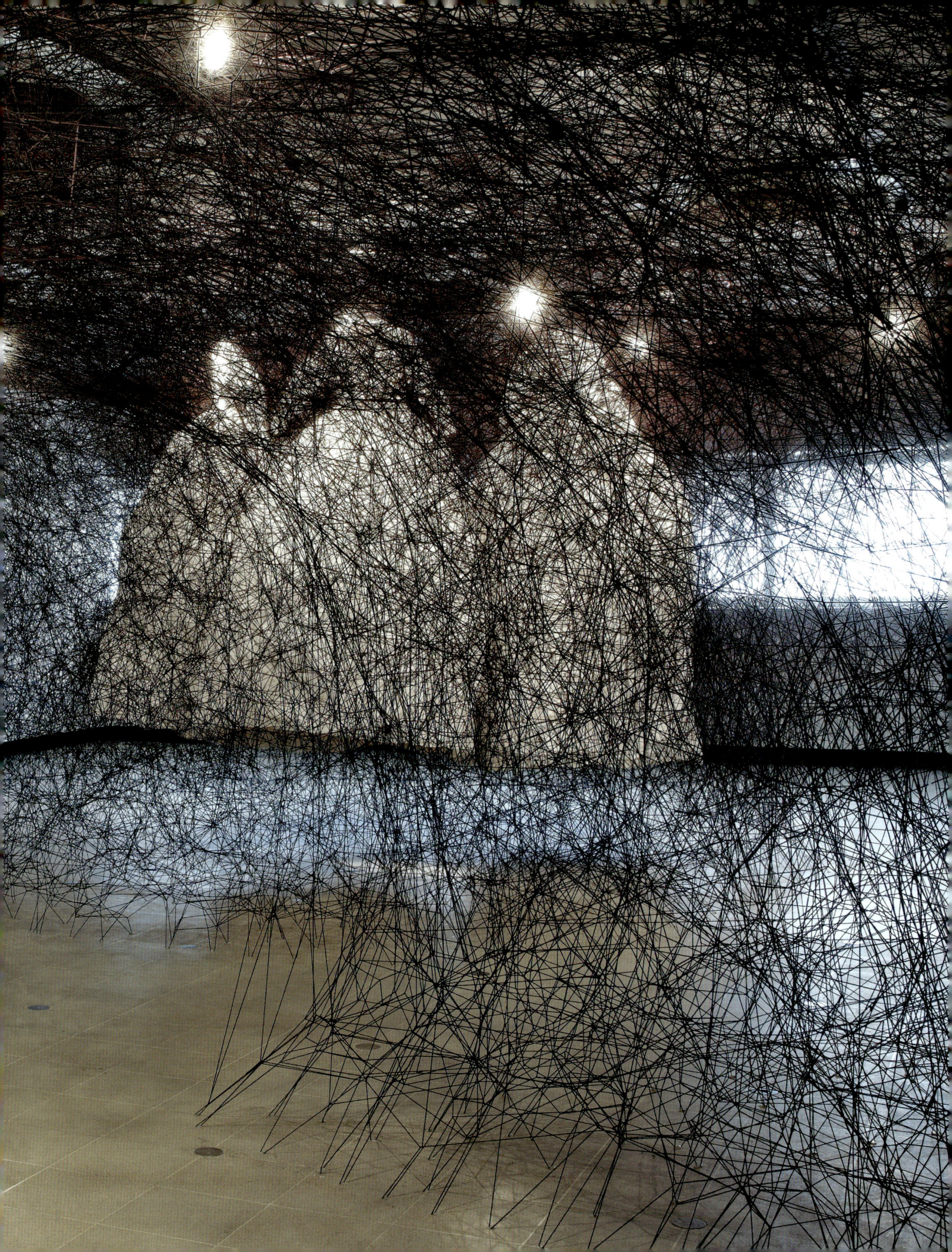

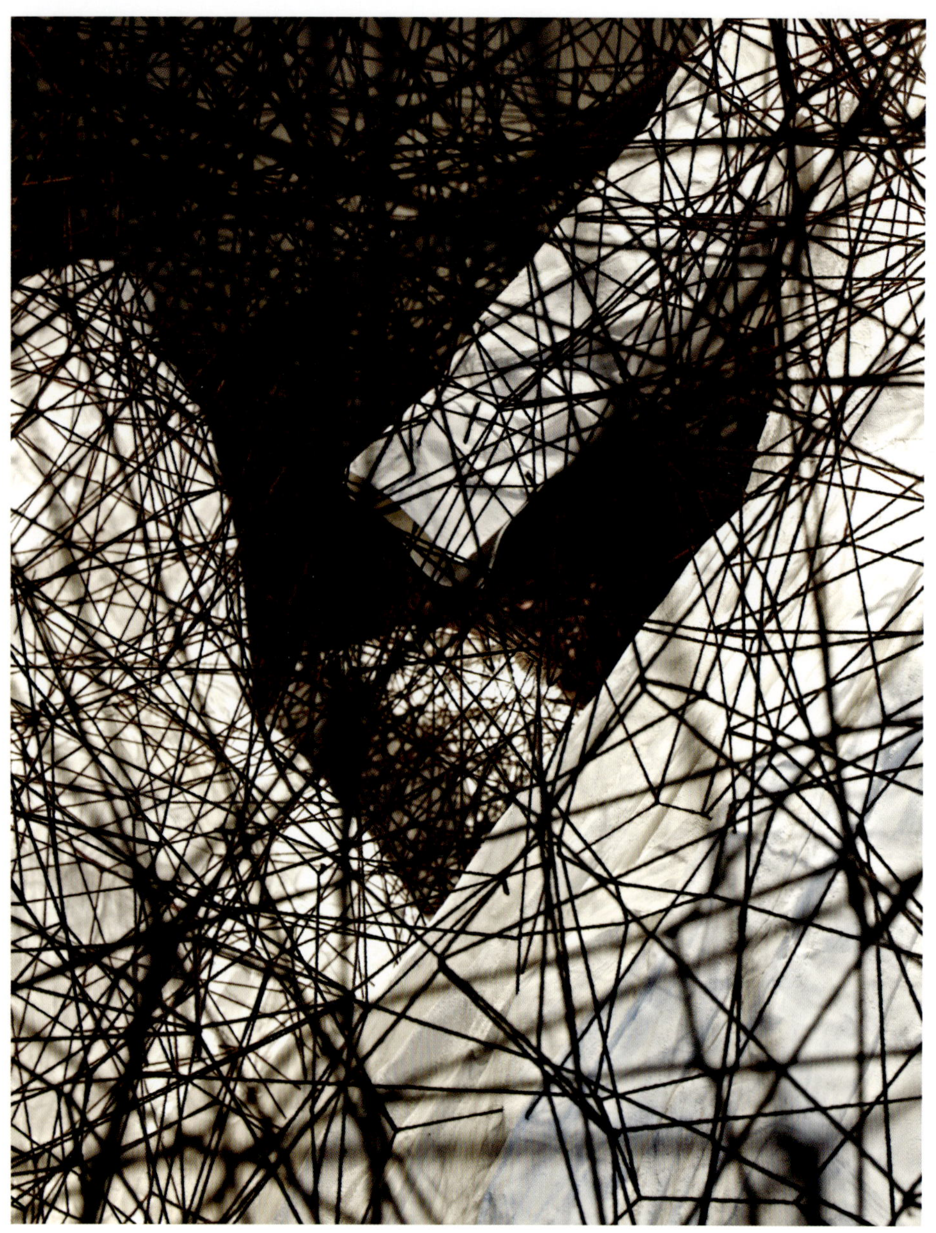

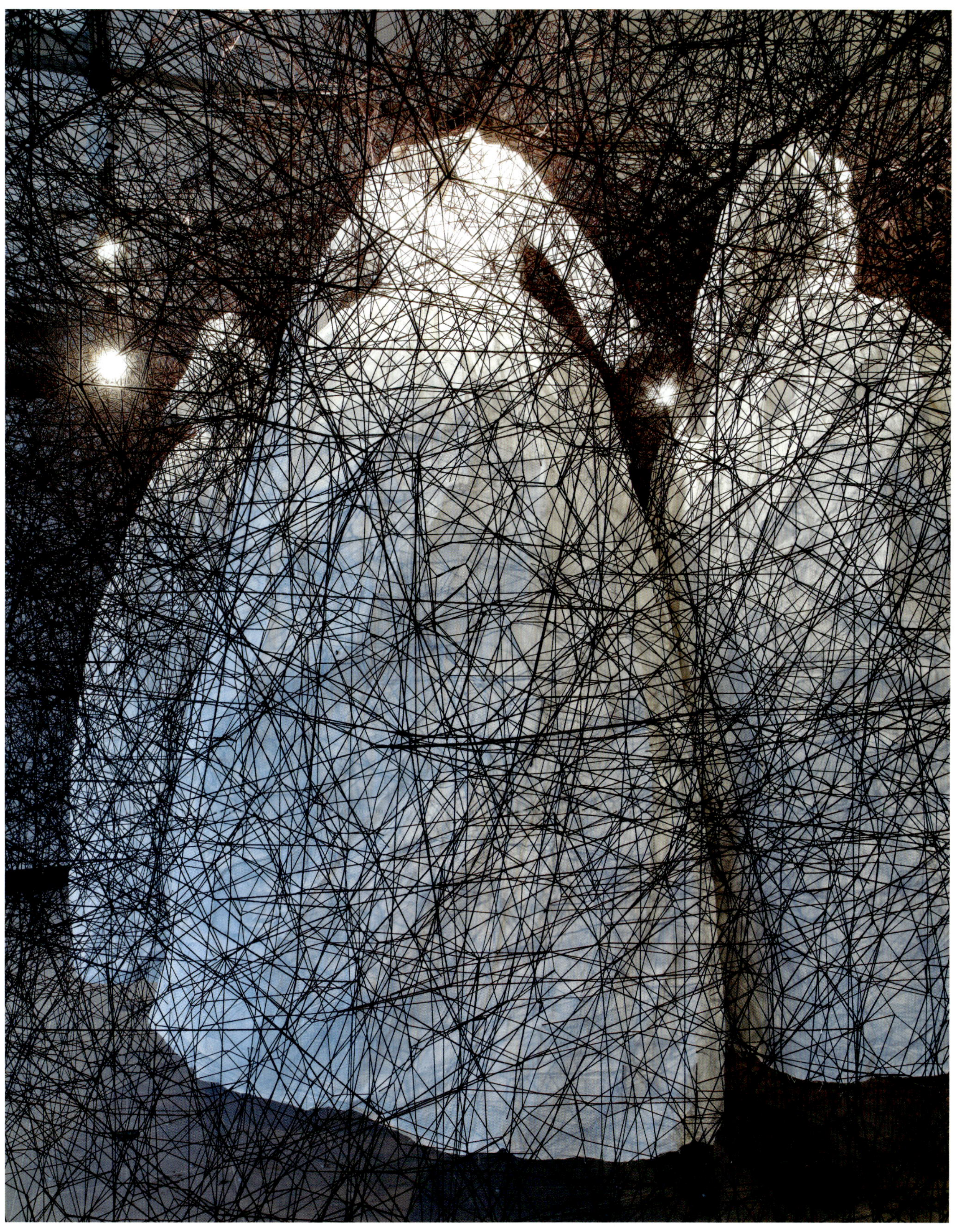

KEITH TYSON

Keith Tyson was born in 1969 in Ulverston, Cumbria, UK. He describes his art as a form of experimentation, comparing his studio to a laboratory and his art works to a series of research projects. Trained initially in mechanical engineering crafts, he went on to do a Foundation course at Carlisle College of Art before completing a degree in Alternative Practice, an experimental course pioneered by the Faculty of Arts and Architecture at the University of Brighton. In 1991 he produced his *Artmachine*, a device that – through its access to many sources of information – provided the artist with random and unpredictable instructions for new works. Five years later, he won the ICA Arts and Innovation Award. In 2001, his works were included in the 49th Venice Biennale, and in 2002 he was awarded the Turner Prize. He lives and works in Brighton, UK.

Jan 2009: Locked Out Of Eden – Viewing
The Children Playing In The Garden
From The Safety Of My Cerebral Fortress,
2009 (detail)

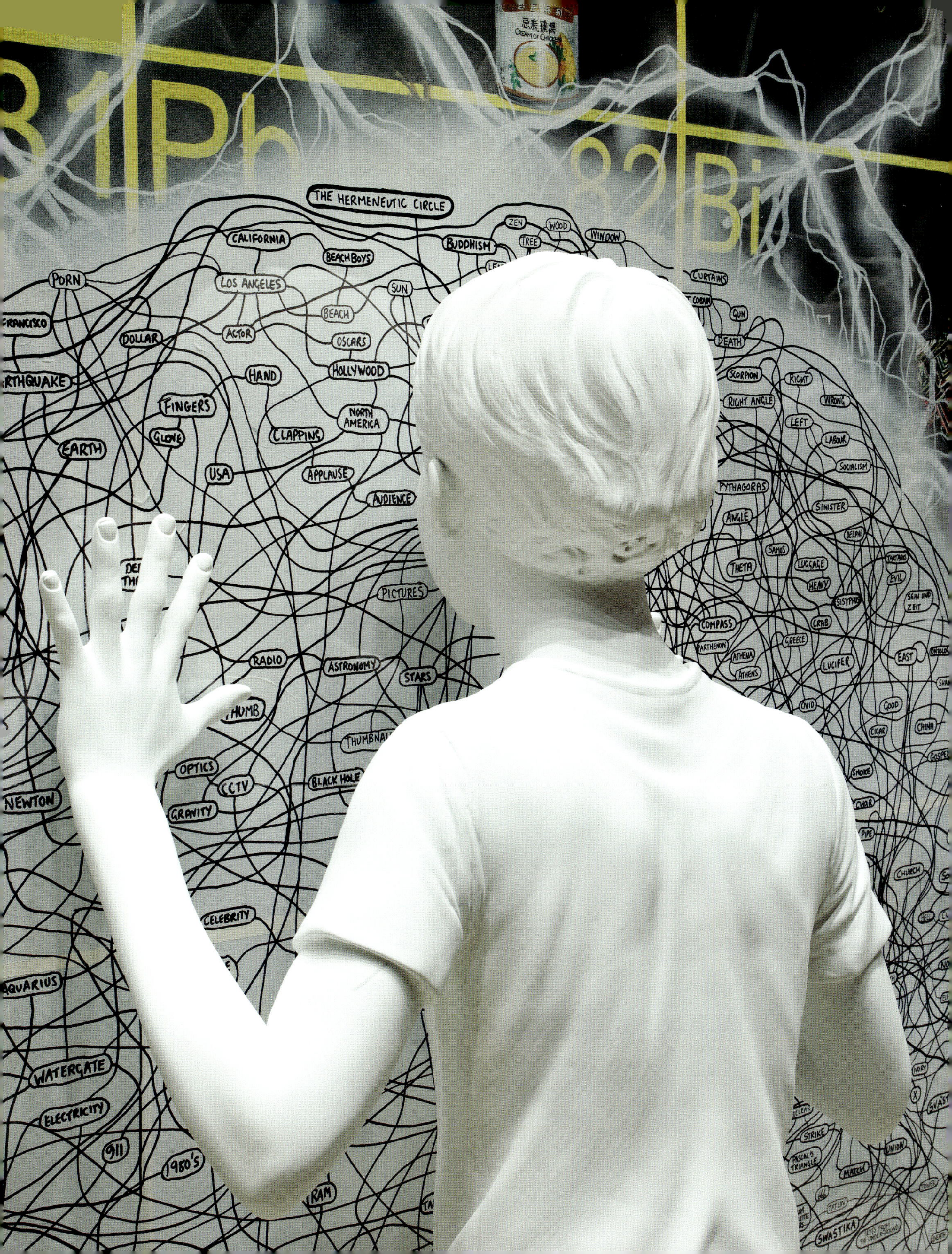
THE HERMENEUTIC CIRCLE
CALIFORNIA
BEACH BOYS
BUDDHISM
ZEN
TREE
WOOD
WINDOW
PORN
LOS ANGELES
SUN
CURTAINS
FRANCISCO
BEACH
COBAIN
DOLLAR
ACTOR
OSCARS
GUN
DEATH
EARTHQUAKE
HAND
HOLLYWOOD
SCORPION
RIGHT
FINGERS
NORTH
AMERICA
RIGHT ANGLE
WRONG
EARTH
GLOVE
CLAPPING
LEFT
LABOUR
SOCIALISM
USA
APPLAUSE
PYTHAGORAS
SINISTER
AUDIENCE
ANGLE
DELPHI
SAMOS
THETA
LUGGAGE
EVIL
HEAVY
SISYPHUS
SEIN UND ZEIT
DEAD
THING
PICTURES
COMPASS
CRAB
RADIO
ASTRONOMY
STARS
PARTHENON
ATHENA
GREECE
LUCIFER
EAST
THUMB
ATHENS
OVID
GOOD
THUMBNAIL
CIGAR
CHINA
OPTICS
BLACK HOLE
SMOKE
NEWTON
CCTV
GRAVITY
PIPE
CELEBRITY
CHURCH
AQUARIUS
WATERGATE
ELECTRICITY
NUCLEAR
STRIKE
911
1980'S
PASCAL'S
TRIANGLE
MATCH
UNION
KRAM
SWASTIKA

Tyson's art has resulted in an extraordinary array of objects, machines, drawings, paintings and immaterial works, such as a series of twelve magically activated spells. For *Walking in My Mind*, he has created an installation combining a sculpture and a sound recording with a massive 21-part *Studio Wall Drawing*. Subtitled *Locked Out Of Eden – Viewing The Children Playing In The Garden From The Safety Of My Cerebral Fortress*, this composite image is a view of a giant brain, bound with barbed briars, surrounded by the fall-out from a massive brainstorm. In this maelstrom of knowledge, the formal grid of the Periodic Table overlays a bewildering accumulation of images, some of which illustrate the chemical elements and some of which refer to the artist's personal history. The sculpture – the figure of a boy with his nose pressed against the wall – seems to be struggling with a Sisyphean boulder bearing a flow-chart describing the development of language.

On the walls on either side of this installation is a selection of *Studio Wall Drawings* dating from the beginning of this century. Begun in 1997, Tyson's *Studio Wall Drawings* is an ongoing series of works on paper. Though they are extremely diverse in style, content and approach, the drawings are all exactly the same size, and correspond to the measurements of a wall in his former studio that he used for day-to-day notes, plans and sketches. Tyson describes the *Studio Wall Drawings* as existing 'in a space somewhere between a map, a poem, a diary and a painting,' and has said: 'the thing I love about art is that, unlike science, it's tolerant of contradictions … I'm a great embracer of complexity, greyness, fuzzy logic. Loose parameters always lead to more interesting results.'

2007–2009: "Walking in Your Mind…", 2009

following page:
Jan 2009: Locked Out Of Eden – Viewing The Children Playing In The Garden From The Safety Of My Cerebral Fortress, 2009

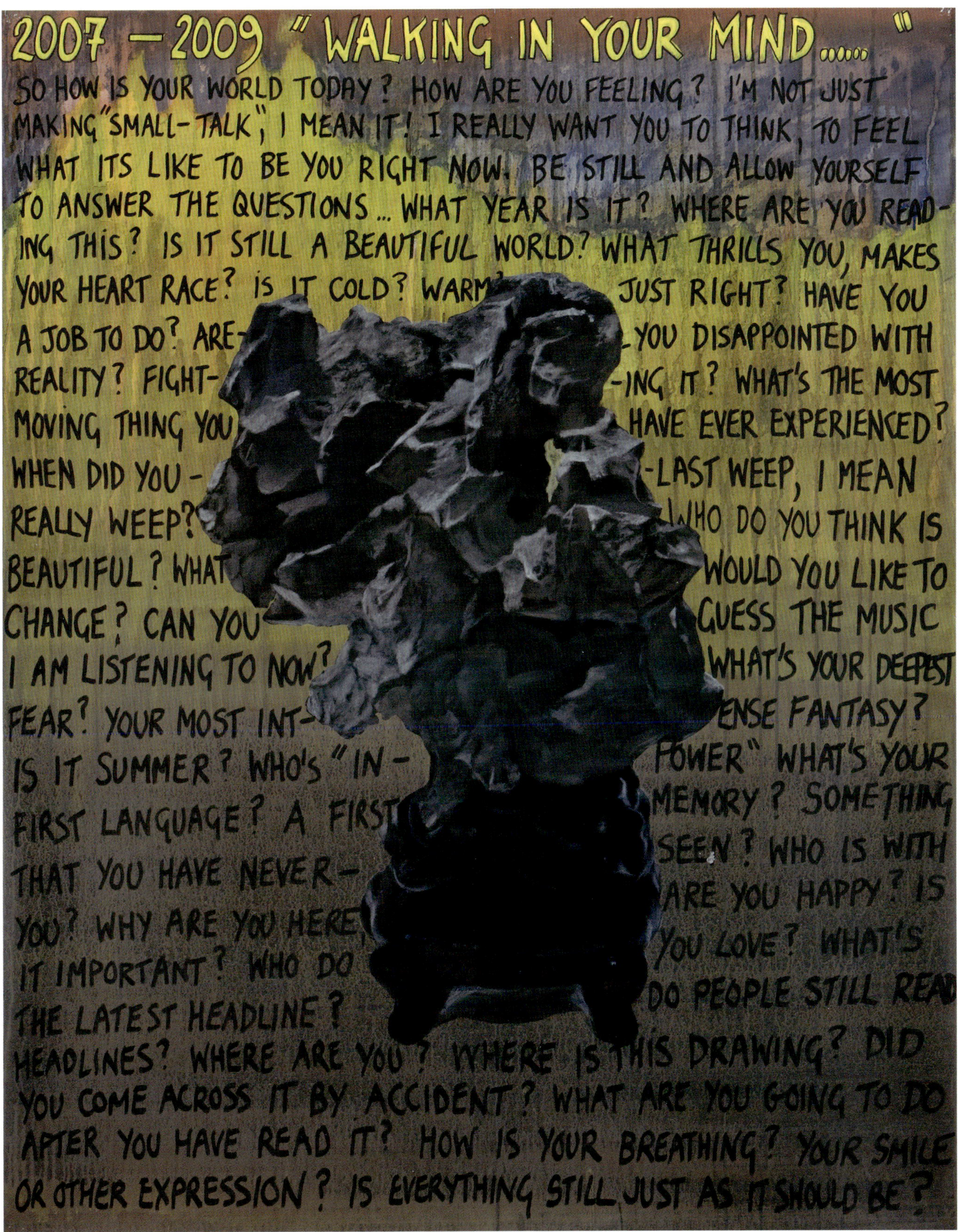

2007 – 2009 "WALKING IN YOUR MIND....."
SO HOW IS YOUR WORLD TODAY? HOW ARE YOU FEELING? I'M NOT JUST
MAKING "SMALL-TALK", I MEAN IT! I REALLY WANT YOU TO THINK, TO FEEL
WHAT ITS LIKE TO BE YOU RIGHT NOW. BE STILL AND ALLOW YOURSELF
TO ANSWER THE QUESTIONS ... WHAT YEAR IS IT? WHERE ARE YOU READ-
ING THIS? IS IT STILL A BEAUTIFUL WORLD? WHAT THRILLS YOU, MAKES
YOUR HEART RACE? IS IT COLD? WARM? JUST RIGHT? HAVE YOU
A JOB TO DO? ARE- YOU DISAPPOINTED WITH
REALITY? FIGHT- -ING IT? WHAT'S THE MOST
MOVING THING YOU HAVE EVER EXPERIENCED?
WHEN DID YOU - -LAST WEEP, I MEAN
REALLY WEEP? WHO DO YOU THINK IS
BEAUTIFUL? WHAT WOULD YOU LIKE TO
CHANGE? CAN YOU GUESS THE MUSIC
I AM LISTENING TO NOW? WHAT'S YOUR DEEPEST
FEAR? YOUR MOST INT- ENSE FANTASY?
IS IT SUMMER? WHO'S "IN - POWER" WHAT'S YOUR
FIRST LANGUAGE? A FIRST MEMORY? SOMETHING
THAT YOU HAVE NEVER- SEEN? WHO IS WITH
YOU? WHY ARE YOU HERE, ARE YOU HAPPY? IS
IT IMPORTANT? WHO DO YOU LOVE? WHAT'S
THE LATEST HEADLINE? DO PEOPLE STILL READ
HEADLINES? WHERE ARE YOU? WHERE IS THIS DRAWING? DID
YOU COME ACROSS IT BY ACCIDENT? WHAT ARE YOU GOING TO DO
AFTER YOU HAVE READ IT? HOW IS YOUR BREATHING? YOUR SMILE
OR OTHER EXPRESSION? IS EVERYTHING STILL JUST AS IT SHOULD BE?

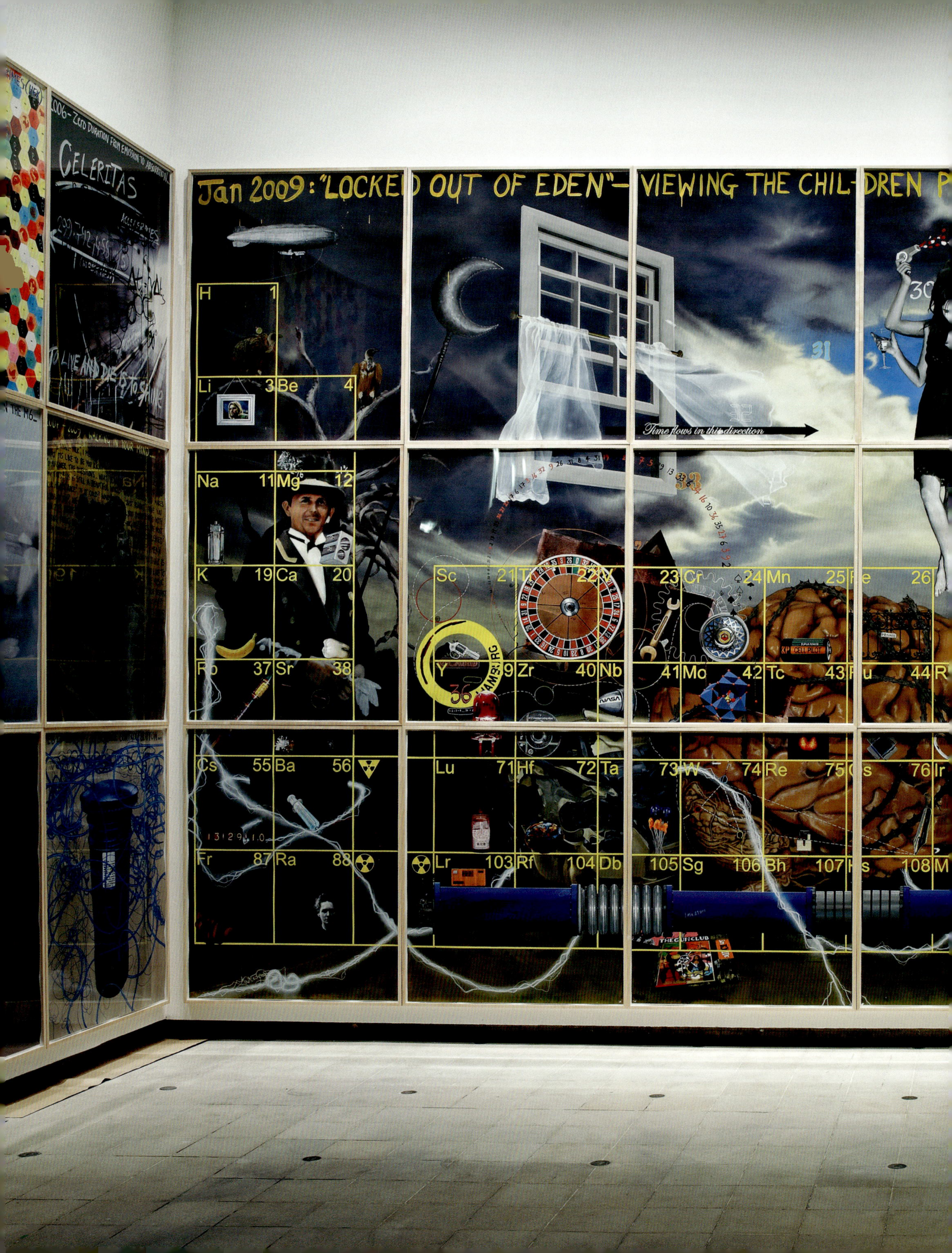
CELERITAS
TO LIVE AND DIE IS TO SHINE
Jan 2009: "LOCKED OUT OF EDEN" — VIEWING THE CHIL-DREN P
Time flows in this direction
H 1
Li 3 Be 4
Na 11 Mg 12
K 19 Ca 20 Sc 21 Ti 22 V 23 Cr 24 Mn 25 Fe 26
Rb 37 Sr 38 Y 39 Zr 40 Nb 41 Mo 42 Tc 43 Ru 44
Cs 55 Ba 56 Lu 71 Hf 72 Ta 73 W 74 Re 75 Os 76 Ir
Fr 87 Ra 88 Lr 103 Rf 104 Db 105 Sg 106 Bh 107 Hs 108
THE CUTI CLUB

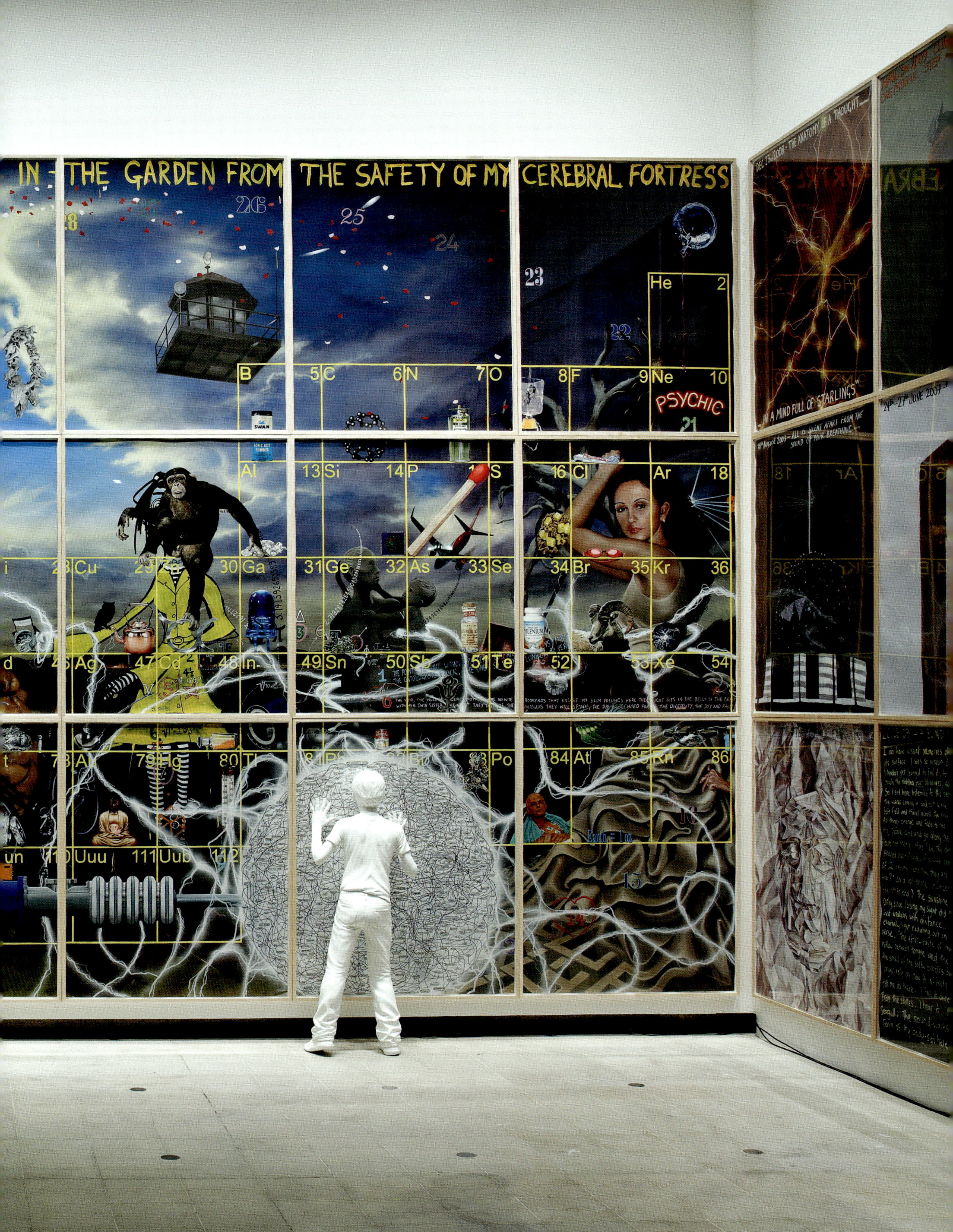
IN - THE GARDEN FROM THE SAFETY OF MY CEREBRAL FORTRESS
PSYCHIC
SWAN

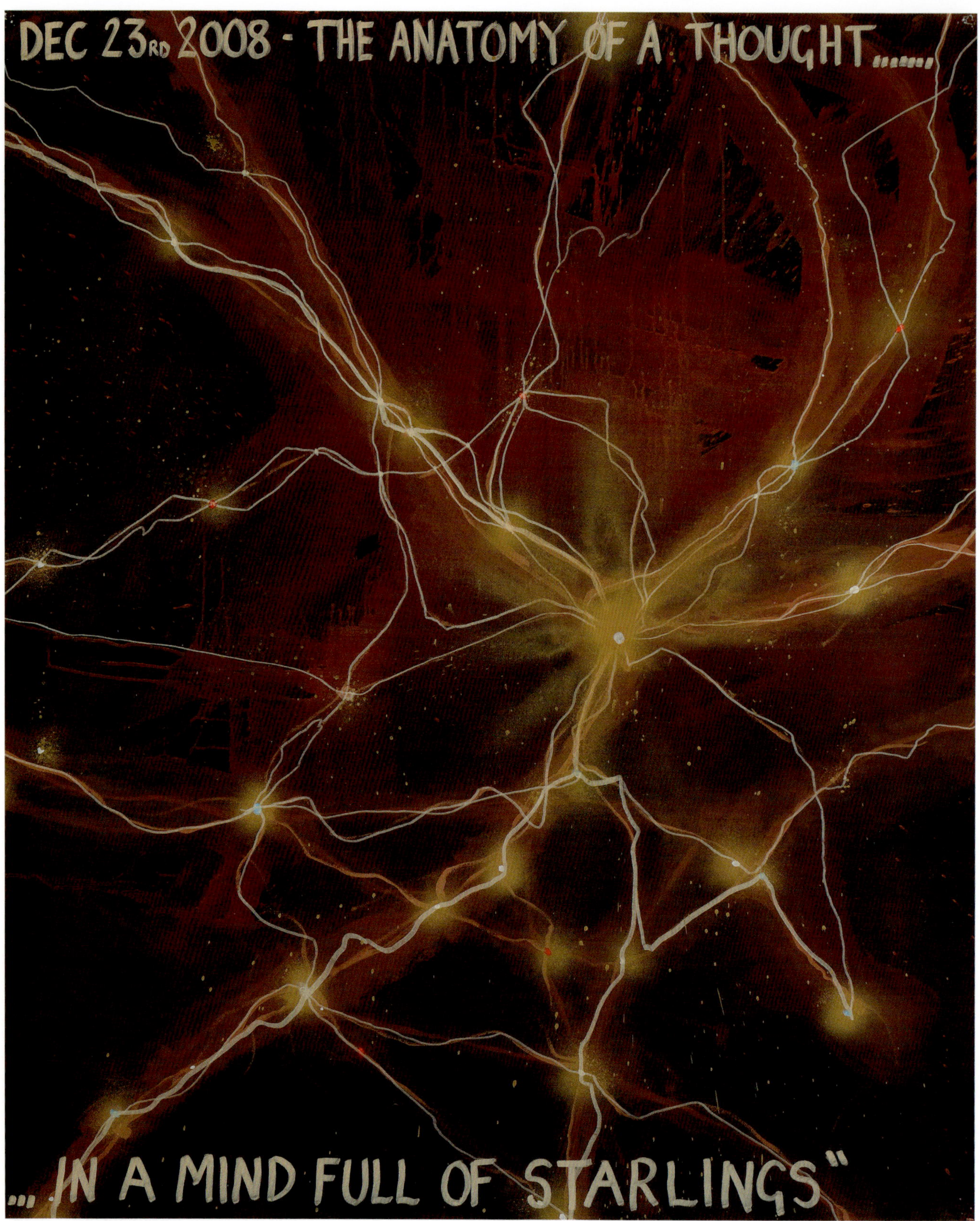

DEC 23RD 2008 - THE ANATOMY OF A THOUGHT.......
"...IN A MIND FULL OF STARLINGS"

19-10-06 – "A DROP IN BLOOD PRESSURE – TIME TO... ...WORK ON AN OPERATOR PAINTING NOTEBOOK"

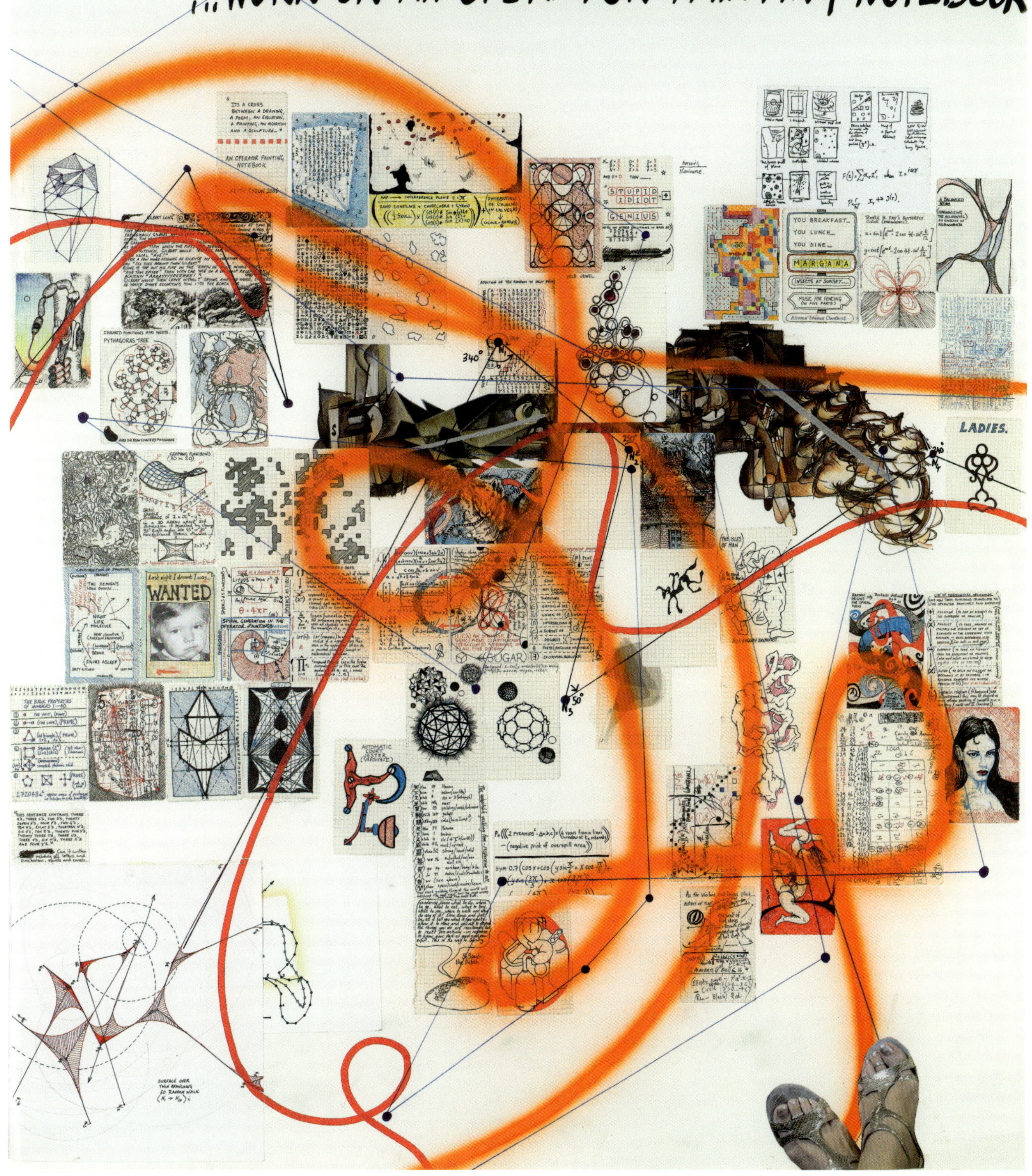

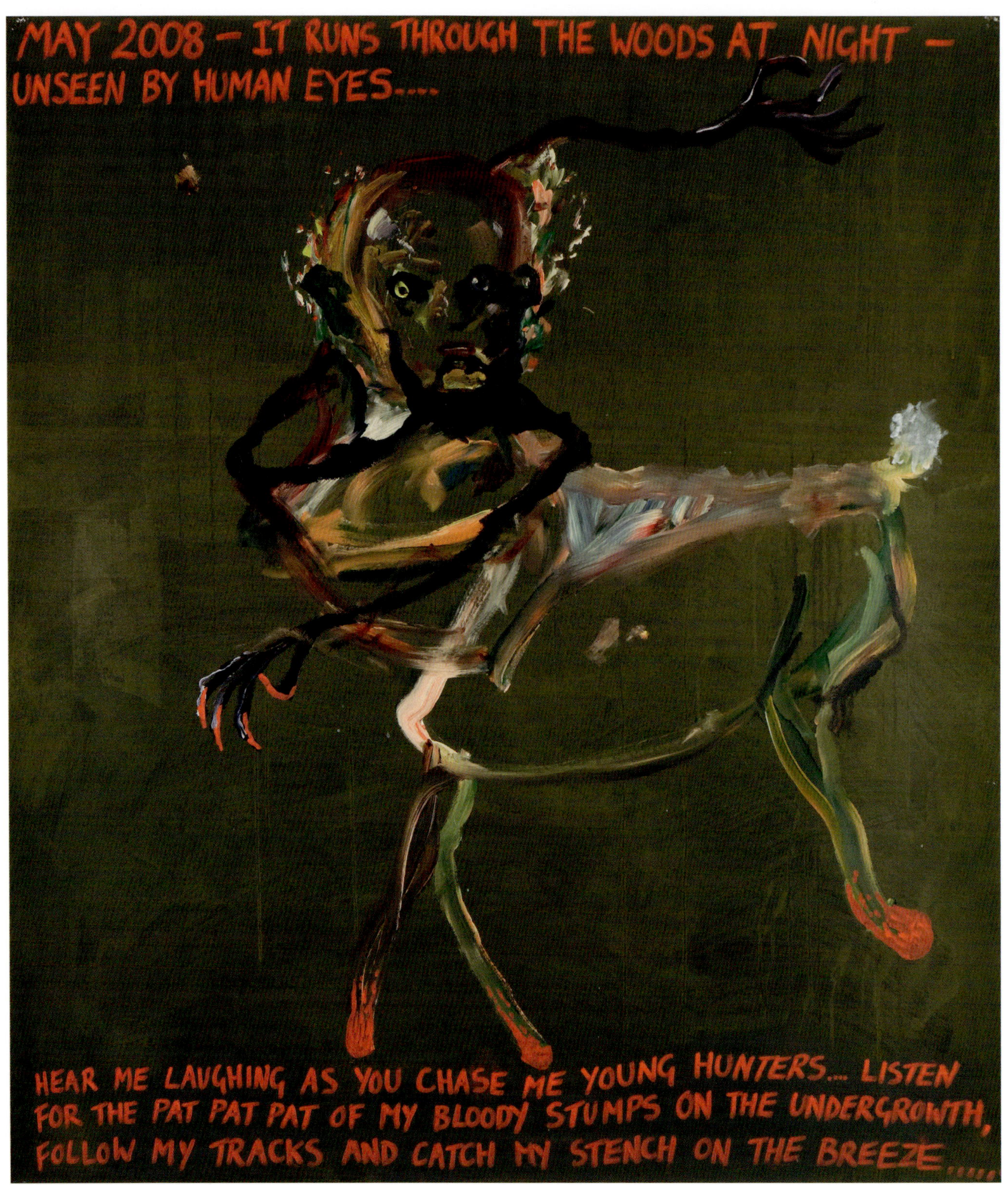

MAY 2008 — IT RUNS THROUGH THE WOODS AT NIGHT —
UNSEEN BY HUMAN EYES....

HEAR ME LAUGHING AS YOU CHASE ME YOUNG HUNTERS.... LISTEN
FOR THE PAT PAT PAT OF MY BLOODY STUMPS ON THE UNDERGROWTH,
FOLLOW MY TRACKS AND CATCH MY STENCH ON THE BREEZE....

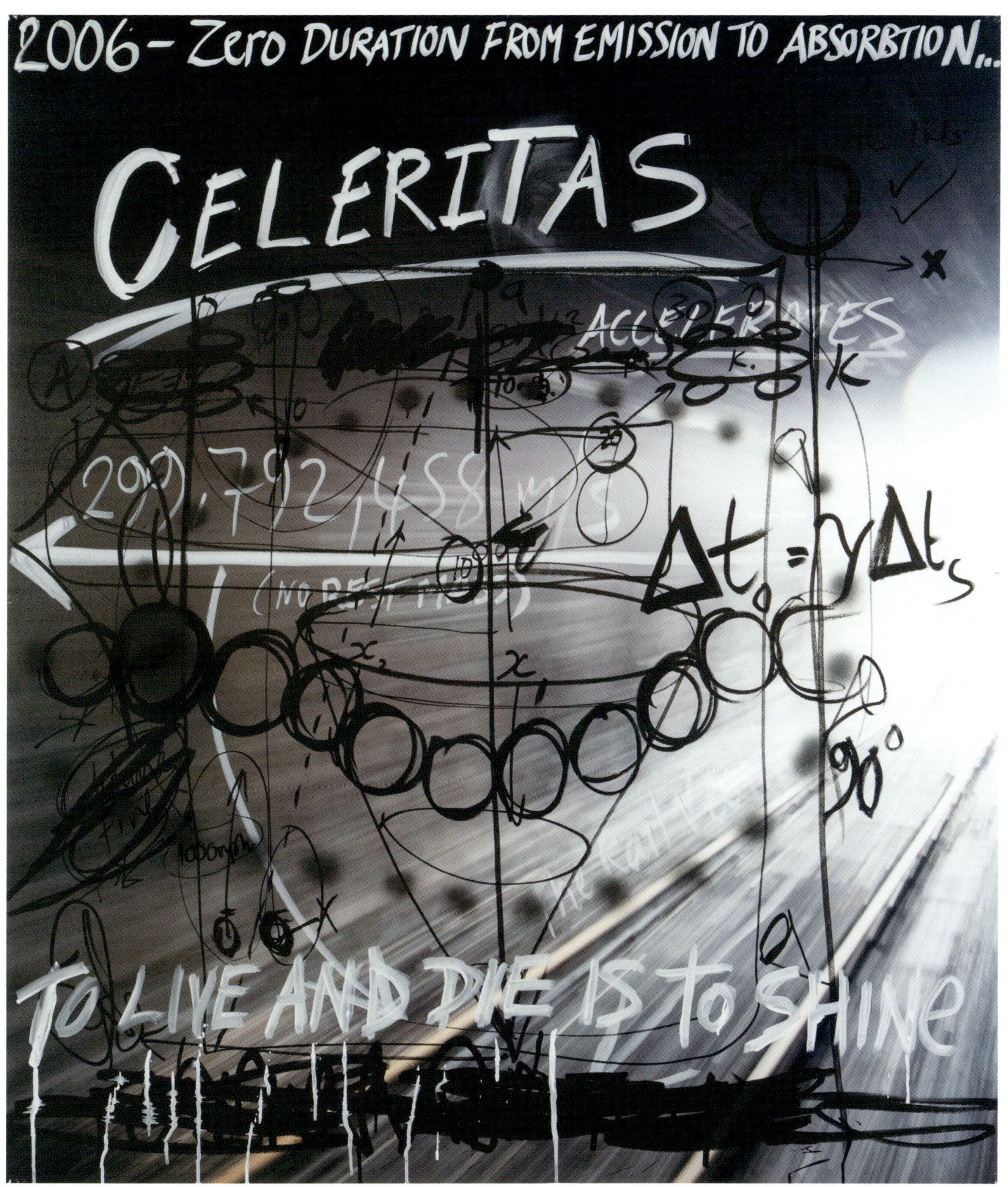

2006 - Zero Duration from Emission to Absorbtion...
CELERITAS
ACCELERATES
299,792,458 m/s
(NO REST MASS)
$\Delta t_0 = \gamma \Delta t_s$
90°
TO LIVE AND DIE IS TO SHINE

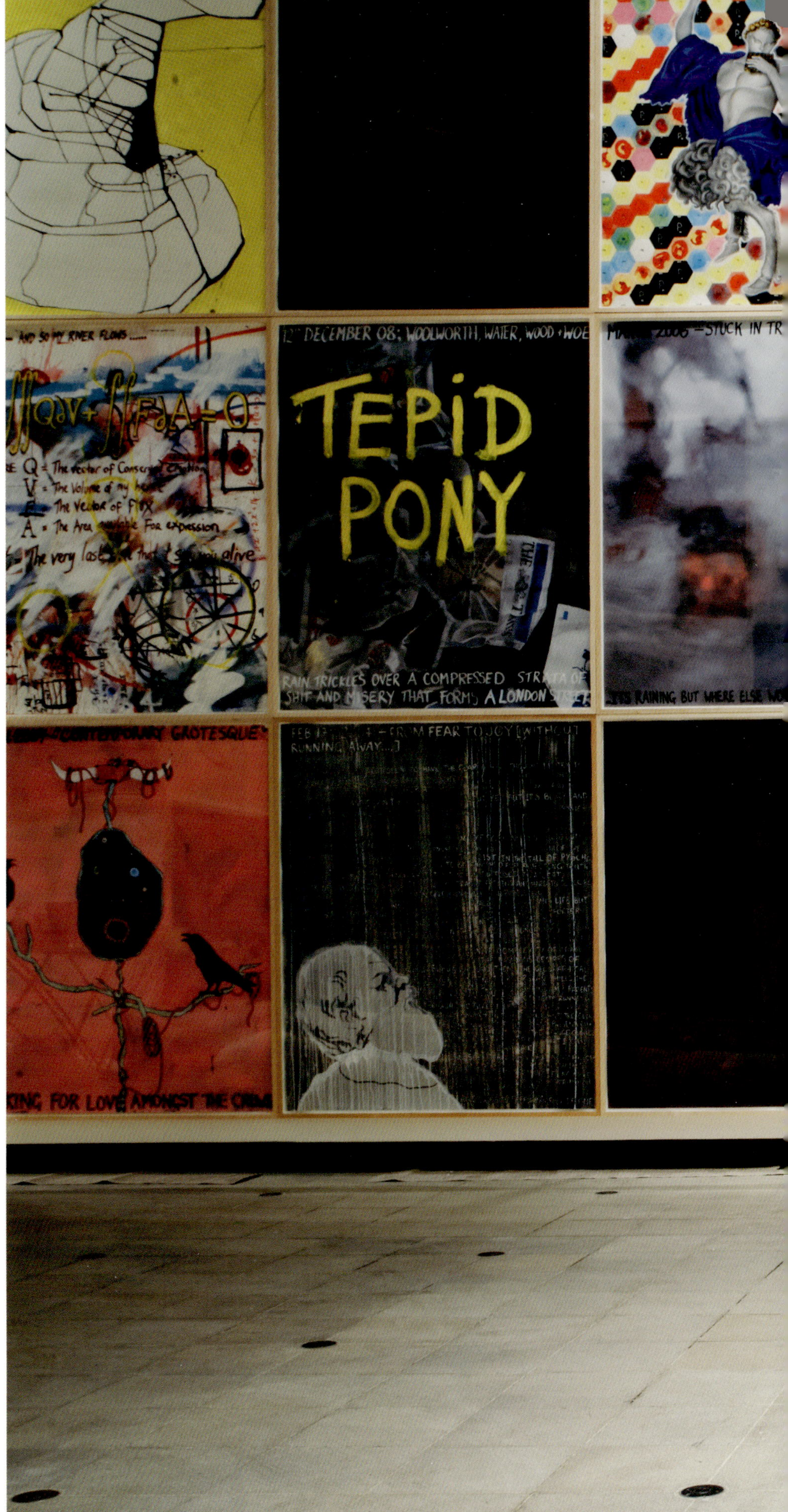

Jan 2009: Locked Out Of Eden – Viewing The Children Playing In The Garden From The Safety Of My Cerebral Fortress, 2009 (detail)

previous pages:
Dec. 23rd 2008: The Anatomy of a Thought…, 2008

19-10-06: "A Drop in Blood Pressure – Time to Work on an Operator Painting Notebook", 2006

May 2008: It Runs through the Woods at Night – Unseen by Human Eyes…, 2008

2006: Zero Duration from Emission to Absorbtion…, 2006

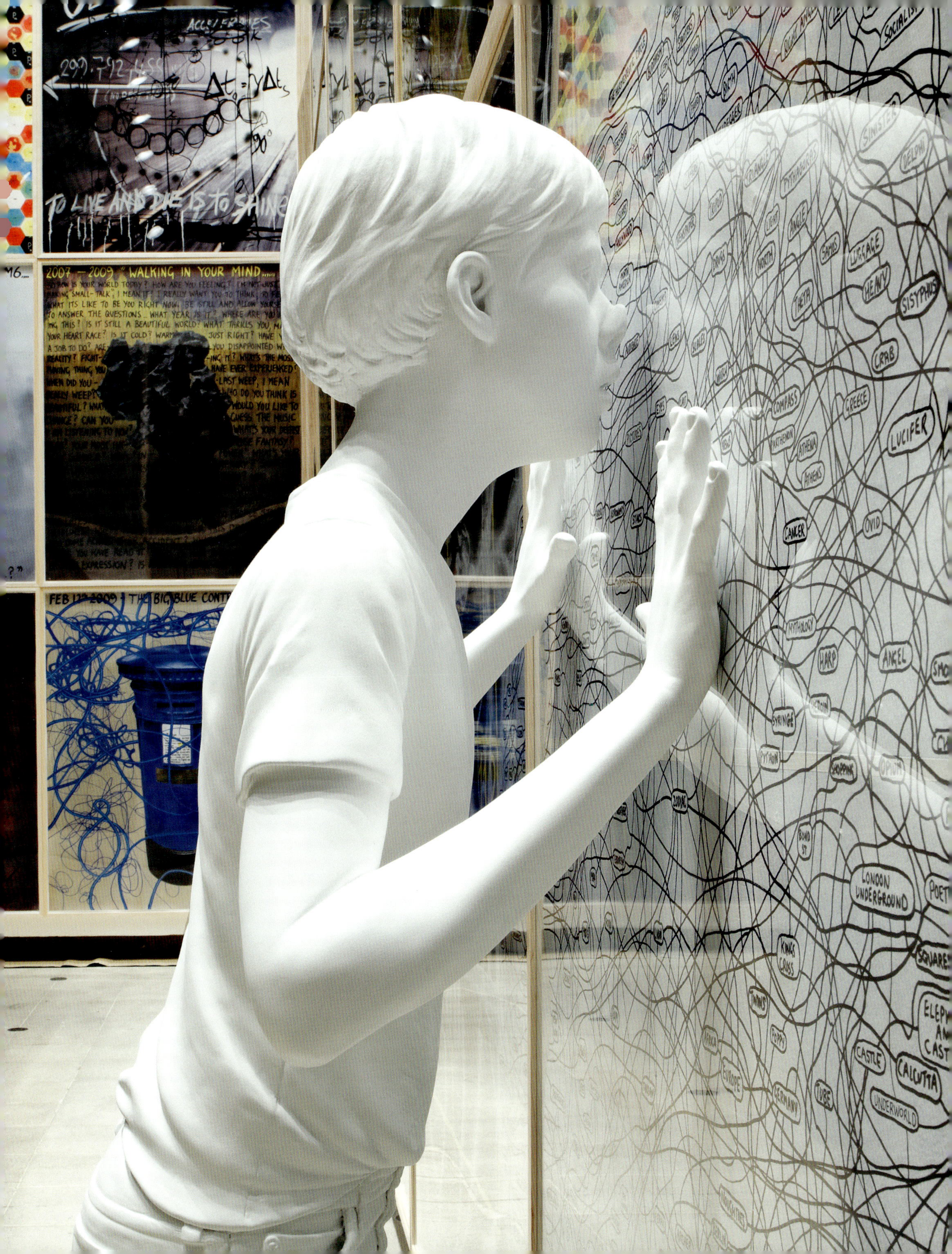

TO LIVE AND DIE IS TO SHINE
2007 - 2009 WALKING IN YOUR MIND
FEB 12 2009 THE BIG BLUE CONT
SOCIALIST
SINISTER
DELPHI
PYTHAGORAS
LUGGAGE
HEAVY
SISYPHUS
CRAB
COMPASS
GREECE
LUCIFER
ATHENA
ATHENS
CANCER
OVID
MYTHOLOGY
HARP
ANKLE
SYRINGE
PYTHON
SHOPPING
OPIUM
LONDON UNDERGROUND
POET
KINGS CROSS
SQUARE
ELEPHANT AND CASTLE
CALCUTTA
UNDERWORLD
TUBE
GERMANY
EUROPE
POPPY
AFRICA

INSIDE THE PAVILION

Brian Dillon

Inside the pavilion we stood and stared. Words fell out of our mouths and floated upwards – words such as 'taut', 'geodesic', 'cripes!' and 'an unprecedented agglomeration of planar fragments'. We professed ourselves, among ourselves, immensely pleased by the structure: the elegance of its twin domes, their amplitude, their glittering armature without and soft shadows within. We admired, loudly, the skill of our native craftsmen and the rigour of our native engineers, whose slide rules had been cunningly wrought by other native craftsmen, overseen in turn by other engineers, no less indigenous nor ingenious. We marveled at the perspicacity and verve of the Exposition Committee – that is to say, at our own perspicacity and verve – in choosing an architect of such ambition and renown to execute the pavilion.

He stood before us now, the architect, some way off among his entourage, gesturing (so I thought) in our direction. We nodded in return, slowly and smilingly, and turned our faces again towards the grey-lit curve above our heads. Certain of my colleagues sighed. A secretary began to sob, and we proffered handkerchiefs approvingly. In sum, we the Committee, inspecting the finished pavilion for the first time, found that it fulfilled our fondest hopes, intimate and official. We felt sure of its eminence among the neighbouring pavilions, here at the soon-to-be-teeming centre of the Exposition. Inwardly, I am not ashamed to say, I thrilled to think of the sinking feeling in the guts of our enemies.

But the day belonged, ceremonially speaking, to the architect and his team. Our small party drifted closer to the knot of draftsmen and apprentices that surrounded him. The architect bowed lavishly at our approach. (Did some among his associates exchange unseemly smiles and then stiffen at the sight of my insignia?) We had interrupted a discourse that he now resumed, to the flutter of notebooks. The building, said the architect, was a creature of its own etymology. *Un pavillon* – he pronounced the word in his native tongue – was at once a tent, a butterfly and that portion of a cut gemstone that lies between the girdle and the point or culet. There were those of both parties who silently mouthed the words 'girdle' and 'culet', but none failed to grasp the properties to which the architect alluded.

We reflected for a moment on the energies so expertly tethered in the fabric and supports of the pavilion, the delicate organic symmetry of the thing, its countless polished facets shining in the sunlight that we had lately left behind, its swelling domes above and the intricate cavities below: there at the mysterious place where the hemispheres met.

The architect's entourage clustered more tightly around the master, their notebooks hoist like tiny sails, as they sensed his lesson breasting urgently an aphoristic wave. We, the Exposition Committee, were already well apprised of the stylishness, profundity and pith of the man's aphorisms, his apothegms or (if you will) his *aperçus*. I myself had been compiling an inventory or album of such, since those fervid days during the commissioning of the pavilion, when with his brisk eloquence he had first won us to his vision. We now drew near and strained to listen. 'In my building', said the architect, 'an object and an idea are trying hard to inhabit the same place.'

The audience whispered. I noticed a handful of Committee members borrow pencils from the staff of the architect's office and write quickly on the backs of their copies of the *Interim Report on the Progress of the Pavilion*, with which document, in my capacity as Artistic Director, I had furnished them that morning. I left the scribbling throng and began to inspect more closely the space around us.

How to convey the splendour of the pavilion, its optimistic air, the accuracy with which the architect had grasped and then expressed, in concrete and steel, our expansive dreams? I have already adverted to the domes. Forgive me, for in truth the architect keenly deprecated the use of the word 'dome', and had banned it from Committee meetings and correspondence concerning the pavilion. Even now, however, my junior staff might sometimes blurt: 'the domes are ravishing … the domes are structural miracles … the domes are the pride of our small but indefatigable nation.' On these occasions, the architect's fury was admirable. 'These are not domes!' he would shout. 'They are lobes, lobes, lobes!'

It was to the substance and design of the lobes that I now turned my attention. The twinned hemispheres were aligned to the east and west of the precise centre of the Exposition site: the point, as is well known, at which our republic is said to have been born with the slaying of a foreign tyrant. Each encircled a floored area of some nine hundred and eight metres, the structure itself rising at its zenith to a height of seventeen metres. The outer surface bristled with a tense cage of steel wire that, at the insistence of the architect, we had learned to refer to as the *caul*. The armature was complex but self-effacing. Inside – that is, at the southern extreme of the eastern lobe, where I now stood – the caul was invisible, so ingeniously had the panels that comprised the burnished concrete shell of the building been fixed in place. My fingers brushed this perfect finish as I followed its circumference towards the point, to the west, where the two lobes met.

In fact, they did not simply abut each other but rather overlapped several metres from their outer edges, so that they formed in the place between a vaulted room – the architect had called it the *fold* – from beneath which the pavilion's famed spectacle, the second pride of our resourceful nation, was soon to be calibrated and controlled. The fold was unlit, a central spiral staircase that led to the control room beneath scarcely visible in the gloom as I entered. A hand gripped my shoulder before I could reach the stairs. I turned to face the architect, who kept his hand there and smiled. 'I have given you a building, but I promise you an *event*.'

★

In the days and weeks following our first tour of the pavilion, we the Committee trained our minds to the subject of the spectacle. It would be, we agreed, extraordinary: that was in the nature, after all, of a spectacle. It would astound our allies, who were fast completing their own, adjacent, pavilions and dreaming of their own displays. It would strike fear in the vitals of our enemies – we pictured the vitals, scoured and sore from the fear – whose requests for pavilion-space at the outskirts of the Exposition we had so decisively turned down. We engaged more engineers, hired more craftsmen and suborned technicians from our nation's peerless academies. Conscripts destined for our colonial wars were diverted to the Exposition site, where they might labour hard into the night, heroically illumined by our inventors' fierce new phosphorus lamps. I sat at my desk in the small hours and buried myself in my *Interim Report on the Success of the Spectacle*.

And yet, we grew fretful and afraid. We had of late heard nothing from the architect. Rumours reached us that he was employed elsewhere, even that he had fled abroad, leaving only his amanuensis and a few apprentices in charge of the spectacle, and was embarked upon the design for an entire city in a far-flung province of an obscure country.

I dispatched my own most trusted assistant to the pavilion, and charged him with inspecting the lower precincts of the fold. What, I demanded to know, was the nature of the spectacle that the architect had promised? Its medium, its cost, its luminance? Its volume, its colour, its velocity? None of which he could report on his return. Only this: that when he had descended the stairs he found the control room empty but for a handful of the architect's entourage, who had regarded him quizzically, perhaps satirically, on his conveying the inquiries of the Committee. And as he left, he said, the stirrings of a great wind at his back.

Within days, a telegram was delivered to my office. 'NOT A SPEC-TACLE STOP A CATACLYSM STOP.' The word, I need hardly mention, perplexed me with its intimations of disaster. My faith in the architect, in his pavilion, in the epochal feat of the Exposition, wavered for the first time as I fingered the document. I pondered, as may be imagined, my own position as Artistic Director. From my balcony, I gazed on the great square at the heart of our gleaming capital, and beyond to the cranes that rose above the site of the Exposition, lately cleared of its shaming and seditious slums, and I trembled. Summoning my secretary, I scrawled a reply. 'EXPLAIN CATACLYSM STOP'.

Messengers began to arrive daily in the square, bearing letters and parcels, curiously postmarked. I convened an extraordinary meeting of the Exposition Committee.

We examined the letters. They were illegible. We seconded scribes, and cipherers from our secret police. The architect's handwriting swam before our eyes. At length, we were able to read. *'The Cataclysm: An Inventory of its Qualities...* A violent geological or meteorological event... Everything is spheres and cylinders... The pavilion is a system of movement... Tunnels like living conduits through the building's substance... I wish to give no guarantees... One might almost say that the body thinks... A political or social upheaval... The hole [sic] must shiver, deliciously, like the Tunnel of Love that summer in... I very sincerely believe that there has been no loss of time and that everything is perfectly under control... The vilest erup-tions... It is fully the equal of many famous continental examples... A pure thought: fleeting, melancholy and tremendous....'

We opened the packages. Blueprints, sketches and photographs spilled out. We summoned our engineers and architects. We called for the physicians, who looked aghast and sent for our most advanced philosopher.

(I myself signed the papers for his release.) We asked these experts to explain the heap of images. It is a prospectus for a pneumatic system, said the engineers, pointing to a drawing of elaborate pipe-work that ended in a great trumpet or bloom of brass. It is a collection of plans for the greatest port city ever seen, said the architects, staring at the same drawing. That is a crude approximation of the human gut, said the doctors dismissively; but this, they cried, pointing to a picture of two pink and lightly veined hemispheres, dotted with tiny numerals: this is extremely promising. It is all merely a map of woe, said the philosopher, clutching his temples.

I dismissed the experts, and addressed the Committee. Gentlemen, I said, we are faced with a type of ambiguity that our most able and audacious thinkers cannot resolve. But we must not falter. For what is Art, and what Nationhood, if not an expanding of our physical and mental horizons? One risks much when commissioning an architect. One puts one's faith, I submit, in Genius. We must now trust in this ageless and ever-reaching entity, the mind of the artist. It is a sky filled with pure and uplifting abstractions, with thoughts swift as zephyrs, impressions that fall like spring showers. But it is an earthy medium too: subject, like the body politic itself, to necessary and enlivening upheavals. The architect, I am certain, has intuitively seized upon our most sublime and our most refined urges. Let us embrace, gentle-men – and here I spread my hands above the papers on my desk – the austere wonder of the cataclysm.

★

It is the day of the inauguration. All about the Exposition, on my orders, work has ceased on the modest buildings of our allies, and their emissaries been seated on the concourse that surrounds the pavilion. At the instigation of the Committee, such of our citizenry as may be trusted to spread word of its splendour have been issued with advance invitations and corralled eagerly towards the entrances to the twin lobes. Between the two queues stand representatives of our sincere and accurate press, rehearsing their encomia to the sounds and sights to come. Adjectives are tested, epithets canvassed, phrases wrought. 'A monument to our national ingenuity … scintillations such as never beheld … void, naked, baffling, serene … to stroll inside the mind of a master'.

We the Committee arrived at dawn. We have been appraising the several innovations lately installed at the request of the architect's office. It is true that we have concerns. We are uneasy, for instance, about the moat that has been sunk around the lobes, describing a figure of eight of still water that prevents close inspection of the caul. The architect's amanuensis assures us that it is a necessary corollary to the cataclysm. We have expressed too our perplexity concerning certain tremors recently reported in the vicinity of the fold, and a rumbling heard in the night, like the starting throes of some huge machine. Inside the lobes, buckets of sand have been placed about, as if in case of fire. The amanuensis nods and smiles, refers us to the architect's impeccable record in matters of safety, intimates that such details as the buckets are merely props to the master's innate sense of theatricality. 'The public, you know, expects....' Our doubts are somewhat assuaged.

The architect arrives with his entourage. The hemispheres are filled: some six hundred citizens in each. We have organized a few preliminaries. A dais has been erected on the concourse, an hour set aside for speeches from the central coterie of the Committee, time enough allotted for the architect's own remarks. To our dismay, he waves aside the uniformed invigilators and rushes towards the entrance to the western lobe. We the Committee follow. Inside, he is recognized instantly; cheers fly from the crowd, and he shakes the hands of several citizens. He raises his arms towards the upper reaches of the lobe and roars: *'the overture!'*

I cannot say for certain how it begins. A sense, perhaps, of fullness in the air around us: a subtle raising of the temperature within the lobe, a pressure of the atmosphere that was not present a moment ago, a sluggishness in the citizens housed there, so that the crowd that pressed towards the architect has slowed now, each body somehow heavier than before. And at the same time a feeling of urgency, of approach. With it the light: a gradual paling of the concrete shell, till its panels are almost white, each segment, even to the most distant above our heads, equally and individually agleam. A great rustling or crackling is heard, as of the unfolding and tearing of vast sheets of paper – it seems to sound from the floor beneath us.

'And now', exclaims the architect, *'mon cataclysme!'* He makes a dash for the entrance to the fold, pursued, I need hardly say, by the full quorum of the Committee. The room, as before, is almost dark. But something glows weakly at its centre. I clutch the balustrade of the spiral staircase; in the depths, a mass of copper pipes, jointed in shining brass, extends beneath the fold and perhaps – there is no time to say for certain – below the entire pavilion.

The architect is gesturing wildly towards the vaulted ceiling above us. Light suddenly falls into the fold. Its central seam has cracked; the two portions of the roof begin to part slowly and noiselessly. We stare at the open sky. Some of my colleagues snivel. For my part, it is the sight of the lobes that I shall never forget, their gentle, magnificent curves rising above me on either side, recalling the still and distant valley in which I was born. Sunlight has warmed the concrete so that it almost blushes. For a moment, a calm such as I have not known since boyhood descends upon me, and the cares of the Committee, the success of the Exposition and the plight of our embattled republic all fall away.

I feel a jolt in the soles of my feet. Something tenses deep in the structure of the pavilion. On the surface, the caul is suddenly alive. The steel cage thrills and appears to spark in the sunlight; the very atmosphere above it seems to shiver. Wires as thick as my wrist start to stiffen and groan. And a new sound overtakes them. It is a slow hiss, like the sound of air escaping a valve, but it rises to a roar as we – that is, the Committee, the architect, his entourage – turn towards its source, which is the spiral stair-case at the centre of the now fully exposed fold. Only the architect, his triumphant cries lost in the noise, grips the balustrade as a hot wind now rushes between the hemispheres, tearing at our clothes, so that we can hardly stand.

Reports have reached my office that the nature of the cataclysm remains enigmatic in the minds of the assembled dignitaries, not to speak of the lesser minds of the citizenry. And yet, it seems that both those who were there and those who read the sublime accounts composed by our native writers have felt, in the weeks since the inauguration, a new ease within and a new alertness to the world without. In the incomparable account of our greatest poet, it is said that the force of the cataclysm sent waves rushing across the moat around the pavilion, and that those waves, though smaller now, are still to be seen, dispatched like subtle messengers from shore to shore.

LIST OF EXHIBITED WORKS

Measurements are given in centimetres, height before width and depth. Works of art are © the artist or the estate of the artist unless otherwise stated. Photos taken by Roger Wooldridge are Hayward Gallery installations and © Southbank Centre, 2009.

CHARLES AVERY

Untitled (Artist's Impression of the Eternity Chamber), 2007
Pencil, ink, gouache and pen on paper
100 x 140
Courtesy of the Government Art Collection, UK
Photo (p. 19): © Crown copyright: UK Government Art Collection

Untitled (Eternity Chamber), 2007
Perspex, Jesmonite, lightbulbs, fan, electric cable, glass, bronze and iron
435 x 180 x 180
Courtesy of the artist and Pilar Corrias, London
Photos (pp. 34, 46): Blaise Adilon, Biennale de Lyon, 2007, Lyon
Photo (p. 47): Roger Wooldridge

Stone-mice, 2008
Stones
Display dimensions 60 x 30 x 100
Courtesy of the artist and Museum Boijmans Van Beuningen, Rotterdam, The Netherlands
Photo (p. 49): Roger Wooldridge

Untitled (As I look into space, I meet the eye of my creator, as she is watching me, as I am in her eye), 2002 – 2009
100 x 75
Pencil and gouache on card
Courtesy of the artist and Galleria Sonia Rosso, Turin
Photo (p. 2): Courtesy the artist

Untitled (Bejewelled Hare), 2009
Taxidermy
75 x 50 x 25
Courtesy of the artist and doggerfisher, Edinburgh
Photo (p. 45): Roger Wooldridge

Untitled (Hat no. 3: Solipsist), 2009
Gouache on card
70 x 110 x 100
Courtesy of the artist and Pilar Corrias, London
Photo (p. 48): Roger Wooldridge

Untitled (Hunter), 2009
Pencil and ink on tracing paper
64 x 45
Courtesy of the artist and doggerfisher, Edinburgh

Untitled (Lionel Leslie's Leviathan), 2009
Pencil, ink, watercolour and gouache on card
140 x 160
Courtesy of the artist and Pilar Corrias Gallery, London
Image (p. 50): Courtesy the artist, Thierry Bal and Pilar Corrias Gallery, London

Untitled (One-armed Snake), 2009
Taxidermy
30 x 15
Courtesy of the artist
Photo (p. 43): Charles Avery and Andy Keate

Untitled (Perspective plan of The Three Trees), 2009
Pencil and ink on paper
101.2 x 81.6
Courtesy of the artist and doggerfisher, Edinburgh

Untitled (Stone-mouse Expedition), 2008 – 2009
Pencil and ink on card
68 x 91
Collection of Keith Wilson

Untitled (The Three Trees), 2009
Pencil, gouache and ink on paper
Three panels, each 170 x 120
Courtesy of the artist and doggerfisher, Edinburgh

Untitled (Tourists in hats), 2009
Pencil, gouache and ink on Paper
56.4 x 75
Courtesy of the artist and Pilar Corrias, London

Untitled (The World as revealed to an itinerant gutter in the diseased eye of a discarded eel), 2009
Pencil and gouache on paper mounted on cotton
150 x 212
Courtesy of the artist and doggerfisher, Edinburgh

THOMAS HIRSCHHORN

Cavemanman, 2002
Mixed media installation
Dimensions variable
Dimitris Daskalopoulos Collection, Greece
Courtesy Barbara Gladstone Gallery
Installation team: Simon Bramwell-Cole, Glynn Davies, Stuart Harris, Lottie Hughes, Jamie Simpson, Alison Wear, Tiff Wear
Photos (except p. 11): Roger Wooldridge
Photo (p. 11): Installation view, Carnegie Museum of Art, Pittsburgh, 2008

YAYOI KUSAMA

Guidepost to the New World, 2005
Mixed media installation
Courtesy of the artist and Victoria Miro Gallery, London / Ota Fine Arts, Tokyo
Photos (pp. 67, 72 – 73): Roger Wooldridge

Ascension of Polkadots on the Trees, 2009
Mixed media installation
Courtesy of the artist and Victoria Miro Gallery,
London / Ota Fine Arts, Tokyo
Photo (p. 71): Roger Wooldridge

Dots Obsession, 2009
Mixed media installation
Courtesy of the artist and Victoria Miro Gallery,
London / Ota Fine Arts, Tokyo
Photo (p. 69): Roger Wooldridge

BO CHRISTIAN LARSSON

The first cut is the deepest and the division of seven, 2009
Mixed media installation with videoed performances
Dimensions variable
Courtesy the artist
Sound recording: Jon Lowe
Photos (pp. 16, 84 – 85): Roger Wooldridge

The piece includes the following works:
Sculptures, all mixed media unless otherwise stated:

Bold, 2009
20 x 20 x 50

The Claw, 2009
60 x 60 x 12

Hellfire, 2009
40 x 60 x 90

Just as you thought it was over, 2009
50 x 30 x 30

The Laws of Babel, 2009
50 x 36 x 15

Nuclear Cancer, 2009
45 x 35 x 50

Storm Hat, 2009
50 x 35 x 55

Suicide Division, 2009
38 x 26 x 35

Walking Stick, 2009
40 x 40 x 110

The Worldhaters's Homesick Blues, Deluxe, 2009
47 x 43 x 17

The Worldhaters's Homesick Blues, Original, 2009
21 x 25 x 14

We Are All Chained to the World, 2009
Dimensions variable
Courtesy the artist and Steinle Contemporary,
Munich, Germany

Drawings, all pencil, acrylic and airbrush on paper:

Ground Control, 2009
150 x 200
Courtesy the artist and Steinle Contemporary,
Munich, Germany
Photo (pp. 80 – 81): Bo Christian Larsson

Revolution Construction, 2009
150 x 132
Courtesy the artist and Steinle Contemporary,
Munich, Germany

Uprising, 2009
150 x 190
Courtesy the artist and Steinle Contemporary,
Munich, Germany

Performance actors:
The Poet: Grahame Edwards
The Worldhater: Michael Good
Mr. Empire: Matthew Miller
Sonuvabitch: Bo Christian Larsson
The Shadow: Richard Parry
The Redeemer: Shaima Al Sitarwi
Sound: Murena
Performance photos (pp. 82 – 83): Jack Goffe

MARK MANDERS

Short Sad Thoughts, 1990
Brass and nails
Each 22.1 x 2.5 x 0.3
Van Abbemuseum, Eindhoven

Fox / Mouse / Belt, 1992
Painted bronze and belt
15 x 120 x 40
Courtesy Zeno X Gallery, Antwerp and
Tanya Bonakdar Gallery, New York
Photo (pp. 94 – 95): Roger Wooldridge

Composition with Broom, 1993 – 2009
Offset print on paper and chicken wire,
mounted on aluminium
121 x 181
Courtesy Zeno X Gallery, Antwerp and
Tanya Bonakdar Gallery, New York
Photo (p. 89): Mark Manders

Nocturnal Garden Scene, 2005
Wood, paper, metal, glass and organic material
160 x 220 x 130
Courtesy S.M.A.K., Ghent
Photo (p. 91): Mark Manders

Still Life with Interconnected Holes, 2006
Sand, hair, porcelain, wool and various materials
17 x 48 x 50
Courtesy Zeno X Gallery, Antwerp and
Tanya Bonakdar Gallery, New York

Livingroom Scene, 2008
Mixed media
300 x 350 x 330
Collection Stedelijk Museum, Amsterdam
Photo (p. 97): Roger Wooldridge

Figure with Wooden Arm, 2009
Pencil on paper
80 x 110
Courtesy Zeno X Gallery, Antwerp and
Tanya Bonakdar Gallery, New York
Photo (p. 96): Roger Wooldridge

Life-Size Scene with Revealed Figure, 2009
Mixed media
139 x 320 x 120
Courtesy Zeno X Gallery, Antwerp and
Tanya Bonakdar Gallery, New York
Photo (pp. 94 – 95): Roger Wooldridge

YOSHITOMO NARA

Yoshitomo Nara + graf (installation by YNG)
My Drawing Room, (bedroom included), 2008
Mixed media installation
301.5 x 375 x 380
Courtesy The National Museum of Modern Art,
Tokyo / Tomio Koyama Gallery, Tokyo
Photos (pp. 102 – 103, 105 – 107): Roger Wooldridge

JASON RHOADES

The Creation Myth, 1998
Mixed media installation
Dimensions variable
Courtesy Friedrich Christian Flick Collection
Photos (pp. 111 – 113, 116 – 17): Roger Wooldridge

PIPILOTTI RIST

Extremitäten (weich,weich) [Extremities (smooth,
smooth)], 1999 / 2009
Audio video installation
Projections, scanners with mirrors, audio system,
seating element and curtains
Courtesy the artist and Hauser & Wirth
Zurich London
With thanks to Thyssen-Bornemisza
Art Contemporary
Video & sound realised with the support of:
Tamara Rist, Anders Guggisberg, Mich Hertig
Installation London: Käthe Walser, Jo Dunkel,
Rachele Giudici, Karin Seinsoth
Photos (p. 119): Roger Wooldridge
Photos (pp. 121 – 125): Ela Bialkowska

CHIHARU SHIOTA

After the Dream, 2009
Mixed media installation
Dimensions variable
Dresses and wool
Courtesy of the artist
© VG Bild-Kunst, Bonn
Photos (pp. 130 – 133): Roger Wooldridge

KEITH TYSON

Studio Wall Drawing: Jan 2009 – Locked Out Of
Eden – Viewing The Children Playing In The Garden
From The Safety Of My Cerebral Fortress, 2009
Mixed media on watercolour paper (21 frames);
glass-reinforced resin; looped sound recording
Overall dimensions 471 x 882
Courtesy of the artist
Photos (pp. 135, 138 – 139, 144 – 145):
Roger Wooldridge

Studio Wall Drawings, 2000 – 2009
Mixed media on watercolour paper
54 frames, each 157 x 126
Various lenders:
Courtesy the artist; Private collection; Matthew
Freud Collection; Collection Michela Moro Journo;
The O'Rourke Collection, London; Collection
Penny Pritzker and Bryan Traubert; Collection
Norman and Norah Stone, San Francisco USA /
Courtesy Thea Westreich Art Advisory Services;
Courtesy Haunch of Venison
Photos (pp. 137, 140 – 143): Keith Tyson

Nov 2000: Section of an Infinite Dam Holding Back
the Terrible Weight of the Abyss

18 Feb 2001: The Diazepam Sketchbook (With Very
Private View in Bedroom Before I Pass Out)

5th March 2001: Intrinsic Subdivision to Point Z

29 Dec 2001: Somewhere Near the Edge of the
Visible Universe...

28th Dec 2001: Welcome Honoured Guest to the
Pewter Fountain

18th August 2003: All is Silent Apart from the
Sound of Your Breathing...

2004: Twenty Four Seven Three Sixty Five Three
Score and Ten...

Feb 17th 2004: From Fear to Joy [Without
Running Away...]

April 19th 2004: A Toral Interface (v.1.1.)
Representing an Isotropic Cluster of Torus
Multiverses Spinning in the Void...

May 6th 2004: Given the Universe is Isotropic it
would be by Implication Infinite...

Sept 2004: The Steel Mosquito... These Trees
Smell of Blood

Oct 2004: "Postcards from the Edge of Reason"
(Pattern, Person or Place)

Aug 03 – Dec 03 – Jan 04 – Dec 04 – Feb 05: "The
Hamburg Hallucinations" (I Wanted your Childhood...)

2006: Zero Duration From Emission to Absorption...

March 2006: Stuck in Traffic on the M6...

May 2006: There he sat Transfixed by the Single
Red Sock... (3 frames)

15th June 2006: Frontiers of the "Organism –
Environment"

12th July 2006: The Movements Through a
Train Window

31st July 2006: Random Walk (+AND-
(L,R,D+RND))...

Aug 2006: The God of Origami...

Aug 23rd 2006: Cell-Organ-Organism-Society-Cell-Organ…

Oct 2006: The Shattered Integer Plane Repairs

19-10-06: A Drop in Blood Pressure – Time to Work on an Operator Painting Notebook

2007: A Retrospective of the Air Above my Head from 1969–2007

2007: The Irrefutable Proof

2007: Sculpture in Black Glass/Steel

2007: Tribute

12th Jan 2007: Contemporary Grotesque. Looking for Love in a Time of Self Hate

15th Jan 2007: Contemporary Grotesque. Looking for Love Amongst the Crows

25th May 2007: Noah the Cowboy

24th–27th June 2007: I Feel Like a Piece of 2 x 4

31st Oct. 2007: Contemporary Grotesque. Looking for Love within the Void

2008 Jan 1st – Contemporary Grotesque. (graphite sculpture): The Deformed Cherub Tree Stump

May 2008: It Runs Through the Woods at Night – Unseen by Human Eyes…

October 2008: And so my River Flows

October 2008: Distribution of Primes (HEX)

12th December 08: Woolworth, Water, Wood + Woe

Dec 23rd 2008: The Anatomy of a Thought… in a Mind Full of Starlings

2007–2009: "Walking in Your Mind…"

2009: Now

2009: The 20 Greatest Moments in History

9 Jan 2009 – Just Winging It! (with a little gravity)…

Feb 2009: This Persistent Lump in your Sea of Tears…

Feb 12th 2009: The Big Blue Control Button

Feb 12th 2009: It's Strange the Things That Come to Mind as one Leaves This Life, Writing the "K" in my Name at School, the Tokyo Skyline, the Smell of Coal Dust and most Bizarrely of all… EXPANDED POLYSTYRENE

March 09: So Then he Dealt the King of Owls… and Instantly the Game Seemed Pointless

April 3rd 2009: Climbing out of the Cravasse One Painful Step at a Time…

15 May 09: Happy Happy Happy Times

20.5.09: A Blind Man on the Beach

June 1st 2009: The Middle One!

Tues 9th June 2009: This Girl, She's Not Me…

11-06-09: Today I Realised the Reversal in the Polarity Between Fact and Fiction

LIST OF ILLUSTRATED WORKS

The following works are illustrated but not exhibited, and listed in the order they appear in the book.

ESSAYS

Chiharu Shiota
Return to Consciousness, 1996
Artist's blood, glass tube and black wool
Dimensions variable
© VG Bild-Kunst, Bonn
Photo (p. 8): Chiharu Shiota

Gelitin
Psycho Hayward, 2008
Collage created for the Hayward Gallery
exhibition *Psycho Buildings*, 2008
Photo (p. 10): Hayward Gallery

Allan Kaprow
Apple Shrine, 1960
Mixed media installation
Courtesy Allan Kaprow Estate.
Courtesy Hauser & Wirth Zurich London
Photo: Robert R. McElroy
Photo (p. 10): © Robert R. McElroy / Licensed
by VAGA, New York, NY
Image courtesy Research Library, The Getty
Research Institute, Los Angeles, California

Gregor Schneider
Haus Ur, 1985 –
Mixed media installation
Courtesy the artist and Sadie Coles HQ, London
© Gregor Schneider / VG Bild-Kunst, Bonn
Photo (p. 12): Gregor Schneider

Paul McCarthy
The Box, 1999
Tables, shelves, chairs, video editing equipment,
tools, drawings, works in progress, sculptures,
sewing machine, audio and video equipment, bicycle,
household utensils and refrigerator
579.12 x 401.32 x 1539.24
Friedrich Christian Flick Collection
Courtesy the artist and Hauser & Wirth
Zurich London
Photo (p. 12): A. Burger, Zurich

Keith Tyson
Dec 1999: 20 Questions, 1999
Mixed media on watercolour paper
157 x 126
Photo (p. 14): Keith Tyson

Charles Avery
Untitled (The Bar of the One-armed Snake), 2009
Pencil, gouache and ink on board
140 x 100
Photo (p. 18): Charles Avery and Andy Keate

Yayoi Kusama
Infinity Net, 1965
Oil on canvas
132 x 152
Photo (p. 20): Yayoi Kusama Studio

Illustration of a neural network (p. 22)
Jurgen Ziewe / Wellcome Images

Mirror Room (Pumpkin), 1991
Installation
Mirrors, wood, papier-mâché and paint
200 x 200 x 200
Collection Hara Museum, Tokyo
Photo (p. 24): Yayoi Kusama Studio

Yayoi Kusama
Untitled, 1939
Pencil on paper
24.8 x 22.5
Photo (p. 26): Yayoi Kusama Studio

Yayoi Kusama in *Aggregation: One Thousand
Boats Show* at the Gertrude Stein Gallery,
New York, 1963
Photo (p. 27): Yayoi Kusama Studio

Yayoi Kusama in *Peep Show – Endless Love Room*
at the Castellane Gallery, New York, 1966
Photo (p. 28): Yayoi Kusama Studio

Chiharu Shiota
In Silence, 2002
Burnt grand piano, burnt wooden chairs, black
wool
1871 x 1645
© VG Bild-Kunst, Bonn
Photo (p. 29): Sunhi Mang

The Memory Theatre of Giulio Camillo
From: *The Art of Memory*
Frances A. Yates
© 2009 Routledge
Image (p. 30): Reproduced by permission of
Taylor & Francis Books (UK)

Mark Manders
Installation view, S.M.A.K., Ghent, 2008 – 2009
Photo (p. 32): Dirk Pauwels

Charles Avery
Coscienza, 2008
Woodcut print, diptych
Photo (p. 31): Charles Avery studio

Yoshitomo Nara
Untitled, 2008
Pencil on paper
65 x 50
Photo (p. 32): Ikuhiro

Ilya Kabakov
The Man Who Flew into Space from His Apartment,
1981/8
Installation
© ADAGP, Paris
Photo (p. 32): © Collection Centre Pompidou,
Dist. RMN / Philippe Migeat

ACKNOWLEDGEMENTS

First and foremost, we would like to thank the artists for contributing such extraordinary work to the exhibition.

Thanks are also due to the following lenders: Collection Van Abbemuseum, Eindhoven; Museum Boijmans Van Beuningen, Rotterdam; Dimitris Daskalopoulos; Friedrich Christian Flick Collection; Matthew Freud; Government Art Collection, UK; Michela Moro Journo; Tom O'Rourke; Penny Pritzker and Bryan Traubert; Stedelijk Museum, Amsterdam; S.M.A.K., Stedelijk Museum voor Actuele Kunst, Ghent; Norah and Norman Stone; and other private lenders who wish to remain anonymous.

We are also very grateful to the following galleries: Marianne Boesky Gallery, New York; Stephen Friedman Gallery, Tokyo; Barbara Gladstone Gallery, New York; Haunch of Venison, London; Hauser & Wirth, Zurich and London; Tomio Koyama Gallery, Tokyo; Victoria Miro Gallery, London; Steinle Contemporary, Munich.

Thanks are also due to: Teresa Kittler and Michael Lewis, Charles Avery studio; Jean-Pascal Flavien; Patrick Peternader, Friedrich Christian Flick Collection; Hideki Toyoshima, Ryo Aoyanagi and Yasumasa Konishi, graf; Bjoern Meyer-Ebrecht, assistant to Thomas Hirschhorn; Romain Lopez and Marc Turlan, Thomas Hirschhorn studio; Etsuko Sakurai, Isao Takakura and Megumi Takasugi, Yayoi Kusama studio; Anna Wondrak, assistant to Bo Christian Larsson; Jean-Pascal Flavien; Rachel Khedoori and Richard Baker, Jason Rhoades estate; Jo Dunkel, Rachele Giudici and Käthe Walser, Pipilotti Rist studio; Tomoko Fujimura, Steffi Goldmann, Satoshi Hoshi and Kiyomi Uozumi, Chiharu Shiota studio; Thyssen-Bornemisza Art Contemporary; Tony Martin, Nick Dowdeswell and Caroline Henley, Keith Tyson studio.

Finally, *Walking in My Mind* was realised through the dedicated work of the Hayward technical team led by Gareth Hughes, Mark King, Miranda Melville, Dave Wood and Ciaran Begley. We wish to thank them, as well as the many others who helped install the exhibition, for their excellent work.

Mami Kataoka and Stephanie Rosenthal